for John Baldwin,
with respect and ~~~~

*The Abbey of St. Germain des Prés in the
Seventeenth Century*

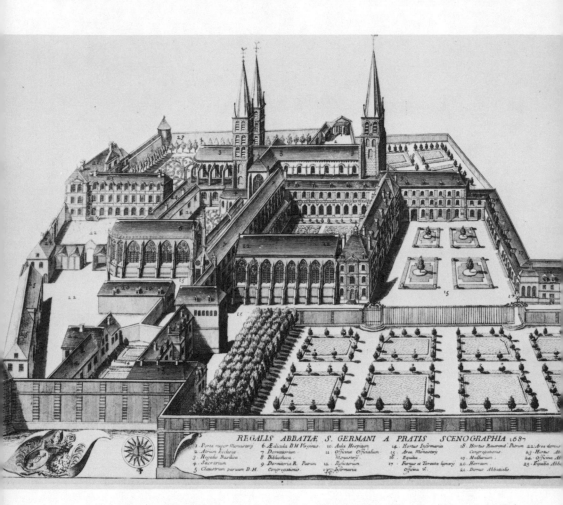

Frontispiece: The Abbey of St. Germain des Prés in 1687. (Source: *Monasticon Gallicanum*, a projected catalogue of all the monasteries of the Congregation of St. Maur; this engraving Bibliothèque nationale, Estampes, 62 B 29136. The same engraving was published later by A. Peigné-Delacourt, *Monasticon Gallicanum* [Paris, 1871], no. 74)

The Abbey of
St. Germain des Prés
in the Seventeenth Century

MAARTEN ULTEE

NEW HAVEN AND LONDON
YALE UNIVERSITY PRESS

Designed by James J. Johnson
and set in Garamond type.
Printed in the United States of America by
Halliday Lithograph, West Hanover, Mass.

Library of Congress Cataloging in Publication Data

Ultee, Maarten, 1949–
    The abbey of St. Germain des Prés in the
seventeenth century.

    Bibliography: p.
    Includes index.
    1. Saint-Germain-des-Prés (Paris, France)
I. Title.
BX2615.P3U44   271'.1'044361   81-2265
ISBN 0–300–02562–9   AACR2

10 9 8 7 6 5 4 3 2 1

Contents

Illustrations

FIGURES

TABLES

GRAPHS

Preface

This is a work of youth, but it has grown tremendously. The author's scholarly debts have grown also, and it is fitting to express thanks to the people who stopped along the way to talk about the monks of St. Germain des Prés.

First, I want to thank my adviser, Orest Ranum. He guided the project from the beginning, gave sound advice, and encouraged me by word and example, carrot and stick. A generation of historians will be grateful to him. Among his colleagues at Johns Hopkins, Professors Robert Forster, John Baldwin, and Harry Woolf also taught me much.

Lewis Spitz at Stanford University was generous and sympathetic at an important time in the writing of the first draft. Marvin Bram likewise supported the research and writing at a later stage. In Paris, Dominique Julia and Emmanuel Le Roy Ladurie provided helpful suggestions. The final revisions were made while I participated in a memorable NEH seminar directed by Stephen B. Baxter at the University of North Carolina.

One close friend whose learning in religious history was always welcome now receives special mention: Ritchey Newton. His comments and collaboration have been rewarding since our first meeting in Paris in 1971.

My family and friends outside the historical profession have contributed much also. Often they were my first readers and listeners. They tolerated this history much longer than I would have on my own. My particular thanks go to Carol Abrams, Marcel and Kathy Vinokur, the Bigelow family, Linda Gasser, Ann Callahan, the Newman family, Pam Camerra, San and Kitty Go, Pierre and Judith Valcke. Finally, I appreciate the conscientious work of the readers and editors at Yale University Press, especially Sally Serafim and Charles Grench.

Now let us turn to history.

Summer 1980

The Abbey of St. Germain des Prés in the
Seventeenth Century

A Royal Monastery in Paris

With many good subjects in French history waiting to be explored, one may well ask why a student would choose to write about the Abbey of St. Germain des Prés. To a modern Parisian, the name "St. Germain des Prés" conjures up visions of a busy square on the Left Bank. There one finds a métro station, a drugstore, restaurants, cafés, and flourishing night life. Not long ago at the Café aux Deux Magots, Jean-Paul Sartre and Simone de Beauvoir spent days and days writing and discussing; on opposite sides of the Boulevard St. Germain at Brasserie Lipp and the Café de Flore fashionable and questionable society continue to gather nightly. "The Faubourg St. Germain," wrote that perceptive observer of *fin de siècle* society Marcel Proust, "like a senile dowager, responds only with timid smiles to the insolent servants who invade her salons, drink her orangeade, and introduce their mistresses." All this activity swirls about an old church tower, an ancient pile of stones, all that remains of a once-great Benedictine abbey. Few passersby bother to visit the interior of the church, although it contains memorials to Jean Mabillon, Bernard de Montfaucon, and René Descartes. Tourists and Parisians alike are more readily drawn to the entertainments of the quarter; the parish church might better be left to the faithful.

For the historian who looks to origins and general causes of events, however, the Abbey of St. Germain des Prés holds greater importance. Named for the bishop of Paris who assisted in its foundation, the abbey is the oldest church in the city. When it was founded by the Merovingian king Childebert in the sixth century, the abbey stood outside the town, next to the royal gardens, facing the countryside. Originally not a parish church, the monastery was built to house the relics of St. Vincent and a fragment of the cross, which Childebert had brought back from a Spanish military campaign. From that distant Merovingian era only a few tombs, perhaps the entranceway and the base of the tower survived into the eighteenth century. Above the doorway was carved a frieze of the Last Supper, and on each side

I

stood four statues. One of these, a mitred figure clad in episcopal robes and triumphing over a demon, appeared to be either St. Germain, the founder, or St. Rémi, who converted Clovis, the first Christian king of the Franks. The other figures supposedly represented Clovis, his wife Clothilde, their son Childebert and his wife, and three other sons who shared the Frankish inheritance.[1] This attribution, which was supported by the monastic scholars Mabillon and Montfaucon, demonstrates that early modern minds closely linked the historical destiny of St. Germain des Prés with the French monarchy.[2] Indeed, the revolution of 1789 that came to sweep away the old regime had devastating effects on the royal abbey as well.

In Carolingian times the enclosing walls of the abbey held a community of over two hundred Benedictine monks and perhaps as many servants. Financial support for them came from the vast lands of the monastery, which stretched far beyond the Parisian region by the ninth century, when Abbot Irminon enumerated the holdings.[3] The abbey was thrice plundered by the Normans, causing one horrified monk to write, "one had never heard speak of such a thing or read anything like it in the books."[4] It survived those disasters and the repeated attacks on its lands by the rapacious nobility of the eleventh and twelfth centuries. Losses suffered during the Hundred Years' War, the Wars of Religion of the sixteenth century, and the civil wars of the seventeenth century were made good in peacetime prosperity. In 1482, Louis XI granted to the abbey the valuable privilege of an annual fair. This Foire St. Germain, which ran for three weeks in February, became an important social and economic event in the Parisian calendar. The abbey's administrative records, which now fill hundreds of boxes at the Archives Nationales, can furnish answers to questions about medieval and early modern agriculture, seigneurial management, and Parisian economy.[5]

St. Germain des Prés was a preeminent privileged institution, estab-

1. Michel Félibien and Guy-Alexis Lobineau, *Histoire de la ville de Paris* (Paris, 1725), vol. 1, p. 32. Citing Thierry Ruinart, ed., *S. Gregorii Turonensis Opera* (Paris, 1699).

2. Jacques Vanuxem, "The Theories of Mabillon and Montfaucon on French Sculpture of the Twelfth Century," *Journal of the Warburg and Courtaulds Institutes* 20 (1957): 45–58; reprinted in Robert Branner, ed., *Chartres Cathedral* (New York, 1969), pp. 168–85.

3. *Polyptique de l'abbé Irminon*, ed. Benjamin Guérard (Paris, 1836–44); also ed. by A. Longnon (Paris, 1886–95).

4. *Analecta Bollandiana* (1883), p. 71; cited by Marc Bloch, *Feudal Society* (Chicago, 1961), p. 55.

5. Marc Venard, *Bourgeois et paysans au XVIIe siècle* (Paris, 1957); Jean Jacquart, *La Crise rurale en Ile-de-France, 1550–1670* (Paris, 1974).

lished before the urban environment, seeking to maintain its private power and yet respond to the needs of its neighborhood. The city of Paris began as a settlement on the islands in the River Seine, and spread in Roman times to the Left Bank—what is now the Latin Quarter.[6] When Clovis and his successors chose Paris as their capital, the population grew. The Abbey of St. Germain des Prés, however, was legally independent of the city as well as physically separated from it. The monastery was exempt from the spiritual jurisdiction of the bishop of Paris under privileges first asserted in the early Middle Ages and later confirmed by the popes of the twelfth century. Civil jurisdictions of city and abbey were also separate; thus the settlement that grew on the periphery of the cloister, the Bourg St. Germain des Prés, was subject only to monastic rule.[7] In the seventeenth century the continuing expansion of the city threatened to destroy the separate identity of this district; what had once been a *bourg* became a *faubourg*, and, after removal of the gates that marked city limits, a *quartier*. With the change from rural to urban surroundings came changes in government: St. Germain des Prés and its neighborhood thus present a model of Parisian development in the age of Louis XIV.

Monastic life at St. Germain des Prés passed through "periods of progress and flowering, and epochs of decadence and decline."[8] The century and a half prior to the French Revolution was undoubtedly one of the better eras. Then the major influence on the spiritual life of the community was the reform of the Congregation of St. Maur. The Maurists brought new monks and stricter interpretations of Benedictine vows—men and ideas that expressed the strength of the French Catholic religious revival of the early seventeenth century. Revitalized by the Council of Trent and revolted by the disorders of the preceding age of religious warfare, the Maurists adhered closely to St. Benedict's Rule and made St. Germain des Prés their headquarters for study and administration, the spiritual and political center of a congregation that eventually encompassed 180 Benedictine monasteries in France.

Why was reform necessary? Prior to the coming of the Maurists in 1631, St. Germain des Prés had recruited its monks independently, probably, like nearby St. Denis en France, drawing novices from well-to-do

6. Pierre Lavedan and Jeanne Hugueney, *Histoire de l'urbanisme (Antiquité)* (Paris, 1966), pp. 399–404.

7. Françoise Lehoux, *Le Bourg St. Germain des Prés depuis ses origines jusqu'à la fin de la guerre de cent ans* (Paris, 1951).

8. Dom A. Dubourg, "La Vie monastique dans l'abbaye de St. Germain des Prés," *Revue des Questions Historiques* 78 (1905): 406.

families of the Parisian region.[9] These young men could look forward to comfortable lives, conveniently close to high society: unreformed monastic life required little education and few sacrifices. Although one abbot, Guillaume Briçonnet II, bishop of Lodève, had forced the monks to accept the reforms of Chezal-Benoît early in the sixteenth century,[10] St. Germain des Prés was not immune to the general monastic decadence of the period. Briconnet and his successors were commendatory abbots, worldly nobles who collected a large share of the income of the abbey but did not participate in its daily religious life. They tended to regard the abbey as a court pension. Cardinal François de Tournon, for example, held the abbey from 1533 to 1562, and acted abusively toward the community; his princely successors, the Cardinal of Bourbon and the Prince and Princess of Conti, were even less interested in the spiritual welfare of the community that provided thèm with income. Buildings and estates fell into disrepair because these noble abbots would not pay for maintenance,. During the Wars of Religion the abbey was even forced to alienate lands in order to pay special taxes. According to the not disinterested Maurist historians, a return to stricter observance after the disorders was beyond the resources of the Congregation of Chezal-Benoît.[11] Pressure for genuine religious reform thus had to come from outside the monastery, from pious civil authorities. The first attempt to force reform on the seventeenth-century monks of St. Germain des Prés met with failure: owing to the disturbed political climate of 1614, Queen Mother Marie de Medici was unable to carry out a national project that would have had the Parisian abbey as its center. Some of the monks left, disenchanted; they would have to seek their conversion to the reformed cause as individuals elsewhere, before they could hope to reform their home community.[12]

Those monks seeking reform naturally looked across the border to Lorraine, then an independent duchy, where another reform had begun in 1598 at the Abbey of St. Vannes in Verdun. These reformers attempted to live according to the letter of the rule of St. Benedict, following the example of Monte Cassino in Italy. To guide the monks in Lorraine, Pope Clement VIII sent a venerable Italian Benedictine who stayed for two years. As

9. Nécrologe de l'abbaye de St. Denis en France, Bibliothèque Nationale, MSS. fr. 8599, 8600. See J. B. Vanel, Les Bénédictins de St. Maur à St. Germain des Prés, 1630–1792 (Paris, 1896), which prints the Maurist necrology, cited herein as Nécrologe.

10. Michel Veissière. "Guillaume Briconnet, abbé rénovateur de St. Germain des Prés (1507–34)," Revue d'Histoire de L'Église de France 60 (1974): 65–84.

11. Dom Edmond Martène, Histoire de la Congrégation de St. Maur, Archives de la France monastique 31 (1928), vol. 1, pp. 6, 23. On these questions, see Terence L. Dosh, "The Growth of the Congregation of St. Maur, 1618–1672," Ph.D. diss., University of Minnesota, 1971.

12. "Dieu ne voulait pas que la réformation des monastères de France commençat par une maison si illustre," Martène, Histoire, vol. 1, p. 23.

the renown of the group at St. Vannes spread, monks at other houses asked whether they might join it, as individuals or as whole communities.[13]

The first French abbey to join the Congregation of St. Vannes was St. Augustin de Limoges, which was reformed in 1613. In this instance, the Parlement of Bordeaux invited the monks from Lorraine: as foreigners, they had to obtain letters of naturalization from the chancellor of France.[14] The reform of an abbey was not a simple matter, since the reformers had to guarantee the rights of all interested persons. All those receiving income or privilege from the monastery had to agree to settlements: papal annates, royal rights of nomination, abbatial revenues, and monastic prerogatives had to be respected. With so many obstacles to overcome, the Vannist reform movement at first made slow progress in France. Dom Adrien Langlois of Jumièges in Normandy, for example, was struck by the piety of the Vannists he met at the Collège de Cluny in Paris in 1613, but his enthusiasm for the reform encountered stiff opposition from members of his own community. Within a year, however, God showed his favor when eight opponents of the reform died, and in 1615 Dom Langlois was elected prior. An order of the Parlement of Rouen prohibited Norman monasteries from joining foreign congregations, but Langlois nonetheless obtained support from François de Harlay, archbishop of Rouen; the Comte de Soissons, commendatory abbot of Jumièges; and the king. Only with their written commitments could the reform proceed.[15]

By 1618 only five French monasteries had accepted the reform of St. Vannes, but in that year the movement received a great impetus. Louis XIII approved the founding of a separate French reformed Benedictine congregation, to be known as the Congregation of St. Maur.[16] French members of the Congregation of St. Vannes were encouraged to join the new group. From a base of thirty-four monks, most of whom had professed reformed vows in Lorraine, the new congregation began a rapid growth. Nine more monasteries were added in the next six years, and by 1621 the Maurists had received papal recognition.[17] In 1630 more than forty religious houses were under Maurist control.[18] Royal favor and monastic per-

13. Petit Précis de l'histoire de la congrégation, Archives Nationales, L 815, no. 26.

14. Ibid., p. 1. Earlier the Congregation of St. Vannes had received royal letters allowing them to settle in France; B.N. MS. fr. 17669, 13 Sept. 1610. Published by Dom Paul Denis, La Cardinal de Richelieu et la réforme des monastères bénédictins (Paris, 1913).

15. Abbaye de St. Pierre de Jumièges, A.N., L 815, no. 17, with copies of the royal letters.

16. Lettre du roi pour l'érection de la congrégation en France, A.N., LL 990, no. 18. See also the response of the Congregation of St. Vannes, A.N., L 815, no. 27.

17. Bulle d'érection; Bulle de confirmation; Fulmination. A.N. LL 990, nos. 21, 23, 27.

18. List of monasteries, A.N. L 814, no. 5; detailed in Martène, Histoire.

sistence were major factors in the reform of St. Germain des Prés itself, which took place in the following year with the approval of Henry of Verneuil, the legitimized half-brother of Louis XIII, who served as commendatory abbot of the Parisian monastery.[19]

The Maurists' takeover of St. Germain des Prés amounted to "the second foundation of the congregation."[20] It underlined the importance of the Parisian abbey, a powerful institution favored by its wealth and location, its renown and friendships. What do we know of the abbey's position within seventeenth-century society? What might a study of its social and economic aspects reveal about the institution, its members and surroundings, and about French society as a whole? To these questions this study is addressed. St. Germain des Prés will be explored as a microcosm, using methods adapted from historical studies of cities and provinces, religious movements and individuals.

In the first part of this study we examine the mature community to appreciate the atmosphere of learned monasticism at St. Germain des Prés in the Maurist period. Then the records of the Congregation of St. Maur as a whole suggest patterns of monastic recruitment and life in a troubled society. Our aim is to discover what kinds of men became monks, how their years in the cloister affected them and the communities to which they belonged. The second and third parts focus on the abbey's economy: although institutional aspects of the history predominate, the Maurist superiors can be observed making decisions in response to general conditions. We consider the range of choices the monks had in revenues from land and borrowing, as well as in expenditures for maintenance of buildings and lands, the monastic community, and spiritual activities. In each of these areas there were trends over the longer term and fluctuations in brief crises so characteristic of seventeenth-century economies in general. The life of an individual monk in the fourth part relates the general picture of population and economy to a well-documented particular case. Finally, we can place into perspective the abbey's spiritual and political contacts with the world beyond the walls. The monks were by no means isolated from local and national politics: the stirring story of their attempts to keep control over ceremonial practice in their neighborhood has connections to Notre Dame de Paris and Versailles. At St. Germain des Prés in the late seventeenth century, scene of regular observance and exemplary scholarship, life in the cloister meant active participation in affairs of the world as well.

Other writers of monastic history have emphasized the interior spiritual life. Commentaries on rules and constitutions, sermons and guides to

19. See part 4, The Monk as Steward.
20. Dosh, "Growth of the Congregation," p. 175.

observance have furnished their information.[21] These sources, invaluable
for the study of spirituality, receive less emphasis in this work, which is
more concerned with the social and economic order of a monastic institution. Without losing sight of the strong religious fervor of the Maurists,
we strive for an understanding of the abbey within its social and economic
context. Frequently, historians have depicted monasteries as outposts of
culture and retreats from the world;[22] yet St. Germain des Prés was a cultural center with a formidable presence in the Parisian urban landscape. In
these surroundings, the notion of retreat may need to be re-examined, and
to this end study of monastic population, economy, and public ceremonial
life is essential.

Fortunately, some works on English monasteries written by Dom
David Knowles and his students at Cambridge may serve as models of organization.[23] From R. A. L. Smith's *Canterbury Cathedral Priory*, we learn
of a community of seventy-five monks that used a central financial system
to control its estates and household expenditures. The monks worked as
agents of the king: they governed with great skill and efficiency, closely
imitating the methods of royal administration. Although monastic discipline was lax just before the monastery was dissolved in the sixteenth century, the Canterbury community showed a strong interest in external affairs.
Meanwhile, the large and wealthy Durham Priory revealed, according to
R. B. Dobson, "the universal aspirations and preoccupations of late medieval monasticism."[24] Zealous monks were aware of tradition, respectful of
education, energetic in administration, and unyielding in defense of their
privileges. A resilience that conquered adversity marked their economy.
Nevertheless, the prior and chapter were at the mercy of the agricultural
market, itself dependent on the weather. The monks at Durham success-
fully maintained recruitment and living standards despite the burdens of
mortality, warfare, and litigation. In intellectual activities the Durham community stood out among the English Benedictines. Histories of monasticism
and defenses of monastic rights manifest their corporate pride.

The French church on the eve of the Revolution of 1789 may have
been as flawed as English monastic observance at the Dissolution, but in

21. Maurus Wolter, *The Principles of Monasticism* (London and St. Louis, 1962);
Cuthbert Butler, *Benedictine Monachism* (London, 1919).

22. R. R. Bolgar, *The Classical Heritage and Its Beneficiaries* (Cambridge, 1954), p.
92. Jean Leclercq, *The Love of Learning and the Desire for God* (New York, 1962).

23. David Knowles, *The Monastic Order in England (940–1216)* (Cambridge, 1940,
1963); R. A. L. Smith, *Canterbury Cathedral Priory* (Cambridge, 1943, 1969); H. P. R.
Finberg, *Tavistock Abbey* (Cambridge, 1951); E. Miller, *The Abbey and Bishopric of Ely*
(Cambridge, 1951); R. B. Dobson, *Durham Priory, 1400–1450* (Cambridge, 1973).

24. *Durham Priory, 1400–1450*, p. 10.

both England and France earlier eras of religious fervor lived in the collective memory as examples of monastic life at its most glorious. If the monks of Canterbury could revere Lanfranc and Becket, and those of Durham, Cuthbert, the community of St. Germain des Prés had its own patrons, Vincent and Germain, and the relics of its Merovingian founders as well. The seventeenth century at the abbey in Paris represented the last glowing era of religious life there, a life that was intimately involved in the surrounding society of Louis XIV. Devoted as any monks could have been, the Maurists could never escape their age. Retreat from the sinful world did not dispense monks from the vicissitudes of old regime demography and agriculture, nor from public ceremonial obligations. As the monks of earlier ages had preserved ancient culture, so the monks of St. Germain des Prés edited secular and religious texts and wrote history supportive of established tradition and power. They were critical scholars, but they readily accepted official subsidies and encouragement; in short, even in scholarship they were well aware of politics.

Histories written by monks themselves remain the best starting points for research on the abbey. The chronological account of Dom Jacques Bouillart, published in 1724,[25] discusses the abbey's relations with powerful persons, building projects, and notable ceremonies. Although his work is not sufficiently critical by modern historical standards, Dom Bouillart did consult the documents and make some perceptive observations. He included a description of the church, a necrology, and a list of works written by his colleagues. Another Maurist, Dom Edmond Martène, wrote eulogies of his brothers in religion and a general history of the congregation, but his superiors thought his work lacked monastic modesty and refused him permission to publish. Consequently, Martène's accounts stayed in manuscript until this century.[26] In favor of monastic censorship it should be noted that his writing is dull, credulous, and repetitive, but his work is indispensable for modern historians of the Maurists. The Maurist history of the city of Paris, compiled by Michel Félibien and Guy-Alexis Lobineau, is also useful.[27] While all these works recognize the importance of scholarship, the *Histoire littéraire de la Congrégation de St. Maur* (1770) of Dom René-Prosper Tassin gives the most comprehensive biographical and bibliographical data on monastic writers.[28]

Modern works about St. Germain des Prés include studies in intellectual history, biography, spiritual and temporal dependencies, Maurist

25. *Histoire de l'Abbaye Royale de St. Germain des Prés* (Paris, 1724).

26. Published in Archives de la France monastique, beginning in 1928 with vol. 31, continued to 1954 in vols. 32–34, 42–43, 46–48.

27. See note 1, above.

28. Brussels, 1770, cited hereafter as Tassin, *Histoire littéraire*.

constitutions and liturgy. Around 1890 Emmanuel de Broglie wrote two volumes on Mabillon and the gatherings of outside scholars held at the abbey on Sunday evenings, and two more on Montfaucon to continue the story to the mid-eighteenth century.[29] A recent critic has described these books as "vivid" but "selective."[30] The 1928 dissertation of Joseph U. Bergkamp on Mabillon appears to have used de Broglie extensively.[31] A more scholarly treatment of Mabillon can be found in the biography by Dom Henri Leclercq,[32] which analyzes monastic correspondence and follows the high standard of Leclercq's earlier articles.[33]

As for social and economic history, Dom Pierre Anger's work on the dependencies of St. Germain des Prés is less satisfactory. It is a catalogue of parishes, religious houses, and lands under the abbey's jurisdiction, but lacks a coherent historical treatment of relations between the abbey and its subjects.[34] For the medieval period, the monograph by Françoise Lehoux on the Bourg St. Germain admirably performs this function as it traces the process of urbanization.[35] Agricultural life around Paris in the sixteenth and seventeenth centuries is the subject of Jean Jacquart's monumental *La Crise rurale en Ile-de-France*; St. Germain des Prés had seigneurial authority in four of the seven estates that he studied.[36] Once again, the pivotal significance of the abbey is emphasized.

The fourteen hundredth anniversary of the founding of St. Germain des Prés was marked in 1959 by the publication of a memorial volume of specialized essays.[37] Dom Jacques Hourlier's article on monastic life in this

29. *Mabillon et al société de St. Germain des Prés au XVIIe siècle* (Paris, 1888); *La Société de l'Abbaye de St. Germain des Prés au XVIIIe siècle: Bernard de Montfaucon et les Bernardins, 1715–1750* (Paris, 1891).

30. David Knowles, *Great Historical Enterprises: Problems in Monastic History* (London, 1963).

31. *Dom Jean Mabillon and the Benedictine Historical School of Saint-Maur*, Ph.D. diss., Catholic University of America (Washington, 1928).

32. *Dom Mabillon* (Paris, 1953–57). See the review by Dom David Knowles, *The Journal of Ecclesiastical History* 10 (1959): 153–73; reprinted in Knowles, *The Historian and Character and Other Essays* (Cambridge, 1963), pp. 213–39.

33. "St. Germain des Prés," *Dictionnaire d'archéologie chrétienne et de liturgie*, vol. 6, pp. 102–50. Leclercq also wrote the articles on "monarchisme" and "Mabillon."

34. *Les Dépendances de l'Abbaye de St. Germain des Prés*, in Archives de la France monastique, vols. 3, 4, and 8, 1906–09.

35. See note 7, above.

36. Paris, 1974. The St. Germain seigneuries are Thiais, Antony, Avrainville, and Monteclin. The last two of these will be mentioned in this work in parts 2 and 4, respectively. An English translation of Jacquart's summary, "French Agriculture in the Seventeenth Century," appears in Peter Earle, ed., *Essays in European Economic History, 1500–1800* (Oxford, 1974), pp. 165–84.

37. *Mémorial du XIVe centenaire de l'Abbaye de St. Germain des Prés* (Paris, 1959), cited herein as *Mémorial*.

collection is a short synthesis.[38] Dom P. Salmon analyzes the Maurist constitutions to explore the leaders' views of asceticism, but he frankly states that he has left aside "l'histoire proprement dite."[39] Essays on Maurist liturgy by Dominique Catta and Hubert Darré are also included. About the same time, the 1958 volume of *Mémoires* of the historical societies of Paris and the Ile-de-France contained four articles on St. Germain des Prés: one on the abbey's medieval stained glass and others on buildings, the courtyard, and plans.[40]

Where these and other publications have furnished information used in this study, they are cited. The Bibliothèque Nationale and the Archives Nationales in Paris are the main repositories of the mountain of documents from St. Germain des Prés, and references to their collections will appear frequently. Yet despite or perhaps because of the mass of material, it remains true that "there is no adequate and critical modern history of the Maurists."[41] Political histories of the congregation, perhaps influenced by the monks' own writings, do exist;[42] but no study combines intellectual, political, social, and economic aspects of the reform. The difficulty of such a project for seventeenth-century French monasticism as a whole is evident. Consequently, this work is limited to the Abbey of St. Germain des Prés. There is a story here, and a history as well. Did this major religious institution, organized for the purpose of praising God, conduct its affairs in rhythm with the affairs of men? Or, in other words, did this abbey conform to social and economic conditions that determined the fate of secular men and corporations? How should this outstanding example affect our views of religious retreat from French absolutist society? To answer these questions, it will be necessary to study the social and economic history of seventeenth-century France, seen large and small, from the vantage point of the royal abbey in Paris.

38. "La Vie monastique à St. Germain des Prés," *Mémorial*, pp. 81–100.

39. "Aux origines de la Congrégation de St. Maur: Ascèse monastique et exercices spirituels dans les constitutions de 1646," *Mémorial*, p. 102.

40. Philippe Verdier, "La Verrière de saint Vincent à St. Germain des Prés"; Hélène Verlet, "Les Bâtiments monastiques"; Françoise Lehoux, "La Cour du monastère"; Roger-Armand Weigert, "Plans et vues de St Germain des Prés," *Mémoires . . . Paris et Ile de France* (1958), vol. 9.

41. David Knowles, *Great Historical Enterprises*, p. 34.

42. Dom Paul Denis, *Le Cardinal de Richelieu et la réforme des monastères bénédictins*; Dosh, "Growth of the Congregation."

PART 1

Monastic Population

1

The Community of 1695

Who were the monks of St. Germain des Prés in the seventeenth century? The names that stand out are those of the great scholars—Jean Mabillon, Bernard de Montfaucon, Thierry Ruinart—pioneers of critical methods of reading charters and inscriptions, editors of the church fathers, learned writers of ecclesiastical and secular history. Some monks of St. Germain fit in this category, while others did not; yet all shared responsibility for regular observance and maintenance of the abbey. Someone had to administer the properties; someone had to lead the community in divine services, to announce and to propagate the word. Someone had to make certain that the candles were lighted and the buildings cleaned, someone had to watch over the library and the garden, the refectory and the dormitory.

Someone at St. Germain des Prés had to fulfill all the normal obligations that arose in any regular religious community. In 1695 Prior Arnoul de Loo prepared a list of monks with their assigned tasks:[1] thus, for St. Germain des Prés at the height of its glory, the community of scholars, the records show who was there and what he did. Through the use of chronicles, minutes of the chapter and the council, correspondence, and literary works, we can reconstruct that community, the individuals and the types who lived in it. In this chapter the governance of the monastery and its particular combination of scholarly and religious life will appear.

As the head of the abbey's administration, Arnoul de Loo may have been in an anomalous position. Prior of St. Germain from 1690 to 1696, and again from 1702 to 1708, he presided over a center of scholarship; yet he had grave doubts about the whole scholarly enterprise. He feared that excessive attention to studies might cause monks to neglect their religious observances. Two monastic writers have even suggested that de Loo formed a scheme to drive the scholar-monks from the Parisian abbey, thus intend-

1. Catalogue des officiers du monastère de St. Germain des Prés, nommé le 2 janvier 1695," Mélanges St. Germain des Prés, B.N. MS. fr. 16866, fol. 162.

ing to disperse the concentration of minds that had been carefully assembled over the preceding half-century.[2] Since de Loo was not a scholar himself, he may have lacked sympathy for study as divine service, complementary to the daily round of the office. His career in the congregation certainly suggested no special interest in learning. He had taken his vows at the typical age of nineteen at the Norman monastery of Jumièges, close to his native city of Rouen. Then he had risen rapidly to superiorship—when he first came to St. Germain, he was only forty-six, yet had already governed for twelve years at three other Maurist houses.[3] His was a respected but severe monasticism, ever conscious of the monks' highest duties: at the end of his life, when he served as superior general of the congregation, he had his personal papers brought to his sickroom and then ordered burned everything prejudicial, critical, and flattering.[4]

Consistent with his view of monastic duty, Prior de Loo prepared a catalogue of officers of the monastery on January 2, 1695, to assign work to all able-bodied monks without regard to their scholarly distinction. Spiritual and temporal matters took precedence over scholarly ones. The government of the abbey was effectively in the hands of the prior and his council, or *séniorat*. There the prior could consult with the monks most experienced in temporal matters. First of all, the prior relied upon his assistant, Jean Gellé, chosen by de Loo and also about fifty years old, with nearly thirty years of monastic experience. Gellé had been a teacher of theology, a missionary to the Huguenots, and a superior himself until continuing attacks of gout had forced him to retire.[5] Because of his great virtue and patience, his fellow monks regarded him as a saint.[6] From de Loo's point of view, Gellé's good nature was fortunately combined with a notable scholarly reputation: he had helped to prepare the Maurist edition of St. Augustine, assisted his colleagues in getting their works published, and was himself engaged in a study of Ivo of Chartres.[7] Gellé, experienced in superiorship and scholarship, respected and liked by his fellows, re-

2. Note in papers of Dom Michel Brial, B.N. MS. fr. 12804, fol. 126; *Nouveau Supplément* (cited hereafter as *N. Supp.*), vol. 1, p. 401; Friedrich Wiegand, "Mathurin Veyssière de la Croze als Verfasser der ersten deutschen Missiongeschichte," *Beiträge zur Förderung der christlicher Theologie* 6 (1902): 274. Cf. Bernard de Montfaucon on Loo: "aussi porté qu'on le puisse être pour nos études." B.N. MS. fr. 17680, fol. 269.

3. *Matricula Monachorum Professorum Congregationis S. Mauri . . . ,* Dom Yves Chaussy, ed. (Paris, 1959), no. 2142; *Nécrologe*, pp. 96–103.

4. *Nécrologe*, p. 98.

5. *Matricula*, no. 2444; *Nécrologe*, pp. 147–48.

6. Edmond Martène, *La Vie des justes*, pp. 171–74.

7. Tassin, *Histoire littéraire*, p. 473; *Nécrologe*, pp. 147–48; letter from Gellé to Edmond Martène, 11 April 1689, B.N. MS. fr. 25538, fol. 8: "If you have some works to print, we have here a bookseller . . ."

mained active in the council until 1714;[8] in the 1690s he contributed greatly to harmonious relations between prior and community.

From its own ranks the community elected Dean Jacques Guillebert, who also served on the council. A native of Pontoise, a river town north-west of Paris, Guillebert had been a monk for thirty-three years; his pre-vious responsibilities included superiorships and the direction of young monks in their studies.[9] At St. Germain, where new members of the con-gregation followed classes in philosophy and theology, Guillebert's sym-pathetic guidance must have been responsible for his popularity. He set an excellent example for the community by showing particular devotion to the Virgin Mary, at whose statue in the chapel he prayed several times a day.[10]

The last two members of the council served ex officio: these were the *procureur*, who represented the community in legal proceedings and nego-tiations; and the *cellerier*, the chief financial official. Jean Barré, the pro-cureur, stayed at St. Germain longer than any other monk; after taking his vows at Vendôme in 1648 he came to St. Germain as a student and stayed until his death in 1716. The necrology of the abbey describes him as "a peaceful man, who did good, of good sense, capable of giving good ad-vice in business matters."[11] Barré was the senior councillor; then already sixty-eight, he remained active in deliberations until he was nearly ninety. The post of cellerier that he had held for so long had been taken over in 1692 by André Olivier, a monk of about forty.[12] Although Olivier had been a monk for only sixteen years, the superiors of the congregation recog-nized his worldly skills. He represented several monasteries and the con-gregation in cases before the Parlements of Rouen and Paris. At St. Ger-main des Prés, "he knew the temporal extremely well"; as evidence of this knowledge we have his treatise on the possessions of the abbey in 1710.[13]

Prior and council were the government of the community, but what kind of community did they govern? Forty-four persons appear on the prior's list. They can be divided into three groups: first, the twenty-four mature monks, all of whom had been ordained and had belonged to the order for at least a decade each; second, twelve younger monks who had come to St. Germain to complete their studies prior to ordination; and

8. *Nécrologe*, p. 148.
9. *Matricula*, no. 2024; Nécrologe, pp. 90–91.
10. Ibid.
11. *Matricula*, no. 1262; Nécrologe, pp. 111–12.
12. *Matricula*, no. 3135; Nécrologe, p. 140.
13. Ibid., "Traité pour connaître l'état des biens. . . ," B.N. MS. fr. 16864; N. *Supp.*, vol. 2, p. 133.

finally, eight lay brothers, who served in material capacities. Several other persons were present but not on the list: monks languishing in the infirmary and the principal officers of the congregation, the superior general and his assistants, accounted for this group. Thus the total religious community at St. Germain des Prés numbered about fifty persons.

The road that led these monks to St. Germain began most often in the dioceses of northern France, where the great cathedrals and Benedictine abbeys inspired many vocations. Two-thirds of the monks of the choir came from Beauvais, Paris, Reims, and Rouen: in these areas centuries of donations by pious kings and lords had made ecclesiastical institutions wealthy and politically important. For the young city-dweller growing up in the shadow of the cathedral, or the peasant's son tilling the lands of an ancient abbey, religious life represented social respectability as well as eternal security. Families were able to protect or even to improve their social standing by sending children into the church. The reasons that impelled young men and their parents to consider the Benedictine Congregation of St. Maur are not difficult to fathom: the prominent role played by monasteries in the community as landlords and ceremonial leaders, the attraction of a secure life of devotion, and the experience of relatives and friends weighed heavily. In the community at St. Germain des Prés in 1695 many monks' lives tell of these influences.

Dom Nicolas de Villeneuve, for example, had two uncles who belonged to the Benedictine congregation; when he and his older brother Joseph were in their late teens, they paid a visit to one of their uncles at St. Germain des Prés. On the way from Orléans to Paris, both boys decided to become monks themselves. Their uncle introduced them to the superior general, who arranged for their novitiates.[14] Dom Benoît de Monceau d'Auxy d'Anvoile, one of ten children in a noble family near Beauvais, joined the Maurists with two of his brothers, although one transferred to the less austere observance of the Oratory.[15] Their family connection with Benedictine monasticism extended back at least as far as the fourteenth century, when their relative Guy II de Monceau ruled as abbot of St. Denis.[16] Simon Langellé, son of a *bourgeois de Paris*, had remarkably strong family ties to the Maurists and to St. Germain des Prés in particular. Three of his older brothers also joined the congregation, and

14. *Matricula*, no. 2581 (Nicolas), no. 2582 (Joseph); the uncles were Grégoire (no. 575), and Ignace (no. 836). *Nécrologe*, pp. 160–62; Martène, *La Vie des justes*, pp. 158–60.

15. *Matricula*, nos. 3769, 3307; Nécrologe de St. Denis, B.N. MS. fr. 8600, pp. 385–86; Martène, *La Vie des justes*, pp. 100–01.

16. *Gallia Christiana in provincias ecclesiasticas distributa. . . .* (Paris, 1715–1865), vol. 7, pp. 400–02; Nécrologe de St. Denis, B.N. MS. fr. 8600, p. 386.

his parents and his sister made generous donations and were buried at the Parisian abbey.[17]

Aside from those whose families were predisposed to Benedictine monasticism, there were others who reasonably chose this style of religious life because they thought it would offer them the proper balance of retreat, devotion, and study. Sometimes their entry into the cloister was preceded by a promising worldly career; they decided to become monks because of concern for their souls, not because of despair in the world. Traces of their past lives persisted in the abbey: Bernard de Montfaucon de Roquetaillade, who came from a military noble family and served for two years with Marshal Turenne, had a brusque and rough exterior that led Mabillon to refer to him as "the Sieur de Roquetaillade."[18] Thierry Ruinart, Mabillon's closest companion in studies, originally intended a career of scholarship in the world—although he was tonsured and a master of arts in his native city of Reims, "he barely knew the world when he became disgusted with it, and searched for a refuge to safeguard his innocence."[19] Yet once assigned to St. Germain des Prés, Ruinart continued his studies and produced monumental histories and editions of texts. Monastic life permitted nonscholarly careers as well: Daniel Deaubonne, a simple monk for more than thirty years, applied his artistic talents to sculpture in wood and ivory, miniature painting, gilding and copper work, and even the manufacture of lenses and microscopes—all of which he sold, with the permission of the superiors, who saw that the money went to the poor.[20] Among the lay brothers, who had been admitted specially for their crafts, there were a carpenter, a cook, and a baker: these more humble servants of the community could not aspire to the rank of monks of the choir, but they manifested their piety in attendance at services, frequent prayer, hard work, and edifying death.[21]

Once he had made the decision to try the monastic life, a young man could begin living at a monastery as a postulant, or candidate for admission. While it was theoretically possible to join the congregation at any monastery, not all of them accepted postulants. Certain houses, however, specialized in accepting and training new monks. The training centers in

17. *Matricula*, nos. 3461, 2944, 2993, 3123; Registre des mortuaires, B.N. MS. fr. 18818, fol. 356. See chap. 4, Borrowing, note 44.

18. *Matricula*, no. 3037; *Nécrologe*, pp. 199–204. See also E. de Broglie, *Mabillon et la société de St. Germain des Prés*, vol. 2, p. 269.

19. *Matricula*, no. 3020; Tassin, *Histoire littéraire*, p. 273.

20. *Matricula*, no. 1700; *Nécrologe*, pp. 104–05.

21. Gilles Allard, carpenter, *Matricula*, Frères convers (F.C.), no. 300, *Nécrologe*, p. 135; Mathieu Tocquigny, cook, F.C., no. 335; *Nécrologe*, p. 158; Marin de Lannois, baker, F.C. no. 348, *Nécrologe*, pp. 64–65.

the Parisian region included St. Rémi in Reims and St. Faron in Meaux. At these monasteries regular communities of experienced monks set the example for younger men and decided on their fitness for monastic life. If a postulant liked what he saw, and if the community approved his vocation, he declared his intention and entered the novitiate, or probationary period. During this time, usually one year, the new monk came under the direction of a master of novices, an experienced monk who helped newcomers learn their obligations. A set of instructions for masters of novices illustrates what was expected: the master was to know his novices well, judge the strength of their vocation, and form and guide them according to the spirit of the rule of St. Benedict.[22] The master had a duty to examine and instruct his novices carefully, to test their physical, mental, and spiritual aptitude for monasticism. Several times during the probationary period, usually at three-month intervals, the community of professed monks at the training center would vote on the continued acceptability of the novices.[23] Only an exceptional young monk like Thierry Ruinart received unanimous approval at both St. Rémi and St. Faron, where the training center was transferred during his novitiate.[24]

The successful postulant who took the habit in his late teens became the novice, and, after his formal profession of vows, the monk of the choir in his early twenties. Although recorded in the matriculation registers as a full member of the congregation, the young monk had not yet completed his training. Unlike the Trappist Abbé de Rancé, who expressed great reluctance to ordain monks for the priesthood,[25] the Maurists encouraged all of their members to follow two years of study in philosophy and theology that culminated in ordination. Even after his ordination the young monk spent another year in *recollection*, rededicating himself to the monastic life by living under the guidance of a director, repeating the exercises and practices of the novitiate.[26] Study and ordination, just as novitiate, were possible at all monasteries; but again the Maurist congregation had designated special centers for these purposes. Thus every year classes of about fifteen young monks came to St. Germain des Prés, where they had the opportunity to learn from the intellectual elite of the congregation: in addition to the standard program of studies, conducted by

22. Firmin Rainssant, "Les Industries du maître des novices," B.N. MSS. fr. 19629. 19630.

23. For examples of votes, see the book of receptions of novices (*frères convers*) at St. Germain des Prés, B.N. MS. fr. 18821.

24. Tassin, *Histoire littéraire*, p. 273.

25. A. J. Krailsheimer, *Armand-Jean de Rancé* (Oxford, 1974), pp. 74, 244.

26. Edmond Martène, *La Vie du vénérable père Dom Claude Martin* (Tours, 1697), p. 44.

monastic teachers, the students received an apprenticeship in scholarly research and writing. If they showed special aptitude, they might be taught
Greek and Hebrew, sigillography and diplomatics—the languages and
techniques necessary for religious and historical studies. Bernard de Montfaucon, himself a graduate of this training system, later commented as a
teacher that "the monks of this class (1696) who understand Greek
rather well . . . can be put to work on manuscripts," and, he noted ap-
provingly, "all are good monks."[27]

To be a good monk: this was what the young should learn and the
old should teach. Prior de Loo emphasized participation and responsibility
to this end. Old and young monks worked together to maintain the material and spiritual aspects of the abbey; the more specific tasks given to
the students appear all the more striking. Perhaps the community could
tolerate the absence from services of one of its seven older confessors, or
assign the task of carrying the relics to others, if Montfaucon and the two
teachers of theology, Pierre Cordier and Henri Bouzenet, were otherwise
occupied. Yet others performed essential services: Brother Jean Plet
awakened the community for matins; Brothers Jacques Bouillart and
Lucien de Norroy rang the bells for the divine office; Paul Bryois and
Gervais Boucicaut carried the lanterns in front of the community. These
men could not easily be missed. The young monks also had charge of the
tombs: those of the Merovingian kings, founders of the abbey; of the
Duke of Verneuil and the Count of Vexin, uncle and son respectively of
the reigning monarch at Versailles.[28] Less pleasant tasks, such as washing
dishes and disposing of wastes, normally done by servants, were also sometimes assigned to monks of the choir. By this means the Maurist superiors
sought to teach humility. Even a scholar like Mabillon, for example, had
as a young monk at Notre Dame de Nogent taken care of the chickens.[29]

To be a good monk meant to be faithful and exact in observing the
rule, to be obedient and helpful in performing the assigned tasks. The
younger monks, whose average age in 1695 was twenty-six, could look
forward to more than thirty years of additional religious life.[30] The more
permanent members of the community, who had already proved themselves hardy souls, had an average age of forty-six, and were to live even

27. Montfaucon to Claude Martin, 10 Jan. 1696, B.N. MS. fr. 25538, fol. 359v; par-
tially cited in the *Nécrologe*, p. 153.
28. Cat. des off., B.N. MS. fr. 16866, fol. 162.
29. H. Leclercq, *Dom Mabillon*, vol. 1, p. 48; cites Martène, *La Vie des justes*, vol.
3, pp. 24–25.
30. Calculated from *Matricula*: n = 12, in 1695, mean = 26, s.d. = 2.61, geometric
mean = 26; at death, mean = 59; s.d. = 17.31, g.m. = 57. See the following chapters
for detailed studies.

longer. Their average age at death was seventy-one, which may seem high
by general preindustrial standards.[31] The main point is that St. Germain
des Prés was a monastery dedicated to regular observance and study in
life, instead of a monastery dedicated to preparation for *death*, like La
Trappe, where the median age of death was under forty, and where more
than half of the entrants were dead within five years of their arrival.[32]
Since the Maurist emphasis was on long and useful life, their lengthy
preparation in study and practice is understandable. The Maurists expected
themselves to exercise scholarly and sacerdotal functions within the context of Benedictine monasticism, and to exercise them for a long time.

Since Maurist monks often completed the novitiate at one monastery,
studied for the priesthood at another, and then served in still other communities, they moved more often than other regular clergy. By their vow
of obedience they were bound to go where the superiors sent them. While
Benedictine monks have traditionally understood the vow of stability to
mean lifelong membership in one religious house, the Maurists applied
the concept to the congregation rather than to the individual monastery.[33]
The more perfect integration of experience in individual communities was
sacrificed to the fellowship of the wider reformed community. Movement
tended to increase spiritual vitality and to uphold regularity of observance.
The active superior might order stricter discipline or a course of studies at
another house when it was appropriate for the individual monk and the
community. The beneficial effect of concentrated effort on scholarship can
be seen in the hundreds of folio volumes researched, written, and edited
at St. Germain des Prés.

As a result of these transfers, only one of the students of 1695 later
died at St. Germain des Prés. Even this monk, Jacques Bouillart, did not
stay in Paris all of the time from his student days until his death in 1726;[34]
he spent some years at the Abbey of St. Nicaise in Reims, where in 1703
he wrote and illustrated the Gradual and Antiphonal.[35] In 1705 Bouillart
returned to St. Germain to serve as sacristan. He then presided over the
redecoration of the church according to his own designs and wrote its
history.[36] Two other monks, promising assistants of Montfaucon, might
have stayed at St. Germain permanently if they had not died early: Michel
Philippe ended his days in 1699 at Jumièges, where he had been sent for

31. Calculated from *Matricula*: n = 24; in 1695, mean = 46, s.d. = 10.91, g.m. =
45; at death, mean = 71, s.d. = 11.40, g.m. = 70.
32. Krailsheimer, *Armand-Jean de Rancé*, p. 92.
33. Cuthbert Butler, *Benedictine Monachism*, pp. 121, 244.
34. *Matricula*, no. 3719; *Nécrologe*, pp. 152–55.
35. *N. Supp.*, vol. 1, pp. 60–61.
36. *Nécrologe*, p. 153.

a change of air and milk treatment; Paul Bryois, chosen to travel to Rome with his mentor to search for Greek manuscripts, died in the course of the mission in 1700.[37]

What happened to the student monks once they became priests? Their life histories suggest three types of monastic careers—superiors, scholars, and ordinary monks. Let us reconstruct one life as a pattern for each of these, following the paths of the Maurists in the late reign of Louis XIV. First, the superior, Benoît de Monceau d'Anvoile, whose noble origins have already been mentioned. In September of 1695 the abbot of St. Germain des Prés, Cardinal Guillaume Egon von Fürstemberg, ordained Dom Benoît.[38] Several months later Bernard de Montfaucon mentioned him as one of the young monks who could help with the preparation of Greek manuscripts—at that time principally the works of St. Athanasius—which were being prepared for the printer.[39] It appears that Benoît de Monceau did not publish any scholarly works of his own; perhaps he sensed that his greater gifts lay in administration. The Congregation of St. Maur included about two thousand monks in 180 French monasteries, and at each of these a prior or abbot governed; consequently, there was a continuing need for competent and politically acceptable superiors. Benoît de Monceau's first position of responsibility was assistant prior of St. Crépin de Soissons, which he held in the opening years of the eighteenth century. His success in this appointive post led the general chapter of the congregation to elect him to a series of priories—first at St. Crépin, then at St. Eloi de Noyon, and finally at St. Thierry and St. Basle, both near Reims, where he served from 1705 until 1717. During this time he showed particular devotion to the task of giving extreme unction—he was always ready to minister to the last needs of his monks and of seculars. An incident from his term at St. Thierry is particularly touching: an epidemic of scarlet fever ravaged the countryside around the monastery. In one village the parish priest and many other inhabitants were already dead when the prior arrived. He took care of those in material need, encouraged the living and visited the sick to prepare them for death. Unfortunately, he caught the disease himself and felt certain that he would die; thus he asked to receive the last rites in the church, in public, among the people he had come to help. But God, "content with the disposition of his heart, yielded him to the tears of the poor,"[40] and he survived. By 1717 Dom Benoît retired from superiorship,

37. Philippe, *Matricula*, no. 3694; Martène, *La Vie des justes*, vol. 2, pp. 150–51; Bryois, *Matricula*, no. 3699; *Nécrologe*, p. 59.
38. Nécrologe de St. Denis, B.N. MS. fr. 8600, p. 385.
39. Letter, 10 Jan. 1969, B.N. MS. fr. 25538, fols. 358–59v.
40. Nécrologe de St. Denis, B.N. MS. fr. 8600, p. 386.

although he was only forty-eight. Political factors may have played a role, however, since he became known for his Jansenist sympathies, described as "love for the truth and its defenders."[41] He went to live at St. Denis, where he took charge of the seigneurial documents, the *censives* and *terriers* of the abbey. His work required him to visit the countryside to collect the dues from the peasantry—even the small *rentes*, under his administration, amounted to "a rather considerable revenue."[42] When he had to leave the monastery on his errands, he took along two hard-boiled eggs, some bread, and a half-bottle of wine for sustenance, but often enough he gave these provisions to the poor he met on his way. In 1723 there was another epidemic, this time of smallpox; again Dom Benoît went from house to house to help the sick, ignoring the danger to himself. Eventually he too fell victim to the disease, and on his deathbed, at the age of fifty-four, he received the sacraments "burning more with the fire of charity than with [the fever] of his disease."[43] His virtue earned him a lengthy account in the necrology of St. Denis and mention in the congregation's book of *The Life of the Just*. While his illustrious ancestry may have been seen as worthy of note, it is clear that his exemplary character counted for more in the memory of his fellow monks.

If there was a dark cloud on the horizon for the student monks of 1695, it came from the Jansenist-Jesuit controversy about grace. The Congregation of St. Maur had already been compromised by declarations of sympathy for the Jansenists, the ideological party that favored strict interpretation of St. Augustine's writings. Dom Gabriel Gerberon, sometime scholar of St. Germain des Prés, had escaped to the Netherlands, where he published inflammatory tracts.[44] The Maurist edition of the works of St. Augustine naturally attracted the critical eye of the Jesuits, particularly when Dom Thomas Blampin included some commentary written by the arch-Jansenist Antoine Arnauld.[45] Despite the vigilance of orthodox superiors, the rebelliousness of the monks increased tremendously after the publication of the papal constitution *Unigenitus* in 1713. Superiors like Dom Benoît de Monceau, who questioned papal authority and joined the appellants, found themselves removed from office and exiled from Paris.

For a monastic scholar, associating with the Jansenists, "the friends of the truth," meant risking the loss of academic freedom, being denied access to libraries, printers, and friends. Dom Edmond Jean-Baptiste Duret

---

41. Ibid.

42. Martène, *La Vie des justes*, vol. 3, pp. 100–01.

43. Nécrologe de St. Denis, B.N. MS. fr. 8600, p. 386.

44. Jean Orcibal, "La Spiritualité de Dom Gabriel Gerberon, champion de Jansenius et Fénelon," *Mémorial*, pp. 151–222.

45. Tassin, *Histoire littéraire*, p. 473.

was a Parisian scholar who suffered for his intransigence. Born in a "très honnête famille" in 1671, he went to school at Jesuit *collèges*, where he learned rhetoric and philosophy, although he practiced a stricter "morality very different from that of his masters."[46] Young Duret placed himself under the protection of the Virgin Mary, and decided to become a monk. After his profession at St. Faron in 1689, he first studied for the priest-hood at St. Denis; there again he came under the influence of a teacher whose views were close to those of the Jesuits. The turning point in Duret's life occurred when he met Pierre Nicole, a leading theologian of the Jan-senist movement. As Duret often repeated the story later in life, Nicole said to him: "My little brother, you are being fooled. If there is one Jan-senist in the world, it is I. I do not believe anything of all that your master has dictated to you in your theses, nor anything that he has made you say is admitted and upheld by the Jansenists."[47]

Afterwards Duret made a careful reading of St. Augustine and came to share Nicole's opinions. In 1699 he started teaching theology at St. Denis and St. Germain des Prés. For thirteen years he led critical attacks on the Jesuits, frequently embarrassing masters and disciples when they presented their theses at Paris. In 1703 Duret made the acquaintance of Mlle. de Joncoux, a pious lady who gave him seventy folio volumes of manuscripts from the Jansenist convent of Port-Royal des Champs. These Duret placed in the St. Germain library for safekeeping. *Unigenitus*, in-tended as the final word of the Church on grace, appeared after Duret had stopped teaching theology, but he joined the appellants and was forced to leave St. Germain des Prés. At first the exile took him only to St. Denis, but when he persisted in his opposition, he was transferred to Beauvais, to Pontoise, to Meulan, and finally to St. Riquier near Amiens. These changes of domicile, although they generally took place over long intervals, sought to remove him from scholarly circulation, certainly from the glittering Parisian learned society around St. Germain. For a monk who had worked for two years with the great Mabillon, who enjoyed public theological dis-cussion with the Jesuits, and who wrote extensive dissertations (many of which remain unpublished), the penalties for his recalcitrance were severe. Yet Duret remained exact in his monastic observance even toward the end of his long life; he bore his increasing infirmity with heroic patience, and died at eighty-six in "sweet and tranquil agony."[48] His scholarly career represents that of a number of appellants. With their forced departure St. Germain des Prés lost much of its distinction, and their absence must in

46. Ibid., p. 730; *Matricula*, no. 3825.
47. Tassin, *Histoire littéraire*, p. 731.
48. Ibid., p. 733.

part explain the dimmed luster of the Parisian abbey as a center of scholar-ship in the eighteenth century.[49]

Superiors and scholars may make an order famous, but that order cannot be devout and exact in observance without the ordinary monks. Less is known, of course, about them: sometimes only the dates and places of their profession and death are recorded, and their characters remain in the shadow of the cloister, beyond all hope of retrieval. This is a sign of their success. When they joined the congregation they became *morts civils*, dead to the world and its vanities. They sought to efface themselves; among them flowed a strong current of opinion that even the most virtuous and learned of their number ought not to be memorialized. Their grave-stones bore no names, only a cross and the date of death; their superiors tried to prevent the publication of biographies and even histories.[50] What information, then, do we have about them? Precious little: Rare is the letter or funeral announcement, thirty or fifty years after student days in Paris. Dom Léger Le Roy wrote from Senlis to Montfaucon at St. Germain in 1727: he would certainly subscribe to the edition of *Monuments of the French Monarchy*, he recommended the bailiff of his monastery, and he sent his best wishes.[51] For Dom Gervais Boucicaut, another St. Germain student in 1695, there is an obituary notice that sheds more light.[52] Dom Gervais was born at Antony, one of the seigneurial possessions of St. Ger-main des Prés. He too had professed at St. Faron in 1688. Although his studies gave him a taste for learning, he read only the scriptures and the church fathers. From his reading Dom Gervais collected material for ser-mons, which he delivered at several monasteries where he handled the ministry to the parish. Thus he came into frequent contact with secular persons. At St. Rémi de Reims, he wrote a description of the laying of the cornerstone of the new cloister in 1709.[53] When his health weakened after thirty-two years of monastic life, he went to St. Denis to retire in 1720. There he lived piously for another quarter of a century. From time to time he would be carried away by his own vivacity, but when he had offended anyone he would tearfully beg forgiveness. Despite his chronic suffering, Boucicaut observed the rule faithfully even toward the end of his life. He

49. See Emmanuel de Broglie, *La Société de St Germain des Prés au XVIIIe siècle: Bernard de Montfaucon et les Bernardins*.

50. See the *avertissement* in Martène's life of Claude Martin: "la grande modestie dont ces pères font profession, ne leur ayant pas permis jusqu'ici de mettre en jour les actions mémorables. . . ." This unauthorized publication earned the author punishment from his superiors, who never approved the printing of his *Vie des justes* and his history of the congregation.

51. Letter, 17 March 1727, B.N. MS. fr. 17702, fol. 2.

52. Nécrologe de St. Denis, B.N. MS. fr. 8599, p. 139; *Matricula*, no. 3762.

53. *N. Supp.*, vol. 1, p. 55.

also wrote the abbey's book of "memorable events" and was still dictating it on his deathbed in 1747.[54] Altogether his was an ordinary monastic life. Gervais Boucicaut neither rose to high offices nor wrote great folio volumes; yet without the years of regular observance that he and hundreds of others gave to the congregation, the glory of the Maurist scholars would have been, in their own eyes, hollow.

"Monks were scholars only in order to fortfy their spiritual life."[55] Scholarship went hand in hand with their observance, so much so that one contemporary wrote of Mabillon, "One is surprised that he can work, keeping to the regular observance as he does during the day."[56] For the monks, as one superior described it, it was a case of rendering unto Caesar (scholarship) that which was owed to Caesar, and rendering unto God (devotion) that which was owed to Him.[57] The international renown of St. Germain des Prés sprang from the scholarly work of a few monks: less than a dozen mature members were officially engaged in literary activity. They may have formed half of the older group at the abbey, but their proportion of the total community was much smaller. The small absolute number of scholars underlines their remarkable productivity, and at the same time points to the fragile nature of the scholarly plant within the congregation. To be successful, scholarship required official support: the superiors had to agree that study, as well as every other monastic activity, "ought to terminate in God, which will happen if you study only in relation to his glory and in the order of obedience."[58]

Scholarly work in groups helped maintain the correct ideals and allowed superiors to control the workers. First, group scholarship presupposed a series of master-disciple relations. From the time of Grégoire Tarisse, superior general from 1630 to 1648, St. Germain des Prés had been the center of monastic scholarly patronage. Dom Luc d'Achery, librarian of the abbey, took on a series of disciples to help him publish gleanings from old manuscripts in his *Spicilegium*. Among these disciples were Hugues Mathoud, Claude Chantelou, Jean Mabillon, and Edmond Martène.[59] This joint effort became a model for others: one or two monks

54. Nécrologe de St. Denis, B.N. MS. fr. 8599, p. 139.

55. Odette d'Allerit, "Comment on travaillait à St. Germain des Prés sous la direction de Dom Claude Martin," *Revue d'Histoire Moderne et Contemporaine* 4 (1957): 212.

56. P. Léonard de Sainte Catherine, cited by Bruno Neveu, "La Vie érudite à Paris à la fin du XVIIe siècle," *Bibliothèque de l'Ecole des Chartes* 124 (1966): 507.

57. Claude Martin to a young monk, 6 Feb. 1690, B.N. MS. fr. 19661, fol. 37. Cf. Jean Leclercq, *The Love of Learning and the Desire for God.*

58. Claude Martin, ibid.

59. Jeannine Fohlen, *Dom Luc d'Achery et les débuts de l'érudition mauriste* (Besançon, 1968), p. 11.

would take primary responsibility for a project, then draw on younger colleagues for help in copying manuscripts, checking references, preparing tables, and proofreading. Along the way the principal author or editor obtained aid from secular librarians and learned men all over Europe. The wide range of research often necessitated visits to Parisian and more distant manuscript collections. While every monk in the congregation learned theology and philosophy for the priesthood, the masters of research at St. Germain also taught their disciples more specialized knowledge. When Mabillon became a master himself, for example, he taught Thierry Ruinart the Greek language, as well as the rules and methods of research.[60] A distinguished master might have several disciples, and these in turn had links to one another and disciples of their own.

The relations among the monks of the 1690s are complex and instructive, for they show the monastic network during its most productive period. Two major scholarly patronage groups were at work. D'Achery, who died in 1685, had built the first of these around the St. Germain library; its leading members were Mabillon, Ruinart, and Michel Germain. They concerned themselves principally with Benedictine history: Mabillon wrote a detailed Latin history of the order, century by century; Ruinart published the complementary work on the acts of the Benedictine saints; and Germain organized studies of the monasteries in France. The second group, working on the Greek fathers of the Church, owed its being to Dom Claude Martin, a Maurist leader whose prestige in the outside world was enhanced by the saintly reputation of his mother, Mère Marie de l'Incarnation, first superior of the Ursulines of Canada.[61] As assistant superior general for several terms from 1668 to 1690, Martin sponsored the Maurist editions of St. Augustine, St. Athanasius, St. Jerome, and St. John Chrysostom. The idea of Greek studies reportedly came to Martin in a conversation with Etienne Deschamps, a Jesuit who regretted that his own order did not have enough trained Greek scholars for an edition of the Fathers.[62] Martin was "a useful counsellor and a powerful protector"[63] to his well-known protégés, Bernard de Montfaucon, Antoine Pouget, Jacques Loppin, and Jean Martianay. Under Martin's influence the first three came together at St. Germain des Prés in 1687, and the following year they produced a volume of *Analecta Graeca*, excerpts from Greek writers. Next the three young Hellenists worked on editions of Athanasius and Chrysostom, while Martianay edited Jerome and wrote translations and studies of the Bible.

60. Tassin, *Histoire littéraire*, p. 274.
61. Martène, *La Vie de Claude Martin*; Tassin, *Histoire littéraire*, pp. 163–76.
62. D'Allerit, "Comment on travaillait," p. 213.
63. Tassin, *Histoire littéraire*, p. 585; *Nécrologe*, p. 201.

Masters and disciples worked best side by side, but the congregation's need for superiors in provincial houses took precedence over joint scholarly projects at St. Germain. When monastic scholars were separated, they wrote to each other to maintain contact: out of this correspondence we can draw a picture of the master-disciple relation. Claude Martin and Bernard de Montfaucon, for example, lived together at St. Germain des Prés only from 1687 to 1690, but both before and after this time they exchanged warm personal letters. Montfaucon, aged about thirty, was stationed at the monastery of La Grasse near Carcassonne when their correspondence began; Martin, who had been a monk for over forty years, wrote from St. Germain. In 1686 the young monk announced his desire to edit the works of St. John Chrysostom, and Martin approved wholeheartedly. Since the annual diet of the congregation would soon provide an opportunity to ask for official sponsorship of the project, Martin asked Montfaucon to write a short sample of his work and to have it corrected by Antoine Pouget and Jean Martianay.[64] By June the master had received the sample: "You have followed well the suggestions that I made to you, except one, that is not to be too bold in your learning and not to make considerable changes without advice."[65]

Martin saw that his disciple needed to learn tact and better Latin: these were themes to which he returned time and again in subsequent letters to Montfaucon. Indeed, his firm guidance is shown in his correspondence with all his disciples.[66] It would be good, he thought, to read some classical Latin every day, not Cicero's orations, which he found too bombastic, but other, less affected works: the critical humanistic Latin of Jacques Sirmond, Marc-Antoine Muret, and Jean Mabillon ought to be the student's goal.

One notices in these authors a correct and light Latin—one that is not overburdened with thoughts, a defect of those who are not well styled in these sorts of works and who want to put in everything they know. It is necessary to show that one is knowledgeable, and to this end one word may sometimes suffice. . . .[67]

64. Claude Martin to Bernard de Montfaucon, 29 March 1686, B.N. MS. fr. 19661, fol. 25.

65. Martin to Montfaucon, 8 June 1686, B.N. MS. fr. 19661, fol. 26.

66. See Martin to Pouget, 2 Oct. 1684 and 26 Oct. 1685, Martin counsels more serious study of Greek and Hebrew, reading as well as grammar. B.N. MS. fr 15793, fols. 49–51; similar advice to Dom Etienne Deschamps, n.d., B.N. MS. fr. 19661, fol. 53; both cited by d'Allerit, "Comment on travaillait," pp. 216–17.

67. Martin to Montfaucon, 20 March 1687, B.N. MS. fr. 19661, fol. 32; cited by d'Allerit, "Comment on travaillait," pp. 218–19. Cf. letters of 8 June 1686 and 1 Feb. 1687, B.N. MS. fr. 19661, fols. 26, 31.

In midsummer of 1686 Montfaucon moved from Carcassonne to Bordeaux, and there he received Martin's letter reporting the superiors' decision on scholarly projects. Martin had called a meeting of Parisian savants to discuss the relative merits of editions of Chrysostom and Athanasius. Almost all of those present ("seven or eight") thought that the monks should work on Athanasius first; thus Montfaucon, Pouget, and Loppin were ordered to begin with him. Mabillon had found some relevant manuscripts on his trip to Italy, but the young scholars would have to take great care to distinguish genuine works of Athanasius from ones incorrectly attributed to him.[68] Martin and Montfaucon corresponded about once a month during this period. The student sent samples of his work and questions, and the master responded with critical notes, suggestions for reading, and editorial hints: "People approve your method, but think that you should add remarks on points of dogma and discipline because these remarks are in fashion at the moment."[69]

Martin was not insensitive to market considerations. He kept a critical eye on his disciples, but when he was pleased with their work, he gave them lyrical praise. "I have received your little abstract, like the smell of a good meal that makes the mouth water, and gives desire to taste the meats. That means," Martin told Martianay, "that I am waiting ardently for your first volume of St. Jerome, which will certainly be a rare and sought-after piece."[70] When he succeeded in bringing young monks to St. Germain in 1687, he could observe and counsel them more closely; he strengthened their linguistic and critical skills, and he helped them to buy or borrow the books and manuscripts they needed.

For three more years the scholars of St. Germain enjoyed Martin's personal guidance. Then, at the general chapter of the congregation in 1690, Martin was elected prior of Marmoutier, a monastery near Tours. With much regret he left Paris for his new post; his disciples were distraught, and one even insisted on going with him.[71] But the others had to stay behind, and for them Martin had words of counsel: "It was a joy for me to be with you, and to support you in your studies, but we must go where God calls us."[72] Claude Martin emphasized the monk's higher obligations. The scholars in Paris could rely on Dom Simon Bougis, assistant superior general, for support: Martin had given him a list of the monastic writers and their projects. For advice on dealing with publishers, he recom-

68. Martin to Montfaucon, 9 Aug. 1686, B.N. MS. fr. 19661, fol. 28.
69. Martin to Montfaucon, 1 Feb. 1687, B.N. MS. fr. 19661, fol. 31.
70. Martin to Martianay, 29 Oct. 1693, B.N. MS. fr. 15793, fol. 84; cited by d'Allerit, "Comment on travaillait," p. 221.
71. Edmond Martène, author of the life of Martin.
72. Martin to Montfaucon, 8 June 1690, B.N. MS. fr. 19661, fol. 38.

mended Dom Jean Prou, depositary of the congregation. Perhaps Martin had a premonition that he would not return to St. Germain des Prés: at any rate, he was already seventy-one years old, and he knew that he would have to give up his active role of master of studies.[73]

Yet Martin's disciples kept him informed of their progress. They sent him abstracts and finished works—Martianay's controversial pieces as well as the beloved editions of the church fathers.[74] For their edition of Athanasius the Parisian monks needed the help of others, and Martin's influence was often persuasive. To mine the rich Vatican archives, for example, Montfaucon wrote to Dom Jean Guillot and Dom Claude Estiennot, the Roman representatives of the congregation. He pointed out the need for a new edition and stated his intention of collating manuscripts and correcting texts. To do this work properly, he asked them to check and copy materials for him in Rome. Montfaucon did not, however, have to worry about whether the Roman agents would help him, for affixed to his letter was a quiet postscript:

> I pray you, my reverend Father, to be so good as to give your support to our workers of St. Athanasius. I shall be obliged to you for it.
>
> Fr. Claude Boistard[75]

Boistard was the superior general of the Congregation of St. Maur. That he spoke in favor of the project testifies both to Montfaucon's influence, probably arranged through Martin, and to the leader's positive attitude to study. References and copies of documents soon flowed back and forth between Paris and Rome. Meanwhile, Jacques Loppin died in late 1693, Montfaucon and Pouget visited the libraries of Reims and Laon in 1694, and six student-monks at St. Germain helped read the Greek manuscripts.[76]

Martin never regretted having brought Montfaucon to Paris.[77] His satisfaction increased with each report on the Athanasius project. Despite the economic crisis of French publishing, Martin hoped that the work would find a reputable printer; this hope was fulfilled when Jean Anisson, printer to the king, contracted for the edition. Now the monks could be

73. Martène, *La Vie de Claude Martin*, gives his birthdate as 2 April 1619 and notes move to Marmoutier, p. 176.

74. D'Allerit mentions the St. Jerome and works of biblical criticism. "Comment on travaillait," p. 223.

75. Montfaucon to Guillot, 12 Nov (1691?), B.N. MS. fr. 17701, fols. 97–98v.

76. Loppin, *Matricula*, no. 2990; research trip, Montfaucon to Guillot, 14 Sept. 1694, B.N. MS. fr. 17701, fol. 48; young monks, note 27, above.

77. "Je ne me repentirai jamais de vous avoir fait venir à Paris . . ." Martin to Montfaucon, 6 June 1690, B.N. MS. fr. 19661, fol. 43.

assured that the work would be well printed, with less difficulty, fewer interruptions, and greater sales.[78] By mid-1695 Montfaucon reported that the first two folio volumes had been printed, but because of "the difficulty of commerce" the editors and publisher resolved to await completion of the third and final volume before beginning sales. They feared that the public would buy only the two volumes of authentic works of Athanasius, leaving the third volume of doubtful miscellaneous pieces sitting on the booksellers' shelves. By selling only complete sets, as Mabillon had done with his St. Bernard, Montfaucon and his team guaranteed a uniform demand for all three volumes.[79]

Montfaucon, for all his bursts of spirit, had a strong sense of scholarly discipline. "We are working diligently, and we must do well in order to make a large Greek and Latin volume in two years. . . ."[80] He told Jean Guillot exactly what he wanted from the Roman libraries; he became impatient when information did not arrive as soon as possible; and he wrote to Estiennot, the senior Roman agent, when Guillot needed prompting.[81] The amount of work may be judged by Montfaucon's contemporaneous description to his patron: "Our brothers in Rome have sent us everything they have been able to find in the manuscripts . . . of the Vatican, and of others . . . . Our brothers, after having transcribed all they could find of St. Athanasius, are working to collect all the passages for my plan."[82] Indeed, Guillot and Estiennot had plenty to keep them busy: about the same time, Antoine Pouget, Jean Mabillon, and Jean Martianay sent them requests for research material.[83] Pouget, for example, wanted documentation about rites and ceremonies of the church; he knew he was asking a great favor, and he would be patient, even if they could only work for him "at [their]

78. Martin to Montfaucon, 16 Aug. 1690, and an undated letter written before the end of 1693, B.N. MS. fr. 19661, fols. 44, 72. Cf. Henri-Jean Martin, "Les Bénédictins, leurs libraires et le pouvoir: notes sur le financement de la recherche au temps de Mabillon et de Montfaucon," *Mémorial*, pp. 273–87. Martin's larger work discusses the political and economic situation of book publishing: *Livre, pouvoirs et société à Paris au XXVIIe siècle (1598–1701)* (Geneva, 1969).

79. Montfaucon to Martin, 31 July 1695, B.N. MS. fr. 12764, fol. 240; printed in *Bibliothèque de l'Ecole des Chartes* 83 (1922), 269–71; Montfaucon to Guillot, 23 Jan. 1695, B.N. MS. fr. 17701, fol. 50.

80. Montfaucon to Martin, 31 July 1695, B.N. MS. fr. 12764, fol. 240.

81. Montfaucon to Guillot, 16 Mar. 1692, 13 July 1693, 7 Mar. 1695, 21 Mar. 1695, B.N. MS. fr. 17701, fols. 46, 47, 53, 56, etc. Montfaucon to Estiennot, 26 July 1694, B.N. MS. fr. 17701, fol. 16. See also the published letters in E. Gigas, ed., *Lettres des Bénédictins de St. Maur* (Copenhagen, 1892–93), vol. 1, letters 59 (25 April 1695), p. 221; and 65 (10 October 1695), pp. 234–38.

82. Montfaucon to Martin, 31 July 1695, B.N. MS. fr. 12764, fol. 240.

83. Pouget to Guillot, 24 July 1695, B.N. MS. fr. 17681, fol. 73; Mabillon to Estiennot, 19 Dec. 1694, B.N. MS. fr. 19649, fol. 272; Martianay to Estiennot, 1 October 1690, in Gigas, *Lettres*, vol. 1, no. 46, p. 165.

leisure, little by little, first one thing, then another. Perhaps if the thing deserves it," he went on, "I could have a collection printed here . . . ;" and the kindness of the Roman workers would not be forgotten.[84]

It may have been easy for Montfaucon, supported by his superiors, to obtain the aid of other Maurist monks. But he needed information from persons outside the congregation as well, for the manuscripts of Athanasius were dispersed over Europe. From Germany, the Netherlands, England, and Italy, men of learning sent Montfaucon their precious treasures. How did he obtain that cooperation? By themselves flattery and dedication might have prompted some members of the republic of letters, but Montfaucon appealed to their self-interest as well. In a typical letter to a librarian of Milan, Montfaucon asked to borrow a manuscript; he and Mabillon, famous throughout Europe, guaranteed its safe return and promised to deliver, postpaid, a finely bound set of the finished work to the lending library.[85] Through this kind of correspondence and exchange, the monks made friendships and acquired valuable material. Yet the enterprising Montfaucon thought that better organized efforts were necessary. He wrote to his patron, Dom Martin, that he had difficulty gaining access to libraries. Recently the Séguier library had been closed, and the monks were able to work in the Colbert Library only because of the kindness of Etienne Baluze, the current librarian. It would be prudent, Montfaucon thought, to collate all the manuscripts in the libraries that were still open. Six monks, working in pairs, could collate three authors at a time and transcribe the best texts. First they would copy the Greek fathers of the church, then the profane Greek authors, and finally the Latin authors. Montfaucon hoped to gather the best materials: "One would make a collection on which one could work perpetually without needing the influence of anyone. And the library of St. Germain des Prés would become the most considerable in the world in this field, without it costing the congregation anything."[86] Of course the purpose of this project would have to be kept secret, so as not to excite envy! The modern scholar, taken aback by Montfaucon's ambition and imperialism, must recall that he faced enormous obstacles in his research: many manuscript collections were carelessly kept; centralized files—even catalogues of printed books—often did not exist; and access to libraries depended on influence and goodwill.

Montfaucon lived in an age when it was still possible to buy or steal ancient manuscripts, and this scholarly opportunity did not escape him either. He would be working, either at the abbey or the royal library, when

84. Pouget to Guillot, 24 July 1695, B.N. MS. fr. 17681, fol. 73.
85. Montfaucon to a librarian, 12 April 1696, B.N. MS. fr. 17701, fol. 161.
86. Montfaucon to Martin, 10 Jan. 1696, B.N. MS. fr. 25538, fol. 359.

treasures from the Orient arrived. Alas, many of these were disappointing to him: one load, he said, contained "hardly anything that did not exist ten times already among the manuscripts of Paris."[87] The problem lay in the ignorance of the buyers, who chose books by their bindings rather than by their contents. This could be remedied only by sending scholars to do the buying. Naturally the irrepressible Montfaucon, the former soldier, volunteered to go to the Mediterranean himself. His proposed itinerary included Florence, Rome, and Venice; then he would make a cruise around the Mediterranean coasts, stopping at Corfu, Cephalonia, Athens, Mount Athos, Constantinople, . . . even Damascus and Egypt before returning via Sicily and Calabria.[88] "This journey should not make one afraid—there is nothing more common at present than people who make it."[89] Can it truly be said that this monk had given up the world when he entered the cloister? If Montfaucon alone had such ideas, he might be considered an aberration in the monastic pattern; and yet his superiors did not reject his proposal out of hand. Claude Martin, "notre père commun,"[90] died shortly afterwards in 1696, before he could see the finished edition of Athanasius published two years later.[91] In 1698 the superiors did send Montfaucon and his pupil, Dom Paul Bryois, on a research trip to Italy. Had the unforeseen deaths of Estiennot and Bryois not kept Montfaucon in Rome as procureur for the congregation, he might well have gone on his dream journey, and the Bibliothèque Nationale would be even richer in oriental manuscripts today.[92]

Group scholarship by nature attracted gregarious individuals. To belong to the scholarly group at St. Germain meant to view the world of learning from a privileged place, and many were the monks who sought permission to live there.[93] When one had to leave St. Germain, even to be

87. Ibid.

88. See Fernand Braudel, *The Mediterranean and the Mediterranean World in the Age of Philip II* (New York, 1972), vol. 1, pp. 103–08, on sailing along coastlines.

89. Montfaucon to Martin, 10 Jan. 1696, B.N. MS. fr. 25538, fol. 359v. He had suggested the trip before, in his letter of 31 July 1695, B.N. MS. fr. 12764, fol. 240, but he was less specific then.

90. Gervais Boucicaut to Edmond Martène, 10 Sept. 1696, B.N. MS. fr. 19661, fol. 62.

91. Martin died on August 9, 1696, *Matricula*, no. 1021.

92. Montfaucon had to be persuaded by Superior General Boistard to take the job. See Boistard's letter of 17 May 1700 in B.N. MS. fr. 17703, printed in the *Nécrologe*, p. 202. Montfaucon's travel diary is now B.N. MS. fr. 19640; his published account of the trip, the *Diarium Italicum* (Paris, 1702).

93. E.g., Alexis Edouard wrote from Redon to Luc d'Achery, 21 June 1651: "J'ai conçu des beaux dessins que j'ai déjà même commencé dans les intervalles de mon loisir, mais ils ne peuvent s'éclore ni se former que parmi les bons livres, tels qu'ils sont en votre belle bibliothèque, et dans la communication avec les doctes. Si vous me pouviez

a superior at another monastery, monks openly expressed their regret and condolences. Consider the case of Pierre Coustant: despite his prayers, tears, and remonstrances, he had to interrupt his studies in 1693, when he became prior of Notre Dame de Nogent: three years later his return to St. Germain brought rejoicing.[94] For those who could not come to the Parisian abbey, correspondence provided the means to participate in its scholarly glory. The volume and quality of the letters are remarkable; if at times they strayed from purely academic subjects to secular and ecclesiastical gossip, the writers were trying to seize the whole atmosphere of learned life and describe it for their distant brothers.

What a correspondence it was! Two monks as well placed as Michel Germain in Paris and Jean Guillot in Rome found enough *nouvelles* to write each other once a week. They rushed to finish letters before the departure of the *ordinaire*, or regular courier; the postage costs rose so high that Depositary Jean Prou complained loudly.[95] But the letters continued to stream back and forth, and the writers themselves expressed concern at their own candor. Certainly the superiors knew about the correspondence, which they thought necessary to scholarly work. Michel Germain even read aloud Guillot's spicy reports during the community's recreation period, "without taking care that there were some sharply critical spirits."[96] Was it consistent with the monastic purpose to revel in the vanities of the world? In 1692, after five years of this news from Rome, Superior General Boistard ordered Guillot to break off his correspondence under threat of being recalled to France. In a last letter to Germain that apparently suffered censorship, Guillot explained that simple jealousy had brought about the ban, and that the reasons cited by the superiors—Guillot's lack of judgment, his rashness, and the possible embarrassment to the congregation—were all excuses.[97] Nevertheless, recognizing his obligation to obey, Guillot kept silent for several years, and Michel Germain died in 1694. At the beginning of 1695, however, Guillot found a new Parisian correspondent—Bernard de Montfaucon. Montfaucon had perfectly plausible reasons for writing to Rome: he needed the material for the Athanasius

---

aider à obtenir cette grâce des supérieurs pour demeurer ou à St. Germain, ou aux Blancs-manteaux, vous obligeriez une personne qui tâcherait de la reconnaître." B.N. MS. fr. 17684, fol. 93; cited by Fohlen, *Dom Luc d'Achery*, pp. 98–99.

94. Edmond Martène to Pierre Coustant, 16 June 1969, B.N. MS. fr. 12804, fol. 117; *Nécrologe*, pp. 127–32.

95. "En particulier, sur les ports de lettre, il était intraitable." *Nécrologe*, p. 79. ". . . des officiers plaignent quelquefois du port des lettres," Montfaucon to Estiennot, 7 March 1695, B.N. MS. fr. 17701, fol. 17v.

96. Montfaucon to Guillot, 4 July 1695, B.N. MS. fr. 17701, fol. 66.

97. Guillot to Germain, 8 April 1692, B.N. MS. fr. 19646, fol. 232.

project. He promised to be more careful than Germain: "As for me, I treat [your letters] with so much circumspection that you need fear nothing similar."[98] Still, Guillot was alarmed when he learned that the correspondence had been discovered by the superiors, although Montfaucon told him that he was getting upset about nothing. True, in Guillot's letter that had fallen in the hands of the superiors, there was some excessive praise that might be interpreted as flattering Montfaucon's vanity; yet the superiors made no move to stop the renewed correspondence, perhaps because they were very pleased with the Athanasius project.[99] When they did delay, censor, or withhold letters, Montfaucon waxed indignant: "I am very angry . . . . It would be annoying if you had sent me something good that was lost."[100]

These scholar-monks had good reason to take an active interest in life outside the cloister. Would contentious books be published or banned? Would their authors be rewarded or punished? Mabillon, Montfaucon, and their comrades were neither exempt from nor indifferent to criticism; they worried about being contradicted, censured, and exiled. State and religion regarded certain ideas as dangerous, and Maurist scholarly ventures such as the edition of St. Augustine often came close to incurring official disapproval. The intensely polemical seventeenth century is reflected in Benedictine correspondence, filled with all the struggles between "defenders of the truth" and spokesmen for orthodoxy, between historical critics and religious traditionalists, and between strict constructionists and moderate interpreters of religious rules. Some of these struggles were bound to involve the monks themselves. In the early 1690s, for example, the Abbé de Rancé and Mabillon had been embroiled in a vitriolic controversy over the value of monastic studies. Afterwards, Dom Estiennot drew the lesson: "one must live in peace even with those who do not wish it."[101] Yet this did not mean more retreat so much as better information. As Montfaucon noted, "Literature is so much like war . . . ,"[102] and one cannot go to war without intelligence.

Some of the St. Germain scholars may have loved the heat of battle more than the light of learning, but all of them, as members of the republic of letters, the international network of scholars, needed the "good intelligence" in which they lived.[103] News of the latest discoveries and

98. Montfaucon to Guillot, 4 July 1695, B.N. MS. fr. 17701, fol. 66.

99. Montfaucon to Guillot, 3 Oct. 1695, 10 Oct. 1695, in Gigas, Lettres, vol. 1, nos. 64, 65, pp. 231–38; also, letter of 23 Oct. 1695, B.N. MS. fr. 17701, fol. 77.

100. Montfaucon to Guillot, 29 Aug. 1695), B.N. MS. fr. 17701, fol. 96.

101. Estiennot to Mabillon, 7 July 1693, B.N. MS. fr. 19644, fol. 122; quoted by Leclercq, Dom Mabillon, vol. 2, p. 574.

102. Montfaucon to Guillot, 14 Feb. 1695, B.N. MS. fr. 17701, fol. 51.

103. "On vit céans en fort bonne intelligence . . . ," Montfaucon to Guillot, 18 April

publications was essential to them: their correspondents in benighted areas, such as Leibniz in Germany, always regretted hearing the news long after everyone else.[104] Thus we can understand the monks' desire to be informed even when not involved—this explains their interest in the great controversialists. When the arch-Jansenist Antoine Arnauld died in 1694, his arguments did not die with him, for his friends published his posthumous works and his enemies attacked his memory in death as violently as they had criticized his views in life. Montfaucon thought the ephemeral pamphlets, the sarcastic and the hagiographic epitaphs, remarkable enough to collect and send to his friends in Rome.[105] The literary critic Adrien Baillet also drew monastic attention for his *Lives of the Saints*: Montfaucon wished that Baillet had not written it, and other monks wrote to Mabillon to ask his opinion of critical studies that cast doubt on traditional beliefs.[106] Pierre Bayle and Richard Simon appeared repeatedly in letters because of their problems with censors. The Huguenot and skeptical views of Bayle practically demanded suppression of his *Historical and Critical Dictionary*. While agreeing with the censors that the book presented a danger to the general public, the monks nonetheless hoped that the chancellor of France would authorize the sale of a hundred copies to "les gens savants."[107]

Should it be surprising that these monks, men of learning in a time that still restricted freedom of opinion, bought and read forbidden books, sometimes without the approval of their superiors? Their scholarly curiosity led them to seek out hidden and suppressed knowledge; the questioning of their own beliefs that resulted from encounters with the unorthodox sometimes had far-reaching consequences. Richard Simon, one-time Oratorian priest turned Biblical critic, could publish his books at Paris only because of the protection of the archbishop, François de Harlay. "In my opinion," declared Montfaucon, "there are hardly any works that have greater need of correction than those."[108] Yet this same Montfaucon schemed to purchase Simon's critique of the New Testament, even when

1695, B.N. MS. fr. 17701, fol. 59; partly cited in Broglie, *Mabillon*, vol. 2, p. 275.

104. ". . . Nous avons le malheur dans ce pays-ci de n'apprendre ces choses que bien tard." Leibniz to Mabillon, 14 April 1867, B.N. MS. fr. 17680, fols. 102–03.

105. Montfaucon to Guillot, 27 June 1695, 11 July 1695, 12 Feb. 1696, B.N. MS. fr. 17701, fols. 64, 67, 88; poems and epitaphs, B.N. MS. fr. 17701, fols. 69–70.

106. Montfaucon to Estiennot, 24 Sept. 1696, B.N. MS. fr. 17701, fol. 32v.; Hilarion Monnier to Mabillon, 15 Jan. 1702. B.N. MS. fr. 17680, fol. 266. Cf. the opinion of P. Léonard de Ste. Catherine in Neveu, *La Vie erudite*, pp. 490–93.

107. Montfaucon to Guillot, 17 Dec. 1696, 31 Dec. 1696, and 14 Jan. (1697), B.N. MS. fr. 17701, fols. 94, 95, 84. Cf. P. Léonard de Ste. Catherine, B.N. MS. fr. 24472, fol. 83.

108. Montfaucon to Guillot, 23 Oct. 1695, B.N. MS. fr. 17701, fol. 77.

Depositary Prou refused to advance the money for it. Booksellers such as Jean Anisson cooperated by supplying and shipping Parisian works in exchange for books from Rome.[109] Despite the censorship of the government and the congregation, the monks of St. Germain des Prés managed to read what they pleased.

But even so, did their unorthodox reading produce any remarkable effects? The community of St. Germain des Prés in 1695 counted only one monk who later carried his doubts as far as apostasy, and his was a special case. This renegade, Mathurin Veyssière, had led a colorful life before joining the order. The son of a trading merchant of Nantes, he left home at age fourteen as a cabin boy on a ship bound for the West Indies. When he returned from Guadeloupe several years later, Veyssière discovered his father in reduced circumstances; he then resolved to join the Benedictine congregation. At Marmoutier, where he pursued his studies, he had Jacques Loppin as a teacher.[110] Veyssière's own scholarly work included participation in the Maurist history of Brittany, a group project subsidized by the estates of that province.[111] By 1695 he had been a professed monk for twelve years. If he was discontented, his fellow monks did not mention it in their letters—until the spring of 1696, when he abruptly disappeared from the cloister. Of course, a monk could simply walk away, but to succeed in his escape, he needed outside help. About the time of Veyssière's departure, Gabriel Groddeck, professor and librarian at Danzig, was visiting Paris. Groddeck became friendly with Montfaucon, who later wrote him a recommendation to Estiennot at Rome.[112] Apparently the Lutheran Groddeck agreed to hide Veyssière for several months at his lodgings; his part in the escape did not come to light until much later, for he remained a learned correspondent of Montfaucon.[113] The Maurists searched widely for Veyssière, even in Italy, where Estiennot investigated rumors of a suspect seen in Florence.[114] But by the summer of 1696 the renegade had made his way to Basel: there he not only rejected his monastic vows but also publicly embraced Calvinism. In later life Veyssière styled himself "de la Croze"; he married and became tutor and librarian at the Prussian court in Berlin. He continued his scholarly work with

109. Montfaucon to Guillot, 7 July 1695, B.N. MS. fr. 17701, fol. 65.

110. *Matricula*, no. 3396; Tassin, *Histoire littéraire*, p. 163; *N. Supp.*, vol. 2, p. 267.

111. Madeleine Laurin, "Les Travaux d'érudition des Mauristes," *Mémorial*, pp. 237–41.

112. Montfaucon to Estiennot, 3 Sept. 1696, B.N. MS. fr. 17701, fol. 28.

113. See the letters in Gigas, *Lettres*, vol. 1, nos. 69, 71, 73, pp. 250, 255, 261–80.

114. ". . . je ne sais si ce ne serait pas Veyssière. Je le fais chercher, mais je n'ai pas encore pu le détenir." Estiennot to Mabillon, 16 June 1696, in Gigas, *Lettres* vol. 1, no. 67, p. 245.

essays and histories, and he always had high regard for the Benedictine order and for Montfaucon in particular, although his own life was happier outside the confines of regular religion.[115] Veyssière asserted that he had left St. Germain des Prés because he feared Prior de Loo would not let him continue with his scholarship, but is it not more likely that monastic life itself was too restrictive for his high spirits? His later works show a remarkable vivacity, as well as an enlightened guiding principle: "The most dangerous of all prejudices is to believe that one has none of them."[116] Other monks willingly suffered reprimands and exile for their religious causes, but remained part of the Maurist congregation; Mathurin Veyssière de la Croze was an exception.

From simple lay brothers to erudite masters of scholarship, from pious chanters to religious rebels, the monks of St. Germain des Prés encompassed a wide range of devotion and divine service. Each of its members had assigned tasks, consistent with his aptitude and station. Yet St. Germain des Prés did not exist in isolation; the abbey was part of the larger congregation of St. Maur, whose headquarters it housed. To understand St. Germain in its proper context, the historian must now turn away from the warmth of individual and collective biographies; the mass of documentation requires a colder statistical treatment of the French Benedictine monks as a whole. From where did these monks come? And what were the patterns of their lives? These questions inspire the next part of this history.

115. *N. Supp.*, vol. 2, pp. 267–68.
116. C. E. Jordan, *Histoire de la vie et des écrits de M. de la Croze* (Amsterdam, 1741), p. 337. See also Wiegand, "Mathurin Veyssière."

2

Demography of the Congregation of St. Maur

The scholars of St. Germain des Prés had been selected from all the reformed Benedictine monks of France. For this reason the social history of the learned Parisian community is inextricably linked with that of the larger group, the Congregation of St. Maur. The act of affiliation of 1631 had continuing consequences—a change from local to national recruitment of monks, and their periodic transfer to and from the abbey. St. Germain des Prés and other Maurist monasteries drew on a pool of thousands of individuals, whose lives are chronicled in the matriculation records.[1] These records allow us to establish the size and growth of the reformed congregation, the geographic origins and movement of individual monks, the age of monks when they entered the cloister, the length of a religious lifetime, and the rate of mortality. In short, the matriculation registers provide the information needed for monastic demography.

The Maurist monks represent a sizable historical population. From 1607 to 1690 inclusive, 3,901 Benedictine monks took vows to the congregation.[2] The demographic study of this group, presented in cold, impersonal tables and graphs, does not have the warmth and reassuring familiarity of individual biographies. Yet by keeping their records the Maurists not only strengthened the ties of membership for themselves, but also simplified our task of reconstructing the basic reality of life and death in an early modern religious community. To understand St. Germain des Prés in the seventeenth century, it is necessary to understand the general demographic pattern of monastic life.

How large was the congregation? The total population actually in the

---

1. The published edition of *Matricula monachorum* is by Dom Yves Chaussy (Paris, 1959).

2. Dom G. Charvin, "Contribution à l'étude du personnel dans la Congrégation de St Maur, 1612–1789," *Revue Mabillon* 46 (1956): 107–14. Charvin used the then unpublished *Matricula* in B.N., MS. lat. 12794–12797, and A.N. LL 994–97.

monasteries was the number of professions less the number of deaths and departures from monastic life up to that time. While the matriculation records give a running count of professions that can be used as an index of recruitment, only adjusted figures can show when growth, stable replacement, or actual decline took place. By studying the monks who joined the Maurist Congregation from its beginnings around 1620 to 1690, population figures were produced; these were checked and extended to 1790 by Dominique Julia.[3] Table 1 and graph 1 summarize the results: Starting from a small base, the congregation enjoyed rapid growth in its first fifty years, then stability around two thousand monks from 1670 to 1760, followed by a slow decline until the French Revolution.

The figures in the table and the steep slope of the graph testify to the explosive growth of the Congregation of St. Maur in its first decades. Professions were running far ahead of deaths: between 1621 and 1630 the population quintupled, and in the next decade it doubled again. In the early years of the reform, manpower was actively recruited to join in the work of religious revival. Each newly acquired monastery needed a con-

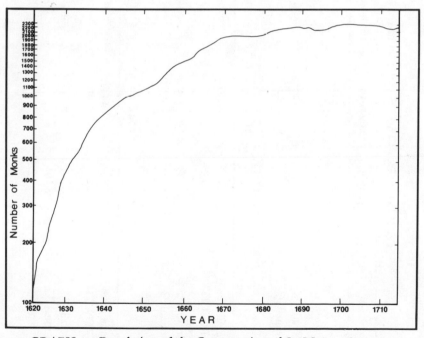

GRAPH 1   Population of the Congregation of St. Maur, 1622–1715

3. M. Julia and I were in contact during the summer of 1976, when he was preparing his article, "Le Recrutement d'une congrégation monastique à l'époque moderne: les Bénédictins de St. Maur," read at the Colloque de St. Thierry, October 1976. I am grateful for his counsel.

TABLE 1 Growth and Population of the Congregation of St. Maur

		1620	1621–30	1631–40	1641–50	1651–60	1661–70
Monks	Population	80	421	840	1098	1472	1907
	Growth		341	419	258	374	435
Rate	Decade %		426%	99.5%	30.7%	34.1%	29.6%
	Annual %		18.1%	7.2%	2.7%	3.0%	2.6%

		1671–80	1681–90	1691–1700	1701–10	1711–20	1721–30
Monks	Population	1987	2146	2222	2178	2145	2087
	GROWTH	80	159	76	−44	−33	−58
Rate	Decade %	4.2%	8.0%	3.5%	−2.0%	−1.5%	−2.7%
	Annual %	+0.4%	+0.8%	+0.3%	−0.2%	−0.2%	−0.3%

		1731–40	1741–50	1751–60	1761–70	1771–80	1781–90
Monks	Population	2065	2111	2101	1896	1764	1646
	GROWTH	−22	+46	−10	−205	−132	−118
Rate	Decade %	−1.1%	+2.2%	−0.47%	−9.8%	−7.0%	−6.7%
	Annual %	−0.1%	0.2%	−0.0%	−0.9%	−0.7%	−0.7%

tingent of reformed monks to take possession of the buildings and to repair the accumulated dilapidation of years of neglect. Since each house added to the congregation brought additional revenue, the superiors could justify rapid expansion of the membership, commensurate with spiritual needs and temporal resources. At times the spread of the reform even required borrowing, but for economic reasons alone the rate of growth could not continue at the initial heady pace. The strain on resources limited the membership.

While graph 1 shows an increasing population at least until the 1670s, the rate of growth was actually tapering off much earlier. The mature congregation strove for a population in line with internal economic resources. Once most of the Benedictine monasteries of France had been reformed, rapid growth through acquisition ended; either there was internal growth or none at all. If the Maurists had stopped accepting novices, their total population would have declined as the remaining members died over the years. Such a pattern can be seen for this period at the Jansenist convent of Port-Royal-des-Champs, where recruitment was forbidden by royal order.[4] As the Congregation of St. Maur collectively reached maturity the number of deaths counterbalanced the number of professions. By the 1670s the net change in population from year to year was occasionally negative.

From a graph of deaths and professions, it is evident that deaths played only a minor role in determining the size of the population during the early decades. Yet in three short periods, the early 1630s, 1650s, and 1660s, the deaths rose sharply before falling back to more normal levels. New peaks in professions occurred in 1635, 1656, and 1664, only a few years after peaks in deaths. Were these tendencies in separate indices related? If the annual number of professions is compared with the number of deaths three years before, there is a marked degree of statistical correlation.[5]

The incidence of death was largely independent of human influence, but there is evidence that the superiors of the congregation consciously adjusted the number of professions. Dom Martène's history notes that many monks died of plague in 1631—eight at Toulouse alone. After prayers to the Virgin the illness ceased and new professions rose dramatically.[6] God had rescued the monasteries when they made themselves more

4. William Ritchey Newton, "Port-Royal and Jansenism," Ph.D. diss., University of Michigan, 1974, vol. 2, pp. 182–93.

5. Correlation of professions with deaths of three years before, 1640–70, R = .73, Standard error = .08. Tendencies in professions appear to lag behind those in deaths because of the time required for an institutional response.

6. Dom Edmond Martène, *Histoire de la Congrégation de St. Maur*, vol. 32, pp. 28–32.

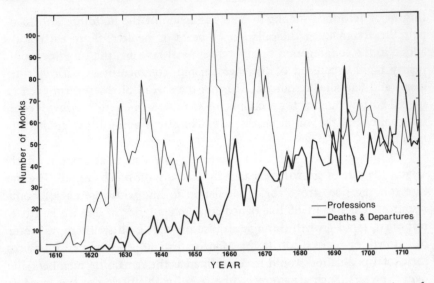

GRAPH 2   Professions and Deaths with Departures in the Congregation of
St. Maur, 1607–1715

receptive to applicants for membership. The memoirs of Dom Bernard
Audebert, assistant to the superior general in the 1650s, mention the leaders' troubled view of the deaths of 1652:

> The heat was very great this summer, and especially toward the
> end, the illnesses were incredible almost everywhere. This was
> felt in several of our monasteries, and above all at St. Denis.
> There most of the inhabitants are dead, and in the abbey there
> were twenty-two sick monks, five of whom have died. The ser-
> vants, and all who were sent to help them, were sick.[7]

The wars of the Fronde were in full swing around Paris, and it was believed that the stay of the court at St. Denis had corrupted the air of that
town. At the same time plague in Toulouse had again increased the number of monastic deaths and reduced the number of novices.

Audebert and other superiors clearly sensed the effects of political
and social conditions. They felt compelled to pray for more young men,
and they saw the sudden appearance of many postulants as the answer to
their prayers. In September of 1653, the Maurists organized a new center
for training novices at St. Denis, "pour ne refuser les grâces du ciel."[8] The
conscious response to demographic crisis is striking: within two years professions were definitely on the rise, from 33 in 1653 to 57 the following

7. Dom Bernard Audebert, *Mémoires*, vol. 11, p. 241.
8. Ibid., pp. 277, 284; need for more monks, p. 296.

year, then to 75, and to 108 (1656). Did the superiors then realize that they had overcompensated for their losses? In following years the downward slope of the professions was as steep as the earlier rise. Perhaps the monasteries discharged some novices who were preparing for final vows, but it is more likely that they permitted these men to continue, and instead closed the doors to new postulants. What is important is the superiors' ability to replenish the population: the crowd of applicants stood just outside the cloister.

More than others in seventeenth-century France, the monks of St. Maur could respond to impersonal demographic forces. The fluctuations of the 1630s and 1650s, when increased mortality led to increased recruitment, were echoed in the 1660s, after another period of general demographic crisis in France.

In considering these changes in monastic population we may ask whether professions and deaths were in step with general trends of the century. Historians of the *Annales* school have accepted grain prices as indicators of general conditions in a predominantly agricultural society.[9] Bad harvests and consequent high prices had a murderous effect on poor people, the overwhelming majority of the nation. Reduced yields often meant that large farmers went bankrupt despite high prices, while landowners and tax collectors had trouble collecting their revenues. Fluctuations in monastic population also coincided with high prices. The revolts of the Fronde (1648–53) and the beginning of the personal rule of Louis XIV (1660–62) saw grain prices reach new highs, four or five times the levels of the 1640s.[10] During the Fronde, marauding armies ravaged the countryside, destroying crops and making people more susceptible to epidemic disease: the result was demographic catastrophe. One-third or even two-thirds of the population died in some villages of the Parisian region: in particular, the year 1652 was marked by *surmortalité*, an extremely high death rate.[11] The early 1660s may have been even worse, as prices rose to the highest level of the century, and the government was forced to import grain from the Baltic. Unlike the monks who could replenish their numbers by accepting more postulants, the general population declined absolutely in these periods.

Viewed against this background, changes in monastic population illustrate the monks' ability to respond to social crises. Peaks and valleys in

9. Pierre Chaunu, "Au XVIIe siècle, rythmes et coupures à propos de la mercuriale de Paris," *Annales, E.S.C.* 19 (1964): 1171–81.

10. Pierre Deyon, *Amiens, capitale provinciale* (Paris and The Hague, 1967), p. 46. Pierre Goubert, *Beauvais et les Beauvaisis* (Paris, 1960).

11. Jean Jacquart, *La Crise rurale*, pp. 681–85.

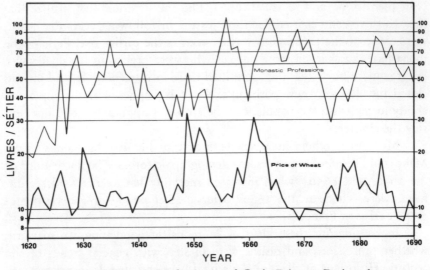

GRAPH 3   Monastic Professions and Grain Prices at Paris, 1620–90

the graph of wheat prices clearly led the lines of monastic deaths and professions during crises: there is also a moderate correlation between general movements in professions and prices. While the figures stop short of
proving lockstep association, they suggest that monastic population was influenced by external demographic trends. Even though they ate well, the
Maurist monks were not immune to the contagious diseases that afflicted
the rest of the French population, weakened by famine and war. As they
noted bad social conditions and the deaths of their colleagues, the monks
sought new recruits—and found them. In responding with resilience, the
Maurists showed conscious control.

Of course, the size and growth of the Maurist congregation did not
depend on the price of grain alone: political and personal factors also
caused monks to leave the cloisters. When Richelieu's project for a union
of the Congregation of St. Maur and the Congregation of Cluny failed, a
number of monks went from one group to the other.[12] The protection of
great nobles and religious enthusiasm affected the membership too.[13]
Transfers occurred back and forth between the Maurists and the Cister-
cians as one group or the other was perceived to have stricter observance.
In the 1650s Dom Audebert asserted that the flow was in the Maurists'
favor.[14] By the 1670s, however, the movement had been reversed, and the
flow streamed toward the Cistercian Abbey of La Trappe in Normandy.

12. *Matricula*, nos. 97, 108, 193, 861. See also Dom Paul Denis, *Richelieu et la
réformes des monastères bénédictins.*
13. Terence L. Dosh, "Growth of the Congregation."
14. "Jadis quantité de Bénédictins ont passé dans l'ordre de Cîteaux . . . à présent

Under the leadership of the Abbé de Rancé, this monastery attracted attention by its extreme rigor. Members of other religious communities came to La Trappe, sometimes without the permission of their superiors.[15] Viewing this situation with alarm, the Maurists appealed to Rome to prohibit monks from leaving their monasteries without written consent of their superior general. On July 1, 1672, Pope Clement X confirmed Maurist authority and ordered the abbot of La Trappe to send back members of other orders who were staying there illegally.[16]

Jansenism, a blend of stern theology, severe penitential practice, and political resistance, also threatened the peace of the Maurist Congregation and the unity of the church.[17] The superiors of the congregation never wavered in their firm opposition to Jansenism: monks were forbidden to read Jansen's works and all commentaries on them, and had to sign formularies condemning the famous five propositions supposedly found in Jansen's *Augustinus*.[18] Official visitors searched for copies of Pascal's *Provincial Letters,* "to tear them out of the hands of our monks and superiors, and to burn them, or at least to lock them away with the heretical and forbidden books."[19] Yet in spite of these drastic measures, the fire of Jansenism would not go out, and the dangerous ideas continued to appeal to certain monks: some, like Dom Gabriel Gerberon, wrote tracts and fled to Belgium or Holland.[20] Here was another reason for departures from the congregation: a few monks even died in exotic Utrecht, headquarters for recalcitrant Jansenists in the eighteenth century.

The geographic origins of Maurist monks reveal regional influences in the congregation. These are best studied in the matriculation records of each monk's native *diocèse*, or area under the spiritual jurisdiction of a bishop. Although they were not necessarily compact or contiguous, nor

---

c'est vice-versa." Audebert, *Mémoires*, p. 278. Cf. Louis J. Lekai, *The Rise of the Cistercian Strict Observance in Seventeenth–Century France* (Washington, D.C., 1968).

15. Annales Congregationis Sancti Mauri, B.N., MS. lat. 12790, fol. 334+. Cf. A. J. Krailsheimer, *Armand-Jean de Rancé.*

16. B.N., MS. lat. 12790, fol. 336.

17. Recent works in English on Jansenism include F. Ellen Weaver, *The Evolution of the Reform of Port-Royal* (Paris, 1978); William Ritchey Newton's work, already noted; and Alexander Sedgwick, *Jansenism in 17th–Century France: Voices from the Wilderness* (Charlottesville, Va., 1977). One important later episode has been chronicled thoroughly by B. Robert Kreiser, *Miracles, Convulsions, and Ecclesiastical Politics in Early Eighteenth–Century Paris* (Princeton, 1978).

18. For St. Germain des Prés, see the Livre des choses mémorables, B.N., MS. fr. 18816, fol. 101 (1664); fol. 110 (1665).

19. Règlements confirmés, 1660, A.N., L 814, no. 25. Earlier prohibitions appear in R.c., 1654, A.N., L 814, no. 12, and in Règlements nouveaux in the same source.

20. Jean Orcibal, "La Spiritualité de Dom Gabriel Gerberon, Champion de Jansénius et de Fénelon," *Mémorial*, pp. 151–222.

always reflective of administrative or cultural realities, the dioceses formed geographic units useful for our study.[21] France had 139 dioceses in 1789 —a few of recent creation, but most were centuries old.[22] There was a major change in diocesan organization in 1626, when Paris was raised to an archdiocese with its own dependencies; later in the century Louis XIV's annexation of Strasbourg brought another important diocese to France.[23]

Generally speaking, the dioceses of northern France were larger and more populous than those in the south. The archbishop of Rouen controlled 1,388 parishes, and his colleagues at Bourges, Chartres, and Limoges had over 800 each; simultaneously, many bishops in the south had only 20 or 30 parishes.[24] In part this can be attributed to patterns of early Christian settlement, but the presence of the popes in Avignon also helped to create the imbalance.[25] Dioceses varied in size, and the numbers of parishes illustrate orders of magnitude of population.

Even with these cautionary remarks in mind, we find the uneven geographic distribution of monks striking. Over 50% of the 2,289 monks who joined the congregation from 1641 to 1680 came from just 12 dioceses.[26] Rouen alone furnished 236 monks, or 10.3% of the total. The next four dioceses in importance—Clermont, Paris, Le Mans, and Limoges —each had over a hundred monks in forty years. Although Clermont and Limoges are in central France, nine of the top twelve dioceses were north of the Loire River. The southern bishoprics and the large cities, aside from Paris, Rouen, and Amiens, made a poor showing. Lyon and Orléans sent fewer men to the monasteries than did Autun, Sées, and Lisieux; Toulouse, Bordeaux, and Nantes were even farther behind. Perhaps owing to the small size of the diocese, Marseille produced only two monks in the whole

21. On dioceses, see Marcel Marion, *Dictionnaire des institutions de la France aux XVIIe et XVIIIe siècles* (Paris, 1923), p. 177; *Gallia Christiana*; and regional studies such as Louis Perouas, *Le Diocèse de La Rochelle de 1648 à 1724* (Paris, 1964); and François Le Brun, *Les Hommes et la mort en Anjou* (Paris, 1971).

22. Marion, *Dictionnaire*, p. 177.

23. Jeanne Ferté, *La Vie religieuse dans les campagnes parisiennes, 1622–1695* (Paris, 1962); Franklin L. Ford, *Strasbourg in Transition, 1648–1789* (Cambridge, Mass., 1958).

24. These figures are taken from *Gallia Christiana* and from the *Almanach Royal* for 1780. Cf. Marion, *Dictionnaire*, and Norman Ravitch, *Sword and Mitre* (The Hague, 1966).

25. "Cum plaucuisset Johanni papae XXII, ecclesias episcopales in Gallia multiplicare, majores dioeceses in duas aut plures scindendo, Pictaviensem in tres divisit partes. . . ." *Gallia Christiana*, vol. 2, p. 1,368. These divisions were designed to increase papal revenues and patronage.

26. Only eleven monks (0.48%) lack diocesan information or were born abroad. The totals for the leading dioceses are: Rouen, 236; Clermont, 124; Paris, 113; Le Mans, 104; Limoges, 104; Chartres, 85; Amiens, 76; Reims, 76; Rennes, 64; Bourges, 59; Tours, 57; Angers, 55.

forty-year period. This pattern of heavy recruitment from the large northern dioceses continued in the eighteenth century with only minor changes: Rennes became the single most productive diocese, and Cambrai and Arras joined the most active list as recruitment in the far north surged upward.[27]

Did the larger dioceses actually have a higher rate of professions in proportion to population? A standard rate that adjusts monastic professions for diocesan size puts the figures in perspective—Arles and Le Puy now head the list, followed by Rennes, Paris, and Orléans. Rouen still appears in the top ten, but in ninth place.[28] The compensation for size reduces northern dominance and shows that some southern dioceses produced more monks in proportion to their population. Local factors certainly influenced the rate of productivity. Is it coincidental that the rate was generally above the median in Brittany and Auvergne, where difficult agricultural conditions may have made families more receptive to the idea of sending their sons into religion? By contrast, although the number of monks from the prosperous north was high, the standard rate was typically close to or below the median: Paris and Rouen are exceptions to this tendency.[29]

It is also likely that Benedictine monasteries exercised some influence over their scigneurial holdings and vicinity. The diocese of Rouen counted 10 Maurist abbeys, Clermont had 6, Paris 5, and Le Mans 7. Membership in a local abbey would have been a natural goal for young men and an attractive social solution for their parents, who could look to the monastery for lifelong care of their children without prejudice to the family status or fortune.[30] A detailed study of 334 monks who took their vows in years spaced evenly from 1630 to 1690 showed that 18.3% joined the Maurists in the same diocese in which they were born. This figure may seem low in comparison with individual monasteries that drew most or all of their recruits from the local population. But the Congregation of St. Maur was not simply a loose federation of autonomous houses: the superiors held centralized power and told the monks where they could take their vows, where they could practice the religious life, and where they could retire to die. Only 10.8% of the monks died in the diocese where they had taken their

27. Julia, "Le Recrutement," p. 16.

28. Rates of productivity (professions per parish per 100 years): Arles, 1.28; Le Puy, .69; Rennes, .60; Paris, .58; Orléans, .48; Tours, .47; St. Malo, .44; St. Brieuc, .44; Rouen, .43; Clermont, .41; Aire, .39; Vannes, .36.

29. Rates of productivity for northern dioceses: Bayeux, .07; Laon, .12; Beauvais, .16; Noyon, .17; Lisieux, .18; Evreux, .19; Avranches, .19; Sées, .23; Soissons, .25; Amiens, .26; Chartres, .26.

30. See Joachim Salzgeber, *Die Klöster Einsiedeln und St. Gallen im Barockzeitalter* (Münster, 1967).

vows; only 12.6% of the monks died in their native dioceses. Although the neighborhood cloister may have been their youthful ambition, few monks were allowed to spend their entire religious lives in one community near their homes: this also was part of retreat from the world.

Training for the monastic life began at designated houses. When postulants did present themselves at St. Germain des Prés, they were sent to the countryside: "On the 19th [of May 1631] Brother Nicolas Gouffette and Jean Pomelot went away . . . to do their novitiate in the Congregation of St. Maur at St. Rémi in Reims."[31] St. Rémi and St. Faron in Meaux, two houses reformed at the beginning of the Maurist movement, were among the most important training centers. From 1621 through 1690, nearly one-fifth of all men who joined the congregation took their vows at these two monasteries.[32] Although the totals for St. Rémi (363) and St. Faron (383) were about the same, the load of novices was seldom equally distributed. No monks professed vows at St. Rémi before 1625 or after 1675, when that center for novices was consolidated with the one at St. Faron.[33] Similarly, no professions occurred at St. Faron between May 29, 1642, and August 25, 1649. Centers for novices could be opened and closed at the will of the superiors: Notre Dame des Blancsmanteaux in Paris, another house that joined the reform in its infancy, was an active center for novices in the 1620s, but professions stopped altogether there after 1633.[34] As noted earlier, the superiors responded to increased mortality in the early 1650s by creating another center for novices at St. Denis en France. In those troubled years, 18 new monks joined there, but none took vows at St. Denis after 1656.

Postulancy, novitiate, and profession—these were the steps toward becoming a monk. Each monastery that trained novices kept records of those who entered, noted their progress, and reported successful completions of the course to the editors of the matriculation registers. These records provide some data for the social origins of the monks. Of course the

31. Journal of Dom Claude Coton, B.N., MS. fr. 16853, fol. 28.

32. Professions at St. Rémi de Reims and St. Faron de Meaux

Decade	St. Rémi	St. Faron	Total	Total P.	Proportion
1621–30	19	43	62	364	17.0%
1631–40	80	35	115	521	22.1
1641–50	67	11	78	402	19.4
1651–60	68	62	130	601	21.6
1661–70	94	68	162	788	20.6
1671–80	35	71	106	497	21.3
1681–90	0	93	93	645	14.4
1621–90	363	383	746	3901	19.1%

33. Tassin, *Histoire littéraire*, p. 273.

34. Martène, *Histoire*, vol. 1, pp. 53–59. See also the documents on the Blancsmanteaux in A.N., LL 1444, and the *Matricula Monachorum*.

superiors who admitted each postulant knew his background, but they did not circulate this detailed information. Once a man had passed through the novitiate and been fully accepted in the monastic community, his standing depended more on his piety than his parentage. No pension or dowry was required of entrants as each was judged on his spiritual promise. The Maurists' willingness to accept vocations from humble men as well as exalted society echoes the practice of Mère Angélique Arnauld at the convents of Maubuisson and Port-Royal.[35] Worldly distinctions were considered vain in the Benedictine cloister; their absence from general congregational records is understandable and reveals something of the mentality of the reform. When spiritual character became paramount after the Maurists came to St. Denis, for example, some unreformed monks dropped out of the cloister and went back to their well-to-do families in Paris.[36] For the Maurists, the proper religious attitude and regular observance outweighed prestigious family connections.

When Maurists did write of their colleagues, they lacked the critical perspective of social historians. Too often they could only tell us that a monk came from "une honnête famille"; they omitted the actual rank or occupation.[37] There is also a risk that prominent families may have received disproportionate attention because their records were more accessible, or because later local historians might find them more illustrious.[38] The *Histoire littéraire de la Congrégation de St Maur*, published by Dom René-Prosper Tassin in 1770, suffers from these problems. Tassin gave no social data at all for 127 of his 162 monastic writers who professed before 1690. In some cases he stated that he had no knowledge of their lives; he merely repeated data from the matriculation registers. Tassin declared that 10 monks came from "honnêtes" or "bonnes familles," and he made some reference to previous religious careers of 3 others. This left only 22 monks to place into social classifications (see table 2). The few monks whose origins were recorded came primarily from the higher strata of society. With such small numbers, Tassin's sample has slight chance of being representative. On the other hand, we could hardly justify rejecting his categories and distribution entirely in favor of the assumption that most monks had obscure origins. Short biographies of Tassin's cases would only illustrate

35. Newton, "Port-Royal and Jansenism," vol. 2, pp. 252–56, gives examples.
36. Nécrologe de St. Denis en France, B.N., MS. fr. 8599, 8600.
37. An example of an early bibliography is Philippe Le Cerf de la Viéville, *Bibliotèque historique et critique des auteurs de la Congrégation de St. Maur* (The Hague, 1726).
38. Some articles on monks from particular regions are quite vague (e.g., Dom Albert Noël, "Les Écrivains champenois de la Congrégation de St. Maur," *Revue de Champagne et de Brie* 5 (1878): 97–114); others are simple lists: Dom Van den Boren, "Bénédictins de la Congrégation de St. Maur originaires du diocèse de Versailles," *Revue Mabillon* 11 (1921): 178–205.

TABLE 2   Social Origins of Monastic Writers (1607–90)

Nobility	8	Prev. Relig. Careers	3
Royal Secretaries	2	Unknown	127
Legal Profession	4		
Military	4	Total writers	162
Prosperous Merchants	3	(out of 3,901 monks)	
"Condition médiocre"	1		
"Bonnes familles"	10		

the limits of our knowledge about a few monks.[39] It is important, however, to study social categories carefully and systematically in order to discern significant differences of wealth and status concealed within such vague categories as "nobility" and "merchant." Nobility and office in the old regime could, of course, be bought; glorious titles and seigneurial holdings that expressed long-held social aspirations often concealed mercantile and petty administrative connections in the previous generation. If the monks whose fathers were merchants tended to come from a wealthy group,[40] those monks of noble origins often carried rank of relatively recent date, or stood just barely on the noble side of the dividing line. On this line we can locate many of the Maurist monks: there is perhaps no better sign of rising status and even faster rising pretensions than the ubiquitous title of *conseiller du roi*, a well-known passageway from commerce to nobility given to many functionaries—and naturally represented among the fathers of monks.

Systematic studies support the conclusion of Dom Paul Denis, a modern scholar: "the majority of the Benedictines of St. Maur belonged to the bourgeoisie; often young men were attracted to the religious life by the edification offered by a monastery of the neighborhood."[41] This opinion, founded on research on the Benedictines from Sées, supposes that young men were free to choose their careers. Some of them did seek the monastic life against the wishes of their parents, yet the parents were as likely to be influenced favorably by the politics of social care and often chose to send their sons to the monasteries.

We have attempted to confirm the findings of Dom Denis by reading

39. These biographies, supplemented by other accounts, can be found in my original dissertation, presented at Johns Hopkins in 1975.

40. The cases noted by Tassin and others at St. Germain des Prés suggest this. Cf. Abbé François Arbellot, "Les Bénédictins de St. Maur originaires du Limousin," *Bull. Soc. Arch. du Limousin* 40 (1893): 644–70; also J.-B. Vanel, *Les Bénédictins de St. Maur à St. Germain des Prés-Nécrologe* (Paris, 1896).

41. Dom Paul Denis, "Les Bénédictins de la Congrégation de St. Maur originaires de l'ancien diocèse de Séez," *Bull. Soc. Hist. Arch. de l'Orne* 29 (1910): 524.

books of professions kept at monasteries where novices were trained.[42] A typical book of professions from St. Rémi of Reims (1634–37) contains 43 postulants' names. All but one came from northern France, and 21% were born in the diocese of Reims itself. Châlons-sur-Marne contributed 6 men, while Paris, Rouen, Soissons, and Troyes sent 3 men each. These dioceses combined furnished nearly two-thirds of the total. The lone monk from distant Saumur in the diocese of Angers was thirty-eight years old when he took his vows in 1635; this suggests that he may have been a mature unreformed monk who decided to join the new congregation.[43] The social origins of only 6 monks are given. The highest office held by a monk's father was procureur in the Chambre des Comptes of Paris, a court charged with conservation of the royal domain, verification of accounts, and tax cases. Lesser officials mentioned include a magistrate of Metz, a tax collector in a small town, and a participant in the royal salt monopoly of Châlons-sur-Marne. One prospective monk was the son of a deceased merchant, and two were already priests at the time they entered the monastery. There was also a sergeant, whose son, a shoemaker, sought to be admitted as a *convers*, or skilled servant. These social origins are consistent with Dom Denis's conclusion, but the exploration is tentative at best. For most monks the desired information is not easily found. The scribe may have recorded occupations and titles of parents only when he felt them noteworthy; monks from ordinary backgrounds were accepted and recorded with no more than the names of their parents and the standard assurance that the postulant had been born in lawful wedlock.

For the eighteenth-century Maurists, Dominique Julia has studied the social origins of 364 monks by going to parish registers. His sample, 8.7% of the monks whose birthplaces can be identified, may still be subject to distortions, in particular to weighting in favor of urban areas. Yet he has supplemented our information on a number of points: first, the monks appear to come from rising bourgeois families who were active in civic life; second, family associations with the Maurists may have predisposed young men to membership in a congregation to which their brothers, cousins, and uncles already belonged; and finally, the parents of monks show a higher literacy than the general population, judged by their ability

42. Profession books from Congrégation de St. Maur monasteries consulted: A.N. L 750, no. 11, Reg. Prof. omnium St. Jean d'Angely, 1630–34; L 750, no. 12, Prof. Frat. Convers. St. Jean d'Angely, 1634; L 750, no. 13, Livre de noviciat, St. Melaine de Rennes, 1634–36; L 750, no. 14, Matric. St. Rémi de Reims, 1634–37; L 750, no. 15, Reg. prof. St. Sauveur de Redon, 1629–31; and A.N. LL 1001, St. Faron de Meaux, 1637–42; LL 1002, Bec, 1628–33; LL 1020, St. Pierre de Jumièges, 1626–36; and B.N. MS. fr. 18820, Prof. des novices convers, St. Germain des Prés.

43. François Cyrille Godin, *Matricula*, no. 648.

to sign marriage contracts.[44] The recruitment of rural monks in the eighteenth century shows "democratizing" tendencies, as the congregation accepted more young men of humble station. But in the seventeenth century as well, the Maurists placed little emphasis on social origins of professed monks; indeed, they congratulated those who avoided mention of their elevated backgrounds. In a highly structured society this monastic nonchalance about social distinctions inside the cloister stands in sharp contrast to an approach to the outside world that placed great value on the friendship of powerful persons. The monks' success in escaping vanity could still be questioned: the striving for harmony of monastic modesty and political realism held particular significance for those at St. Germain des Prés.

When monks took their final vows, they also reported their ages.[45] In the seventeenth century the most frequently reported age was 19, and the median age was 21. Several samples show over 75% of the monks' ages between 17 and 25 at the time of profession. Most of the recruits were thus young men, although at the beginning of the reform an appreciable number of older recruits did play an important role.

Both regulations and social patterns account for this distribution. Following the decrees of the Council of Trent in the sixteenth century, monasteries were not allowed to accept final vows from novices under 16. Yet the Maurists seldom took men at the minimum age, and even those who professed at 17 formed less than 5% of the total. Benedictine monasticism required both a level of education above that of the general population and a psychological commitment for life; it is likely that few young postulants possessed the necessary qualities. Apart from educational and spiritual reasons, the congregation had sound demographic reasons as well for giving preference to older applicants. Diseases of infancy and childhood still took a heavy toll of younger postulants, who were not yet past the age when sudden illness might carry off all but the hardiest individuals. Indeed, there was a greater risk to the congregation that young boys would die during or soon after their period of training. By contrast, those who had demonstrated their ability to survive by living for a few years longer outside the monastery, perhaps even in a hazardous career, gave greater promise of making a lasting contribution to the congregation.

A few years in the world invariably provided a strong test of health. For groups of monks who entered the congregation later, the incidence of death was clearly lower than for those who entered at younger ages. This difference can be attributed only to the experience of the intervening years,

44. Julia, "Le Recrutement," pp. 29–30.
45. Their ages were recorded in *Matricula*, and studies in parish registers have confirmed their accuracy. Julia, "Le Recrutement," p. 4.

when the outside world saw the disappearance of weaker men who probably would not have survived the rigors of monastic life that dispatched their cloistered counterparts. The median age of death, rate of mortality, and life expectancy at specific ages all favored the worldly group.[46]

Median Age of Death for Profession Age Groups

Age of Profession	16	17	18	19	20
Median Age of Death	44	54	58	59	63

Were these demographic facts known to monastic superiors in the seventeenth century? Probably they had only a vague notion, reflected in their preference for more mature novices; but some early modern people did know. These calculations are based on the work of Antoine Deparcieux, an eighteenth-century pioneer in actuarial demography.[47] Working from the matriculation registers of the Maurists, Deparcieux took two samples of monks—one of those professing 1607–69, and another of those dying 1685–1745. The professions in the first sample were made at the beginning of the reform and during its period of greatest growth, when there were proportionately more older men taking vows. The reform began with an established order and soon attracted recruits from other religious groups. Some experienced Benedictine monks, the unreformed *anciens religieux* of monasteries taken over by the Maurists, began their religious lives anew as novices in the Congregation of St. Maur. Men who came to the monasteries from worldly occupations were also older than postulants who had just completed their secondary studies. In the early years of the reform over 40% of the monks joined when they were 25 or older, but by the 1640s this group represented less than 20% of the total, and in the mature population the percentage of older men entering dropped to about 10%.

Proportion of Older Men Taking Vows

	25–29	30–39	Over 40	Total 25+
1607–29	19.3%	14.8%	6.3%	40.3%
1641–51	10.8	6.8	2.0	19.5
1661–66	7.5	3.0	1.0	11.5
1675–83	7.5	4.5	0.5	12.5
1692–99	8.5	1.0	0.3	9.8

N = 2,000, selected groups of 400

46. Even a comparison of monks who entered at 19 with those who entered at 20 shows the advantage in life expectancy of the older group: at age 20, $e_{x(20)} = 38.7$, vs. $e_{x(19)} = 37.5$. Details of these calculations can be found in the original dissertation.

47. Deparcieux, *Essai sur les probabilités de la durée de la vie humaine* (Paris, 1746, 1760).

Let us construct a hypothesis that will explain the changing age distribution of the entering monks. The Benedictine reform got its start during the reign of Henry IV, the leader of national reconstruction after the Wars of Religion. After the decadence of the sixteenth century, the reformers sought to restore strict monastic observance. The novelty of the reform at first attracted many mature individuals who were moved by piety to leave their corrupt cloisters or to retreat from the evils of the world. The greatest growth of the new congregation came during the early years of the personal rule of Louis XIII. In that turbulent era the desire of the devout to see monastic life as an alternative to the world may have been strengthened: the spiritual vitality of this Catholic revival shines through the hundreds of religious houses founded by "a generation of saints."[48] Religious communities that had lost their members and their spirit were reformed and revived, and monasteries that had fallen into ruin were rebuilt.

Twenty and fifty years later the proportion of younger men among the entering monks rose markedly. Eventually nine-tenths of the entrants were below the age of twenty-five, the legal age of majority in most French provinces. Instead of mature individuals who gave up established social positions to struggle for monastic reform, the newer members of the mature congregation were young men who did not fully enjoy their civil rights—who could neither inherit property, nor acquire goods, nor give evidence in court.[49] During the reign of Louis XIV, more monks came as a result of parental influence, while earlier in the century the older men had been responsible for founding and expanding the congregation. By the time that internal order was restored in the state, however, the monastic congregation had developed its own discipline and rigidity. Professional mobility from external careers to religious life first slowed and later practically ceased. This may have been the result of tightened regulations and hardened attitudes: transfers to other religious orders were forbidden, and those who dared to sympathize with the Jansenists were forced to return to orthodoxy or to flee the country. The regulations of the congregation became increasingly complex to cover the smallest details of daily life; yet regulations by themselves were not enough to keep the community together. When the founding spirit faded, when a young monk's commit-

48. Orest Ranum, *Paris in the Age of Absolutism* (New York, 1968), pp. 109–31.

49. Pierre Goubert, "Legitimate Fecundity and Infant Mortality in France during the Eighteenth Century," *Daedalus* 97:2 (Spring 1968): 595. François Olivier-Martin, *Histoire de la coutume de la prévôté et vicomté de Paris*, revised ed. (Paris, 1972), vol. 1, p. 185.

ment to obedience weakened, monastic practice could not uphold the ideal: departure from the congregation was the result. Indeed, many more monks left the congregation when the reform was firmly established, after 1660, than at the beginning. The initial population with its greater proportion of older entrants apparently had more internal solidarity, a quality to be expected in founders. Those younger monks who came later, sometimes recruited suddenly in response to crisis mortality, might have tried to maintain the forms of observance, but lacked the inner confidence to persevere in them. Finally, the strictness of the established group may have discouraged others outside it from giving up their careers for religious retreat, then in disrepute with the higher levels of French administration. Louis XIV had had enough of adventurism in religion; his minister Colbert, ever eager to suppress idleness and increase French productivity, sought to limit the religious orders. In 1664, Colbert was already proposing "to reduce sweetly and unnoticeably the monks of both sexes," and in the following year he considered the legal aspects of raising the minimum age of profession to twenty-five, "to make religious vows more difficult."[50] The effects of hardening attitudes within and governmental restrictions without, combined with mortality, can be seen in the age distribution of the congregation.

Mortality, the ultimate demographic factor, also played a role in monastic population. We have seen the congregation's response to *crisis* mortality; using the same data collected by Deparcieux we can determine their *normal* mortality by making standard life expectancy tables. Deparcieux calculated the life expectancy for both monastic samples, and then compared the monks with other early modern populations. From the table and graph it is apparent that monks at first had longer life expectancy than the general population: a monk aged 20 could expect to live to age 58, while a man of the world could look forward to only 56.[51] In middle age, however, the balance of mortality shifted to favor people in the world. That is, a greater proportion of the cloistered group survived to middle age, but then they died in greater numbers than other old people. Deparcieux suggested an explanation for this.[52] First, while all of the popula-

<hr>

50. *Lettres, instructions et mémoires de Colbert*, Pierre Clément, ed., vol. 6 (Paris, 1869), pp.lvii–lviii. See also Dosh, "Growth of the Congregation," pp. 212–26. The age was raised to 21 in 1768; see Julia, "Le Recrutement," p. 10.

51. The worldly sample is of Dutch rentiers, a more representative sample than rentiers of the French crown, who had the highest life expectancy of any group in Europe. Marion, *Dictionnaire*, p. 483. Canons of Ste. Geneviève and nuns also appear in table 3.

52. Deparcieux, *Essai*, pp. 84–85.

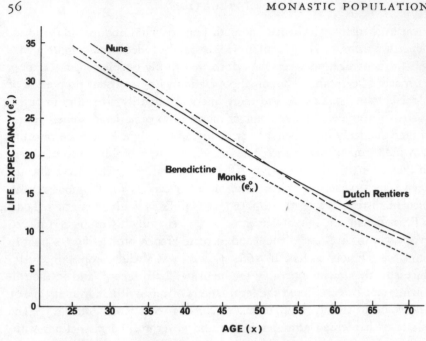

GRAPH 4   Life Expectancy of Early Modern Populations

tions he studied were selected to favor healthy individuals, the religious populations were more carefully chosen. Not only were prospective monks examined to make sure that they were free of external infirmity, but also they swore an oath attesting to their internal soundness. Furthermore, superiors could check the health of young men during their novitiate, before the profession of final vows. Still, after fifteen or twenty years of abstinence, fasting, chanting, waking, and other bodily mortification, even the strongest monks suffered failing health. And while the monk who lived to an advanced age was not necessarily released from the rigors of observance, the aged man of the world could surround himself with comfort. Therefore, although some individual monks might become very old, as a group they did not enjoy life expectancy as high as that of the general population.

How reliable are these figures? Generally speaking, life expectancy in early modern times was closer to 25 or 30 than to 60.[53] But figures for general populations that start at birth are depressed because they include infant mortality. By contrast, those who survived infancy and childhood could expect to live long even by modern standards. Progress in medicine

53. Jacques Dupâquier, "Sur la population française au XVIIe et XVIIIe siècle," *Revue Historique* 239 (1968): 62–66.

TABLE 3   Comparison of Abridged Life Tables

| Age | Life Expectancy of: | | | | |
| | | | | Nuns of | |
	Monks "A"	Monks "B"	Canons SG	Paris	Dutch Rentiers
20	38.33	38.50	36.50	40.17	36.25
25	34.67	35.00	33.00	36.67	33.25
30	30.83	31.42	29.42	33.17	30.50
35	27.42	27.67	26.08	29.67	28.33
40	24.00	24.00	23.00	26.25	25.50
45	20.58	20.50	19.67	22.92	22.33
50	17.25	17.17	17.00	19.50	19.42
55	14.33	14.17	14.33	16.25	16.75
60	11.67	11.33	11.50	13.25	14.08
65	9.00	8.75	9.08	10.83	11.58
70	6.67	6.50	7.08	8.42	9.17
75	5.00	4.83	5.17	6.25	6.83

had little effect on demographic characteristics in the seventeenth and eighteenth centuries. In sum, the figures for Maurist monks appear quite reasonable in comparison with those of underdeveloped countries today, where the populations are mathematically similar.[54]

Our calculated monastic life table will also yield a probable age distribution.[55] If the congregation had taken exclusively young men when it was growing most rapidly, nearly half of the monks would have been under thirty; but in fact the acceptance of older novices tended to spread the distribution. The truest picture is provided by the mature congregation—the distribution shown in graph 5, with about half of the monks under thirty-five. As a group the Maurists were aging: from a base of active reformers with little shared religious experience, the congregation evolved to a stable community with longer and more conservative experience. Among other religious groups, aging had a telling effect, especially if they could not recruit new members: both the nuns of Port-Royal-des-Champs and the unreformed monks of St. Germain des Prés lost their spiritual vitality.[56] As these restricted communities moved toward extinc-

54. Ansley J. Coale and Paul Demeny, *Regional Model Life Tables and Stable Populations* (Princeton, 1966): *Methods of Estimating Basic Demographic Measures from Incomplete Data* (United Nations, 1967). Nathan Keyfitz and Wilhelm Flieger, *Population: Facts and Methods of Demography* (San Francisco, 1971). Henry S. Shryock, Jacob S. Siegel, et al., *The Methods and Materials of Demography* (Washington, D.C., 1971).

55. Cf. Keyfitz and Fliegel, *Population*, p. 213: "We can use a given life table along with an arbitrary rate of increase to see to what age distribution a population would tend. . . ." Also in Coale and Demeny, *Methods*, p. 14.

56. Compare Newton's treatment of the decline of Port-Royal, "Port-Royal and

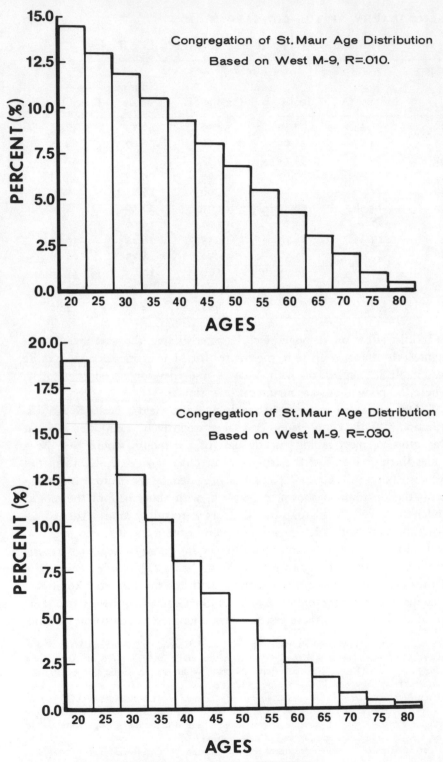

GRAPH 5   Monastic Age Distribution

tion, their concerns shifted from the perfection of interior spiritual ideals
to the observance of exterior legal forms.

Did the Maurists suffer a similar fate? No, because the congregation
had only reached maturity, not passed into decline. Some of the original
reforming spirit had gone—public attitudes had changed, and monastic
attitudes changed also. Yet the population remained remarkably stable well
into the eighteenth century.[57] Far from being a period of decadence, the
late seventeenth century was the epoch of greatest glory in Maurist scholarship; many of those who would do the best work joined the congregation
at that time. These men came from all over France to study at the Parisian
headquarters, St. Germain des Prés. It is time now to turn to that community, to discover how it managed its temporal and spiritual affairs in
the age of Louis XIV.

Jansenism," vol. 2, pp. 200–09. Part 4 of this study treats the unreformed monks at St.
Germain des Prés.
    57. See table 1 and Julia, "Le Recrutement," p. 7.

PART 2

Monastic Revenues

3

Regular Income

If only the financial records of St. Germain des Prés existed for the seventeenth century, our knowledge of the abbey would still be considerable. Study of these records reveals how the abbey managed its lands in the Parisian region, how it participated in capital markets, and how it spent its money. Alongside the religious purposes of the monastery must be set the financial activities of a powerful corporation, a separate legal entity that owned property and made contracts. Its affairs were separated into two autonomous divisions: the *manse abbatiale* and the *manse conventuelle*.

The manse abbatiale provided income for the commendatory abbot, who held his office as a favor and pension from the king. Since the monks had lost the right of election during the Middle Ages, the abbots of St. Germain des Prés were usually high churchmen, counsellors, or relatives of the reigning monarch. Certainly the seventeenth-century abbots fit these categories. From 1623 to 1668, the abbot was Henry de Bourbon, bishop of Metz and duke of Verneuil, proudly described by the sacristan as "natural son of King Henry IV, natural brother of King Louis XIII, and natural uncle of King Louis XIV."[1] He enjoyed cordial relations with the monks; he simply took his share of the revenues and left responsibility for the governance of the abbey to a prior chosen by superiors of the congregation. From time to time the monks sought political support from Verneuil, a powerful protector at court; as long as he held the abbey, he watched over their interests. His successor as abbot, Jean Casimir, had a chequered career as Jesuit, cardinal, and king of Poland. When he took up exile in France, Louis XIV gave him the abbacy as a court pension. Although Jean Casimir was beset by financial difficulties during his brief tenure, he made efforts to attend religious services and achieved a measure

1. Sacristie, B.N. MS. fr. 18818, fol. 200.

of respect and popularity among the monks.[2] After Casimir's death in
1672, Louis XIV did not immediately appoint a successor. Instead he took
the revenues for himself and left administration to Paul Pelisson, an experienced financial agent who had served under Fouquet and Colbert.[3]
Pelisson and the monks worked together to preserve the privileges of the
abbey and increase its income. Relations between them were generally
good during the seventeen years that the monastery remained under royal
administration. Then, in 1690, Louis gave it to Cardinal Guillaume Egon
von Fürstemberg, bishop of Strasbourg and proven servant of absolute
will. Again blessed with a powerful protector, the monastery won back
lost privileges, and despite financial difficulties the abbot and monks
strengthened their positions under princely abbots in the early years of the
eighteenth century.

Since the religious community is the focus of attention here, this
study will concentrate on the manse conventuelle, the endowment which
provided income for the monks. By itself a substantial enterprise, the
manse conventuelle had an annual income that ranged from 60,000 to
100,000 *livres* between 1660 and 1700. The monks kept accounts according to a model suggested by the Congregation of St. Maur. They recog-
nized that "good administration of the temporal contributes much to the
spiritual."[4] The cellerier, a regular monk of the choir, took care of the
bookkeeping. While other monks might be moved from house to house,
continuity in office was the rule for the celleriers, whose stay at St. Germain
des Prés tended to be lifelong. In the Maurist seventeenth century, Dom
Romain Rodoyer took over the office from Claude Coton, in 1631 one of
the unreformed monks; Rodoyer served until he died in 1652, and was
succeeded by Jean Barré, whose term lasted forty years.[5] The cellerier's
duties included collecting amounts owed to the abbey by its tenants, and
in this work he occasionally employed other monks and lay brothers as
assistants.

Each year the receipts were recorded in a chronological journal. Ordinary and extraordinary items of income were kept separate: contractual
rents and customary payments fell in the first category, while the second
included arrears in rents, loans, and gifts to the monastery, as well as

2. Casimir's financial difficulties are mentioned in Choses mémorables, B.N. MS. fr.
18816, fol. 128; a loan guarantee for him was approved, Actes cap., B.N. MS. fr. 16857,
fol. 20. His piety is praised in the Sacristie book, B.N. MS. fr. 18818, fols. 229–30.

3. See the chapter on Pelisson in the book by Orest Ranum, *Artisans of Glory*:
Writers and Historical Thought in Seventeenth Century France (Chapel Hill, N.C.,
1980).

4. Dom Bernard Audebert, *Mémoires*, p. 293.

5. *Matricula*, nos. 465, 1262; Cf. J.-B. Vanel, *Nécrologe*.

proceeds from sales of lands and rights. The monks noted quarterly totals, and, as might be expected, most of the income came to the abbey in the third and fourth quarters of the year, after the harvest. At the end of the year the monks drew up a *Compte général* listing the expected income from leases, foundations, offices, and priories. The cellerier then checked the items in the journal against this general account. When obligations went unpaid, they appeared as deductions from the total of expected revenues. After extraordinary items had been added, and reductions in rents and dues subtracted, the monks knew their net income. They kept separate accounts of agricultural products delivered directly to the abbey and sold by the monks.

An overview of the abbey's revenues in the late seventeenth century (graph 6) suggests the grandeur of the institution. At a time when an un-reformed monk received a yearly pension of 500 livres, and when a servant might be paid 60 livres annual wages plus room and board, the monastery had revenues running into tens of thousands of livres. By the third quarter of the century total income typically exceeded 70,000 livres per year: by the 1690s totals of 90,000 livres and more were common.[6] Although year by year comparisons can be misleading because of irregular payments from tenants and lenders, moving averages clearly establish the favorable situation of the abbey (graph 7). Even after allowing for devaluation of the currency, the income of the monastic properties increased significantly between 1660 and 1720: conservatively capitalized at thirty times annual income, the manse conventuelle rose in market value from two million to over four million livres.[7] To the ordinary income must be added revenue from the sacristy, from gifts, loans, and new foundations. Despite the difficulties created by tenants in arrears and a substantial debt, St. Germain des Prés was still one of the richest monasteries in France.

On balance, the community bought both urban and country property around Paris in the seventeenth century. The monks themselves made a

TABLE 4   Land transactions, 1631–1710 (manse conventuelle, livres)

	Paris	Country	Total
Purchases	287,059	698,068	985,127
Sales	144,700	319,425	− 424,125
		Net Gain	+ 521,002

6. Comptes, A. N. H5 4274–H5 4279.

7. On capitalization, see Marc Venard, *Bourgeois et paysans au XVIIe siècle*, pp. 48, 72.

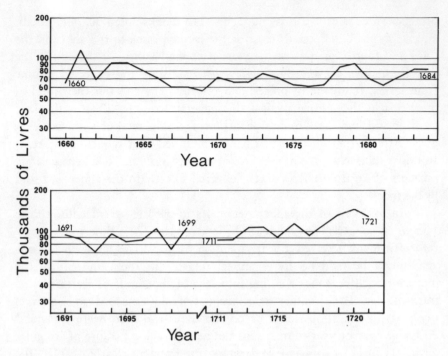

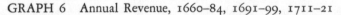

GRAPH 6   Annual Revenue, 1660–84, 1691–99, 1711–21

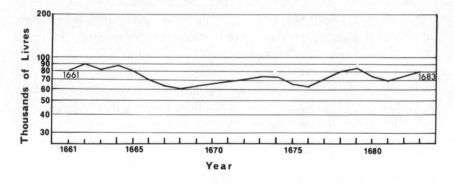

GRAPH 7   Moving Average of Annual Revenues, 1661–83

summary of their purchases and sales between 1631 and 1710: besides 200,000 livres spent on new buildings and improvements at the abbey itself, the manse conventuelle paid 985,127 livres for properties; after deducting sales, the monastery nevertheless became half a million livres richer in land.[8] How were the monks able to enrich themselves in the

8. Biens de l'abbaye, B.N. MS. fr. 16864, fol. 57+; printed in Dom Anger, *Les Dépendances de St. Germain des Prés*, vol. 3.

course of the "tragic" seventeenth century? In an age of economic stag-
nation and even decline, where did they find the capital needed to under-
take their expansion? To answer these questions a closer study of monastic
finances is appropriate.

The largest proportion of ordinary monastic income came from agricultural property. Most of it had been in the possession of the monastery
for centuries: some lands mentioned in the *Polyptique* of Abbot Irminon
in the Carolingian era were still producing income for the monks nine
hundred years later. Even those parts of the manse conventuelle that had
been alienated and were no longer farmed by the monks or their tenants
continued to owe seigneurial obligations to the abbey. At their seigneuries
of Thiais and Choisy, for example, the monks still held 120 hectares of
domaine réserve that could be let on short-term contracts; yet their "vaste
censive" over the alienated lands beyond brought them a whole catalogue
of rights and privileges.

> On these lands the monks levied major and minor tithes as
> *curés primitifs*; and, as seigneurs, the ground-rent in money
> [*cens*], a seigneurial tax in kind [*champart*] on the arable, and a
> vine tax [*vinage*] on certain vineyards. At every change of
> ownership they collected mutation fees [*lods et ventes*]. Over
> their tenants they exercised all rights of justice, high, middle,
> and low. Contracts were signed before their notary and recorded
> by their registrar. The oven and the wine-press used by the in-
> habitants belonged to [the monks]. Weights and measures were
> inspected, controlled, and stamped by their fiscal officer. They
> collected a *forage* tax on retail sales of wine and a *roulage* tax on
> all loaded vehicles crossing their seigneurie. On the Seine River,
> they had fishing and wreckage rights, and the ferry that made
> the crossing at Choisy belonged to them. Each year, "on the last
> day of August, the eve of St. Leu and St. Gilles, the saintly pa-
> trons of the said church of Thiais," all the heads of household
> of the two villages and the hamlet of Grignon had to appear in
> person at the "general assizes" held by the Provost, to recognize
> the seigneurie of the monks.[9]

The stewardship of these scattered lands, the exact and insistent observa-
tion of rights and privileges, could not be done effectively from Paris by
the religious community; thus the monks appointed *fermiers*, local agents
who undertook to pay the abbey a fixed sum in exchange for complete

9. Jean Jacquart, *La Crise rurale*, p. 68.

seigneurial responsibility. This system assured the monks regular income for the term of the lease, usually nine years; the fermiers in turn had the necessary independence to manage and perhaps even to improve the properties. Nevertheless, the abbey's income did vary with agricultural conditions. A poor harvest on the farms could mean reduced income for the monks because some fermiers might be so destitute that they could not meet their obligations. Floods, droughts, and military campaigns had devastating effects on the crops, and the higher grain prices in bad years did not adequately compensate fermiers for reduced yields. Monastic revenues, which show some correlation with the trend of grain prices,[10] were probably more influenced in difficult times by the supply and demand for loans. When the fermiers were unable to pay the rent, the monks were immediately pressed to find ways of delaying payment to their own creditors or borrowing money; as for the fermiers, the monks had to decide whether to reduce their rents and bear with slow payers, or to seize their personal property and offer the leases to others.

This did not preclude the development of long relationships between the abbey and its fermiers. At the seigneurie of Avrainville, which has been extensively studied by Marc Venard and Jean Jacquart, the fermiers drawn from the Harineau and Grégoire families held leases for more than a century. These were the dynasties of "coqs de village," the more enterprising peasants who amassed responsibilities and properties piece by piece; initiative in farming, inheritance, and marriage were their means, increasing wealth and prestige their ends. The Harineau fortunes received impetus from a lease of 1507, under which the family obtained the management of 14.2 hectares of monastic land at Avrainville.[11] This lease was unusually generous in that it farmed the property for two lifetimes against a fixed rent in kind. By 1550 the rent was very low compared to that of other lands, and the Harineau were able to use their savings to buy other properties in the same censive: the Harineau of the seventeenth century, their descendants, became the largest peasant property owners of the seigneurie.[12] But during this time the family had not given up their role as agents of St. Germain des Prés—from father to son the responsibility passed. From 1608 to 1617 Pierre Harineau shared the lease with Jean Grégoire; then Jean Harineau took over from 1622, receiving renewals in 1631, 1640, and 1649. Table 5 summarizes the information found in the contracts.[13]

10. Correlation of three-year moving average with wheat prices at Paris (annual averaged figures, from M. Baulant and J. Meuvret, *Prix des céréales extraits de la mercuriale de Paris* (Paris, 1960–62), vol. 2, p. 135): R = .69; s.e. = .11.
11. Jacquart, *La Crise rurale*, p. 157.
12. Ibid., p. 461.
13. Venard, *Bourgeois et paysans*, pp. 93–107; Jacquart, *La Crise rurale*, pp. 509–11.

For the Harineau family, the first half of the century was marked by regular renewals of their lease. The rise in rent from 1630 to 1648, reflecting rising property values, may be attributed to population pressure, increased demand for land, and successive devaluations. Another study has found that between 1633 and 1653, landed revenues rose 29%, prices rose 53%, and the livre suffered a devaluation of 33.5%.[14] To improve their worsened position, the monks and other landowners raised the rents, but these increases became counter-productive. On the eve of the civil wars of the Fronde, in 1648, Jean Harineau agreed to a substantial increase in the rent for Avrainville, the contract to take effect the following year. Unfortunately, the devastation of the Fronde left him unable to fulfill the conditions. The monks sued Harineau for damaging buildings, removing gates, and failing to plant trees as agreed; they further contended that he led a scandalous life and had abused his office as the abbey's agent.[15] All these charges were made against a man who had dealt with the abbey for over thirty years! Blaming the troubled conditions, Harineau sought remission of the rent for 1652 and 1653. Although the monks granted a reduction of 400 livres, by St. Martin's Day, the traditional November settlement date, 1653, Harineau owed them 2,282 livres 2 s. 6 d. back rent and 600 livres for damages to the estate. In these circumstances, the monks

TABLE 5   Leases of the Seigneurie of Avrainville

Date	Fermier	Annual Rent
1631	Jean Harineau	700 livres
1640	Jean Harineau	800 livres
1649	Jean Harineau	1,100 livres (not finished)
1653	Denis Grégoire	1,100 livres*
1662	Denis Grégoire	1,200 livres
1671	Louise Poullain	1,100 livres*
	(widow of Grégoire)	
1679	François Guillaume	1,300 livres*
1689	(difficulty obtaining renewal; *fermier* died just after lease began)	
1693	Robert Rufray	1,100 livres
	(died 1695; lease continued by widow)	
1701	Louis Brière	1,100 livres*
1712	Louis Brière	1,100 livres
1722	Louis Brière	1,100 livres

*Minor changes in conditions of the lease, generally in favor of the tenants.

14. Jean-Marie Constant, "Gestion et revenus d'un grand domaine aux XVIe et XVIIc siècles," *Revue d'Histoire Économique et Sociale* 50:2 (1972): 165–202.
15. Jacquart, La Crise rurale, pp. 510–11.

broke the lease, confiscated some of Harineau's personal property, and found a new tenant. But Jean Harineau was not completely reduced to poverty by this loss: he still owned more than twenty hectares of land in the seigneurie, and the influence of his family continued—the new fermier, Denis Grégoire, was the son of the Jean Grégoire who had worked with the Harineau in running the estate before. Jean Harineau's daughter was also Denis Grégoire's mother-in-law; thus were the bonds of family joined and the continuity of administration assured.[16]

The later history of the seigneurie of Avrainville is equally illustrative of general trends in administration. Under Denis Grégoire, a period of reconstruction and relative prosperity took place. In general, rents in contracts signed around 1660 rose to the highest level of the century: the lease on Avrainville was renewed at another increase. From 1667 to 1674, however, there was a catastrophic fall in the price of grain, and leases renewed during this period show a downward adjustment. By this time Denis Grégoire had died, and his widow took over the responsibility for the estate. About 1679–80 there was another time of recovery: at Avrainville the rent was raised again and the changes in terms, while more favorable to the tenant, did not make up for the increase. "This doubtless explains why at the end of the lease the monks seem to have had difficulty renewing it."[17] A fall in grain prices had begun in 1685, and reductions as well as bankruptcies of tenants were the order of the day. Suffering from low grain prices, high rents that resisted the general tendencies of prices to decline, and increased wartime taxes, the fortunes of the great fermiers went into eclipse until the "belles années" of the eighteenth century.[18] The nominal stability of rents at Avrainville from 1693 to 1722 does conceal a decline from devaluations of the currency, but for the fermiers to have remained prosperous, further declines would have had to take place. The rents on small pieces of property even show a contrary tendency—to increase: Venard has theorized that while the larger tenants were becoming poorer and more reluctant to sign contracts, simpler peasants could always be found to work the small lots, even though it may have been economically disadvantageous to them.[19] At Thiais and Choisy the rents were somewhat lower, perhaps because the seigneurial tax was so high (13% of the harvest); yet there too the peasantry continued to participate in the system, trying to make ends meet through human ingenuity in the face of an unfavorable general economic situation.[20]

16. Ibid., p. 511.
17. Venard, *Bourgeois et paysans*, p. 95.
18. Jacquart, *La Crise rurale*, p. 715.
19. Venard, *Bourgeois et paysans*, p. 103.
20. "Théoriquement, aucune de ces fermes n'était économiquement capable de faire

What happened at Avrainville, Thiais, Choisy, and other lands of St. Germain des Prés also happened on other properties of the Parisian region. The rents of the abbey of St. Denis, for example, rose sharply in the 1630s and 1660s; although they peaked in the late 1670s, they declined later.[21] In practice the theoretical stability of monastic income promised by nine-year leases was subject to long-term fluctuations: the rent specified in each contract was influenced by agricultural conditions at the time the lease was signed. The Compte général of the monks records the annual income anticipated from the leases. Consistent with Venard's findings, and with the smoothing effect of periodic renewals of long-term leases, there was little variation from year to year in the anticipated income from 1661 to 1675. The trend-line of this income shows a slight decline over the long term, a decline which accelerated between 1675 and 1680.[22] Unfortunately, the lack of receipt books for later dates makes it difficult to draw conclusions about the severity and duration of the decline. On the basis of the preceding fifteen years' data, however, it is reasonable to suppose that only minor variations took place in total expected revenue.

What did fluctuate considerably, on a year-to-year basis, was the regularity of payment of the rent. The monks actually received on time much less than the specified amounts. Seldom, even in years of good harvests, was more than 45% of the rent paid before the end of the

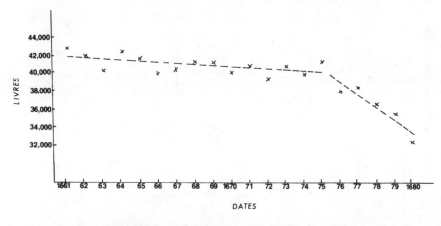

GRAPH 8   Trend-line of Ordinary Receipts

face à ses obligations." This is Jacquart's conclusion after calculating all charges. *La Crise rurale*, pp. 380–81.

21. B. Veyrassat-Herrer and E. Le Roy Ladurie, "La Rente foncière autour de Paris au XVIIe siècle," *Annales, E.S.C.* 23 (1968): 541–55.

22. The slope of the regression line changes from −0.12 (1661–75) to −1.40 (1676–80). See the accompanying graph.

calendar year for which it was owed. When the fermiers received very low prices for their grain, the percentage of the rent paid on time fell to 25% or less, as was the case from 1668 to 1672. A graph of these figures shows peaks and valleys similar to those of the Baulant-Meuvret price series for grain sold at the Halles of Paris, and linear regression indicates a moderate correlation of percentages and prices.[23] In its general outlines this association should not be surprising, since in normal times higher grain prices meant more income for tenants and monks. During the disastrous years of the Fronde, however, it is probable that the ruin of the countryside left few fermiers with substantial amounts of grain to sell; consequently, their net income may have been lower, and the amount available to pay the monastery smaller than in years of lower prices but greater yields.

Yet one must not assume that rents remained unpaid. Unless they were totally ruined, the tenants eventually paid their arrears, and St. Germain des Prés shared this experience with other estates.[24] Payments were frequently made in the year after they were due: arrears acquired an important place in the receipts, and often overshadowed the rents paid on time. Of course, these figures may have been influenced by independent variables such as the perseverance of the monks in collecting rents and the reluctance of the tenants to pay them. The total of arrears collected each year depended on these and other factors: it does not appear to have a direct or a delayed relationship to grain prices.

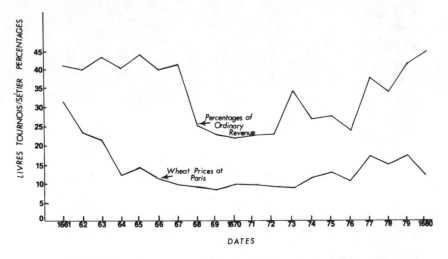

GRAPH 9   Percentages of Ordinary Revenue and Wheat Prices

23. With the St. Martin prices, R = .62, s.e. = .14 between 1661 and 1679.

24. Failure to pay occurred in only 3.7 percent of the cases studied by Constant, "gestation et revenus."

Direct sales of agricultural products accounted for, on the average, one-third of the total income of the monks. The average ratio of this source of income to the combined income from ordinary payments and arrears was .70, but in some years it fell to less than one-half or rose above 1.0. One might expect that the volume of direct sales would closely follow the Baulant-Meuvret price series, but in fact there was practically no correlation.[25] Nor was there any consistent relationship between income from this source and lease income. The explanation may lie in greater human factors in sales of produce. Since the monks exercised control over products sold directly, they could use sales to balance their accounts. In years of hardship, they might divert grain from the open market to the poor or to the monastery itself. In this trading activity the monks of St. Germain des Prés followed the practice of their medieval English counterparts. Although the monks of Durham, purchasers of grain, were absolutely at the mercy of the market and had a vested interest in low cereal prices, those of Canterbury in the thirteenth century used a balance of sales and purchases of crops to see them through the year.[26]

Extraordinary income other than arrears appears under the heading *casuel*. The receipts of the sacristy, drawn from collection in the church, fell in this category because they were not specified, contracted sums like lease income. These voluntary contributions show some negative correlation with wheat prices, suggesting that when prices were high, popular support of religion took second place to popular spending on food: when grain prices were low, people gave more money to the church.[27] Although major construction and renovation in the abbey church required additional financing, the collections did furnish the monks with more than adequate funds for ordinary maintenance.[28] Most of the time between 1660 and 1680 the casuel was little more than the sacristy, and it contributed less than 10% of the total income. Only when the monks sold property or borrowed money did the casuel assume a more important role. When the Maurists considered building projects or acquisitions, they did not have to base their decisions on current agricultural conditions: they had the freedom to use borrowed money—additional, readily available, extraordinary income.

25. $R = .14$, s.e. $= .22$.

26. R. B. Dobson, *Durham Priory, 1400–1450*, pp. 265–68; R. A. L. Smith, *Canterbury Cathedral Priory*, p. 132.

27. $R = - .49$, s.e. $= .17$.

28. Cf. receipts, A.N. H5 4275, 4279, and expenditures, A.N. H5 4274, 4276. See part 3, Monastic Expenditures.

4

Borrowing

When the monks of St. Germain des Prés found their current income in-sufficient to meet their needs, they had to borrow money. Because of the abbey's wide landholdings and its closeness to the Parisian financial mar-ket, the monks seldom had difficulty finding lenders; indeed, there were times when borrowers with equally good security were in short supply. Four features of monastic borrowing will be considered here: first, the abbey could borrow on favorable terms; second, the supply of capital was adequate to support building projects and purchases of land; third, the monks were able to refund older loans with newer ones at lower interest; and fourth, the group of lenders to St. Germain des Prés represented an interested constituency whose dealings with the abbey were mutually ad-vantageous.

The Parisian capital market of the seventeenth century is imperfectly known. Borrowers and lenders alike shared a reluctance to accept the con-cept of interest.[1] Owing to religious prohibitions, loans had to be dressed in "legal clothing that was simultaneously subtle and transparent."[2] Money could not be lent at interest, but income could be sold: in a typical *rente constituée* of this period the contract involved a transfer of capital and regular payments of interest. Yet to the seventeenth-century legal mind, the transaction was a completed sale: pledging property as collateral, the borrower sold an annual income to the lender in exchange for the capital. Thus the purchase price of the rente was the principal of the loan, and the annual income was the interest. In theory the lender could never demand repayment of the principal, but in practice he often requested it. If the

---

1. Some of this material appeared in my article, "Perspectives on French Interest Rates in the Seventeenth Century," *Proceedings*, Western Society for French History 2 (1975): 2–11.

2. Pierre Goubert, *Histoire économique et sociale de la France*, ed. E. Labrousse et al. (Paris, 1970), p. 343.

borrower fell behind in his payments, the lender could seek legal recourse and seize the property placed as collateral. The borrower had an advantage in that he was free to repurchase the rente whenever he wished by reimbursing the principal and accumulated interest; repeated refunding might be especially advantageous in periods of capital oversupply and falling interest rates. These constituted money rentes had evolved from pure property rentes; however, the property stood only as security for the loan.[3]

Two types of money rentes were in common use for private borrowings—*rentes perpetuelles* and *rentes viagères*. The first of these resembled modern loans with an eventual obligation to repay the principal, though at no specified date. Rentes viagères, on the other hand, were life annuities—in exchange for his capital, the lender received annual income as long as he lived. The annuities became extinct upon the death of the lender or his designated beneficiary, but rentes perpetuelles could be passed down as heritable property.

The government decreed the maximum interest rate on rentes perpetuelles and thereby also sought to influence the rate on annuities, where credit-worthiness played a smaller part than the age and health of the lender. Interest was expressed in *deniers*, the fractional parts of the principal paid each year. For example, denier 12 was equivalent to 8.3% (1/12 of the principal), and denier 20 to 5.0%. These numbers are reciprocals of the interest rate; consequently, the higher the denier number, the lower the percentage rate. At the end of the sixteenth century private rentes at denier 12 were common. Royal ordinances in the seventeenth century, however, proclaimed progressive reductions: the rate fell to denier 16 in 1601, to denier 18 in 1634, and then to denier 20 in 1665—a fall of more than one-third. Louis XIV, who pursued so many schemes for enriching France, announced the last reduction in order to obtain "the great benefits that the circulation of money produces," and to oppose the "excessive profits returned by constitutions of rentes, which may give rise to idleness and prevent our subjects from devoting themselves to commerce, manufactures, and agriculture."[4]

Was this attempt at economic regulation effective? An absolute monarch might want to set interest rates by fiat, but independent economic forces probably had greater effects on the Parisian money market. To confirm this point, we must make a careful study of private accounts and notarial contracts, where the constituted rentes were recorded. For St.

3. On the evolution of these *rentes*, see Bernard Schnapper, *Les Rentes au XVIe siècle: histoire d'un instrument de crédit* (Paris, 1956).
4. Edict of December 1665, in F. Isambert et al., eds., *Recueil des anciennes lois françaises* (Paris, 1821–33), vol. 18, no. 471, pp. 69–71.

Germain des Prés we have the monks' internal discussions of loans, their account books, and finally the notarized contracts, most of which can be found in the files of Philippe Le Moine, the notary who handled the abbey's transactions. The contracts are particularly useful because they give names, titles, and addresses that allow us to reconstruct the monastery's external constituency, its financial and perhaps also political supporters.[5]

First of all, the records show that money was almost always readily available to the abbey. The monks regarded borrowing as an opportunity as much as a necessity. When funds were needed—or, as often, when eager lenders presented themselves, proposals were discussed at meetings of the séniorat, or council, where the prior and his close advisors could consider delicate matters with discretion. Once a favorable decision was reached, the community as a whole gave its approval in a meeting of the chapter. St. Germain des Prés and all other reformed Benedictine houses in France had to ask permission from the superior general of the Congregation of St. Maur before the contracts could be drawn. Philippe Le Moine was the notary for most of the mid-century acts, and occasionally they were registered at the Châtelet as well.[6] Once the cellerier received the funds, he was required to furnish the lender with receipts showing how the money was used.

In the early 1640s, when wheat prices were high and credit was tight, lenders demanded an interest rate above the legal maximum of 5.5%. Since rentes drawn up before the reduction of 1634 could still be transferred at the 6.25% rate, lenders naturally turned to these instruments. A vigorous traffic in forged older obligations suggests that this means was employed to circumvent the legal maximum.[7] Despite these indications of general difficulties, St. Germain des Prés borrowed 10,800 livres in 1641 at 5.5%, and in 1643 obtained another 36,000 livres at 4.5%, nearly two percentage points below the going rate. The first loan was actually an obligation of the Abbey of St. Denis en France, which repaid the lender; he then transferred the money to St. Germain des Prés. The Parisian abbey used the money to repay another lender, M. Morot, *bourgeois de Paris*, and to make improvements at the seigneurie of St. Germain lès Couilly.[8] The second loan came from Nicolas de la Haye, a canon of Noyon, and

5. W. R. Newton and J. M. Ultee, "The Minutier central: A Research Note," *French Historical Studies* 8 (1974): 489–93. See W. R. Newton's dissertation, "Port-Royal and Jansenism," where this point is made with considerable effect.

6. Minutier central, Etude CX, 7 juin 1640–15 oct. 1676. Châtelet, Insinuations, series Y (both at A.N.).

7. Pierre Deyon, *Amiens, Capitale provinciale*, p. 314.

8. Actes cap., B.N. MS. fr. 16852, fol. 234; A.N., M.C., Etude CX, 97 (23 avril 1652), quittance de rachat.

was used to repay other loans at 5.5% and 6.25%.[9] In neither case is there any evidence to suggest a "friendly" donation at favorable rates; if anything, the abbey was doing the lenders a favor by taking their money. Little of the total went into landed improvements, as most repaid older loans at higher rates. As a result, the abbey saved over 400 livres per year in interest.

For private individuals, using borrowed money to buy land was usually unprofitable, since the cost of interest exceeded the landed income. For those who already owned land, wholesale mortgaging of estates to raise money was one sure way of losing them, as the nobles of the sixteenth century discovered when they borrowed from commercially astute families like the Séguiers.[10] Although St. Germain des Prés had been forced to alienate lands in order to pay special taxes during the Wars of Religion, the abbey reserved the right to buy back these properties. Thus for the monks, borrowing in order to acquire more land was feasible, since both their purchase price and borrowing cost were below market. As seigneurs who had the right of first refusal on lands offered for sale in their jurisdiction, the monks could take advantage of distress sales. As members of a corporation with solid assets, they could borrow on more favorable terms.

The significance of these advantages is apparent. In 1637 Dom Claude Coton, the agent for St. Germain des Prés, studied the repurchase of the barony of Cordoux, which had been alienated during the sixteenth century.[11] Dom Coton estimated the price at 70,000 livres, and feared that the land in its present state would not return enough revenue to pay for the costs of borrowing. Active management would be required to make the operation show a profit. With this in mind, the community decided to buy back the land, using 50,000 livres from the sale of an urban garden and 11,000 livres borrowed at 5.5%. Two-thirds of this money came from the Parisian President Duvelot, and the rest from a priest at the Collège de Lisieux.[12] Over the next five years the repossessed seigneurie and its improvements cost 63,000 livres.[13] When Coton himself went to Cordoux as fermier, he immediately raised the income by one-third in 1640, and by

9. Actes cap., B.N. MS. fr. 16854, fol. 78; A.N., M.C. Etude CX, 97 (29 nov. 1653), permission to reimburse; CX, 199 (24 Jan. 1658), and CX, 200 (6 Juil. 1661), quittances de rachat.

10. Denis Richet, "Les Séguier: une famille de robe à Paris du XVIe au XVIIIe siècle" Thesis, University of Paris, n.d. Cf. Jean-Louis Bourgeon, Les Colbert avant Colbert (Paris, 1973).

11. A more detailed account of these transactions can be found in part 4, The Monk as Steward; only the overall economic aspects are considered here.

12. Actes cap., B.N. MS. fr. 16852, fols. 130–32, 140.

13. Biens acquis, B.N. MS. fr. 18864, fol. 54; Actes cap., B.N. MS. fr. 16852, fol. 158.

1654 the annual revenue had risen to 6,750 livres, up 57% in 14 years.[14] This meant an 11% return on capital, nearly 13% on the abbey's own investment, considering the leverage provided through borrowing. We can understand why, despite disturbed conditions in 1649, the monks chose to purchase the fief of St. Maur with 6,000 livres borrowed from Jean-Baptiste de Conte, dean of the Cathedral of Paris.[15]

Lenders obviously had confidence in the monastery, for even in difficult times they were willing to lend it money at bargain rates. In 1648 and 1649 the abbey used more than half of its 68,400 livres borrowing to repay older loans. Perpetual rentes at 5.5% were replaced by others at 5.0%, or by life annuities at 10%. These were advantageous to the abbey if they became extinct within twenty years, a point generally assured by the age and infirmity of the lenders. Borrowing at St. Germain des Prés reached all-time high levels in 1652 and 1653, when the chroniclers wrote most plaintively: "The lands and farms of this monastery being entirely ruined by soldiers and abandoned by fermiers, the community no longer receives any of its extraordinary revenues. . . . There is no money at all in the monastery, not the slightest hope of receiving any payments for a long time. . . ."[16]

But of the money borrowed, over 152,000 livres, or nearly 85%, went toward refunding existing loans. That some of these new loans provided no interest advantage to the abbey may indicate that it was the creditors rather than the monks who were hard-pressed and requested repayment. Since the abbey was not required to repay on demand, its willingness to help must have been appreciated. In 1648, for example, Jean Bilaine, a Parisian bookdealer, requested repayment of 2,000 livres; in the following year, François de Verthamont, conseiller du roi, asked for repayment of 8,000 livres.[17] The abbey obtained the money from a canon of Notre Dame. Or there could have been other reasons for repayment: M. Solomon "made himself difficult" in 1653, probably by refusing to lower the rate of interest on his rente; he was repaid with money from a jeweller who agreed to 4.5% instead of 5.0%. As the scribe noted, "Without in-

14. Actes cap., B.N. MS. fr. 16855, fol. 180; A.N., M.C., Etude CX, 97 (11 Nov. 1654). Because the livre was set in 1654 at the same silver content as in 1641, this figure represents growth in constant terms over that period. M. Baulant and J. Meuvret, *Prix des céréales*, vol. 1, p. 249.

15. Actes cap., B.N. MS. fr. 16855, fol. 81; A.N., M.C., Etude CX, 97 (27 Sept. 1653), rachat; the loan contract dates from April 17, 1649.

16. Actes cap., B.N. MS. fr. 16855, fol. 134.

17. Actes cap., B.N. MS. fr. 16855, fols. 66, 73, 76. François de Verthamont, *trésorier* à Bordeaux, later *maître des requêtes*, lent the abbey at least 26,700 livres between 1641 and 1653.

creasing the interest we profit from 3,000 livres [additional] capital,
which the community needs badly."[18]

The general increase in borrowing between 1661 and 1663, brought
on by bad agricultural conditions, caused the going rate on new rentes perpetuelles to rise to 5.5%.[19] During the same period, however, St. Germain
des Prés refunded 36,000 livres borrowed at 5.0% with new loans at
4.5% and 4.2%. In 1661, two rentes of 18,000 livres each were refunded
to Mme. de Berault and M. de la Haye; funds to replace them came from
three other lenders.[20] Four years before the edict of Louis XIV, proclaim-
ing the 5.0% interest rate in 1665, this abbey borrowed nearly 57,000
livres at even lower rates, and only 10,050 livres at that rate. Of the three
rentes at 5.0%, two may have been accepted only out of charity to the
lenders—the nuns of the Holy Sacrament and an orphaned nephew of one
of the monks.[21] As other historians have suspected, the edict thus served
only to ratify an existing economic fact—money was available at lower
rates.[22] When the monks decided to recover the alienated seigneurie of
Valenton in 1664, they had no trouble finding 33,800 livres at 4.2%. "We
shall borrow as much as necessary," noted the secretary of the chapter.[23]

Substantial refunding of debts occurred in 1665 and in the early
1670s. Sometimes the monks had to consider the political consequences of
repaying their loans. In 1671 the bailiff of the Faubourg St. Germain, an
officer of the abbey, proposed to lend money at 4.5% to the community,
which could then repurchase a rente at 5.0% owed to Thierry Bignon,
maître des requêtes. But the monks were reluctant to accept: the offer was
practical only "supposing that the said Sieur Bignon would not be angered,
since experience has shown that such reimbursements are very odious to
powerful persons who do not desire them, and denounce as enemies and
opponents those who owed them the rente."[24] Bignon was a man of influence—his brother was *avocat général* in Parlement, and his father and
father-in-law had held the same post. To repurchase the rente was to cause
an upheaval in his portfolio, and to risk breaking a tie with an important
Parlementaire family that also controlled the royal library. The Bignons,

18. Séniorat, B.N. MS. fr. 18819, fol. 38.
19. Deyon, *Amiens, capitale provinciale*, p. 314.
20. A.N. H5 4274, mises, 1661; H5 4275, casuel, 1661; Actes cap., B.N. MS. fr.
16856, fols. 159, 162. A.N., M.C., Etude CX, 200 (6 juil. 1661), de la Haye.
21. "Conclu qu'il falloit recevoir laditte somme" (of the money from the nephew).
Actes cap., B.N. MS. fr. 16856, fol. 163. The rente from the nuns is listed in A.N. H5
4275, and in A.N., M.C., Etude CX, 199 (14 mars 1661).
22. "Les décisions réglementaires françaises . . . ne faisaient que ratifier l'evolution
réelle." Goubert, *Hist. écon.*, p. 344.
23. Actes cap., B.N. MS. fr. 16856, fol. 169; Séniorat, B.N. MS. fr. 18819, fol. 103.
24. Séniorat, B.N. MS. fr. 18819, fol. 19.

patrons of intellectuals, employed scholars as tutors and secretaries in their
hôtel; St. Germain des Prés, a center of monastic scholarship, could ill
afford to lose their friendship.[25]

This naturally raises the question, "Who were the lenders?" On
rentes viagères they tended to be older persons, ecclesiastics with private
property and others who did not have to provide for heirs. St. Germain
des Prés felt some obligation to take rentes viagères from its own unreformed monks: on a proposed rente from Dom Nicolas Gouffette the
scribe noted, "We shall receive his money at 10%, even though the thing
is not very advantageous."[26] When persons outside the abbey proposed
these loans, the monks evaluated them more carefully, sometimes rejecting
their offers because the terms were not favorable enough. Among the unsuccessful lenders were a young man who refused to take a lower interest
rate "because of his age," and a nun of Chelles with extra money to invest
after she had been reimbursed for a public loan, a rente on the Hôtel de
Ville.[27] An infirm man aged sixty-six proposed a life annuity with his wife
as the surviving beneficiary, but the monks found "that the wife is not so
advanced in age as has been represented to the community," and that offer
was also rejected.[28] Naturally, in considering life annuities, the community
looked more favorably upon lenders whose age and poor health gave hopes
of early termination.

The monks tried to borrow with some assurance that these loans
would be extinguished in less than twenty years, because annuities that
continued longer were generally more expensive than ordinary loans.
Based on typical interest rates, an annuity that ran for thirty years was 500
livres of interest per 1,000 livres of principal more expensive than an ordinary loan: this meant a difference of 20% in total costs.[29] Also, ordinary

25. Bruno Neveu, "La Vie érudite à Paris," pp. 432–511. See also Newton, "Port-
Royal."

26. Actes cap., B.N. MS. fr. 16852, fol. 207. This loan was later repaid, "pour avoir
de la paix," according to the council book. Séniorat, B.N. MS. fr. 18819, fol. 31. Note
also that this unreformed monk held several such loans—A.N. M.C., Etude CX, 199 (8
fév. 1658), for 3,000 livres; and CX, 199 (7 juil. 1660), 4,000 livres.

27. Actes cap., B.N. MS. fr. 16855, fol. 95; MS. fr. 16857, fol. 126.

28. Séniorat, B.N. MS. fr. 18819, fol. 55.

29. Given the current interest rates, the period during which life annuities (*rentes
viagères*) are less expensive than ordinary loans (*rentes perpetuelles*) can be calculated
as follows:

I_v = rate on annuities $\qquad$ (Normally, $I_v > I_p$)
I_p = rate on ordinary loans
Time in years T = $\dfrac{1}{I_v - I_p}$

The total paid on a loan is found thus (without compounding):

For *ordinary loans*: $\qquad\qquad\qquad$ For *annuities*:
$\quad$ Total = Principal + ($I_p \times P \times T$) $\qquad$ Total = $P \times I_v \times T$

loans could often be reimbursed and refinanced at lower rates to produce even greater savings. Problems for the abbey arose, therefore, when lenders lived longer than expected at the time a life annuity was made.

Indeed, some of the lenders profited handsomely from their longevity. Madeleine Darville, countess of La Grange Palaiseau and granddaughter of an avocat général of the Parlement of Paris, lent the abbey 7,000 livres on a life annuity in 1656, when the money was used for the seigneurie of Courbetin and for repayment of an ordinary loan.[30] Later the countess made a donation requesting that prayers be said for her deceased sister, a nun. But thirty years passed before the lender herself died and was buried in the abbey. At the time of her death she was about eighty years old; that would have made her about fifty when she lent the money. Yet she had received 175 livres quarterly for the rest of her life.[31] Jean Galeot, a priest and doctor of the University of Paris, also lived long and invested wisely. In 1654, while aged fifty, he lent 5,600 livres to the abbey at 7.14% on an annuity; thirty years later he too was still collecting payments of 400 livres per year.[32] Both of these lenders had effectively insured themselves against the risks of an uncertain economy, which included a falling interest rate.

The opposite conditions applied more often, when buyers of annuities made little financial profit in their dealings with the abbey. Another priest, Jean Fagot, living in the Rue St. Victor, offered in 1649 to convert an ordinary loan of 8,000 livres at 5.00% to an annuity capitalized at 7,200 livres at 5.56%.[33] His annual income would thus be the same. He offered to reduce the normal difference in interest rates because he wanted to name his sister, Damoiselle Jeanne Fagot, as the surviving beneficiary. The abbey agreed to these terms because the proposed rate on the life annuity with two beneficiaries was no higher than the prevailing legal rate on perpetual loans—and eventually the obligation would become extinct. Subsequently, Jean Fagot drew the annuity until his death in 1661; starting in October of that year, his sister, by then married to a M. Godefroi, received payments. Madame Godefroi was still alive and benefiting in 1684.[34] Up to that time she and her brother had collected 14,000 livres, whereas an equivalent ordinary loan, even assuming refinancing to take advantage of

30. Actes cap., B.N. MS. fr. 16855, fol. 236, 23 mai 1656; A.N., M.C., Etude CX, 97 (26 juil. 1656).
31. Actes cap., B.N. MS. fr. 16855, fol. 239, 21 juin 1656. Reg. des Mortuaires, B.N. MS. fr. 18818, fol. 355, 19 avril 1656. Comptes, A.N. H5 4274, H5 4276.
32. Actes cap., B.N. MS. fr. 16855, fol. 168, 13 juil. 1654, fol. 178, 23 sept. 1654.
33. Actes cap., B.N. MS. fr. 16855, fol. 84, 26 juil. 1649; Insinuations du Châtelet, A.N. Y 186, 3533, 30 juil. 1649.
34. Comptes, A.N. H5 4274. Jeanne Fagot had also lent the abbey 4,000 livres on a rente constituée from 1649 to 1654: A.N., M.C., Etude CX, 97 (28 mars 1654). Jean Godefroi was Commandant des Gardes du Corps du Roi. Comptes, A.N. H5 4276.

lower interest rates, would have cost the abbey over 18,000 livres.[35] Even after thirty-five years of payments while general interest rates were declining, in 1684 another forty years would have been required to make the total cost of the annuity higher than that of a regular loan.[36] The original terms were thus so favorable to the abbey that one assumes the lender had pious motives for providing his funds and expected only a modest return during his lifetime.

By contrast, those involved in the traffic in rentes perpetuelles were more active investors, whose income from royal offices and trade was more than adequate for their level of consumption, and whose surplus funds went into capital accumulation. Faced with a shortage of suitable investments, the equivalent of an oversupply of capital in an underdeveloped society, the enrichening officials and merchants lent money at falling interest rates and needed no royal guidance to follow the long-term downward trend. Parlementaires, masters of requests, members of the lesser courts such as the Chambre des Comptes and the Châtelet, royal treasurers, advocates, and bourgeois de Paris can be identified as lenders to St. Germain des Prés. The merchants include a dyer, a grocer, a jeweller, and a fishmonger.

With some lenders and their families the monastery enjoyed financial relationships lasting twenty years and longer. The bourgeois de Paris brother of one monk lent at least 37,500 livres between 1640 and 1655; when the abbey was pressed for funds in 1653, he offered an additional 6,000 livres of principal to lower the interest rate from 5.5% to 4.5% on one loan.[37] Again the monks gained capital without increasing the burden of annual interest payments. Nicolas de la Haye, the canon of Noyon who had lent 36,000 livres in 1643, provided further loans of 4,000 and 6,000 livres between 1649 and 1653; the monks repaid half of his largest loan in 1658, then made further payments to his heirs in 1661 and 1666.[38] The Verthamont family, another group of St. Germains des Prés creditors, had enriched themselves through careers in royal finances; their members included two masters of requests, an archdeacon of Josas (associated with the archbishopric of Paris), and a canon of Notre Dame. All of them were conseillers du roi, and they were related by marriage to the d'Aligre

35. This assumes refinancing at the same time as other loans with the interest rate falling to 4.17%.

36. This is figuring the differential between 4.17% and 5.56%. An actual rente constituée, however, would probably have been refinanced with interest close to zero during John Law's system.

37. Actes cap., B.N. MS. fr. 16854, fol. 34; Séniorat, B.N. MS. fr. 18819, fols. 44, 58. Note a gift of 10,000 livres to provide for a daily mass in perpetuity, A.N., M.C., Etude CX, 200 (22 déc. 1661), Charles Brachet, brother of Benoît Brachet, C.S.M.

38. See note 20, above. The 1666 refund went to the namesake, another Nicolas de la Haye, also dean and canon of Noyon, A.N., M.C., Etude CX, 200 (15 mars 1666).

family, even more prominent in French officialdom. In the early 1650s they lent St. Germain over 60,000 livres to repurchase older, more onerous obligations.[39] As a conservative investment, the rentes of St. Germain des Prés could be held for years, even by a single individual. Over a decade beginning in 1661, Jacques Vigneron, *tailleur du roi*, made loans to the abbey totaling 44,800 livres. Some of this money was repaid to his estate in 1672 and 1679, but the final settlement did not take place until 1697.[40]

That St. Germain des Prés was a solid Parisian institution inspiring confidence, that it could borrow from the Verthamont, the Talon,[41] the Bignon, and other moneyed Parisian families, is clear enough; but it does not appear to have had the tight supporting network of family and economic connections that surrounded the Abbey of Port-Royal des Champs.[42] There the Jansenist faithful required ideological commitment to the convent as well as financial support. This commitment could be shown by retreating from the city and living at Port-Royal, by sending children to its schools and daughters to its community, and finally by being buried there. St. Germain des Prés drew its monks from all over France, as they were selected for scholarly work by the Congregation of St. Maur; therefore it lacked the regional character of Port-Royal, a character that was strengthened further by strictly applying the vow of stability to the community. Despite these handicaps to the formation of a politically significant constituency, St. Germain actively sought the favor of powerful persons, and there are indications that the abbey inspired generous sentiments among those associated with it. The maître d'hôtel of Abbot Henry of Verneuil lent the community 18,000 livres in 1661, then an additional 6,600 livres in 1664; when he was near death in 1667 he donated 12,000 livres to the abbey, and he was later buried there.[43] The case of Jacques Langellé, bourgeois de Paris, is exceptional; he sent four sons into the Congregation of St. Maur, lent

39. See note 17, above, on François de Verthamont. The notarial contracts show the capital transfers. Antoine, Archdeacon of Josas, lent 14,700 in 1654, A.N., M.C., Etude CX, 97 (18 and 19 mars 1654). Michel, Baron de Breau, *maître des requêtes* and husband of Marie d'Aligre, lent 18,000 in 1658, CX, 199 (24 jan. 1658), and rachat, CX, 200 (13 juin 1661). Jean-Baptiste, canon of Notre Dame, obtained by transfer a loan of 1,000 livres, rachat, CX, 155 (8 août 1665).

40. A.N. H5 4275, casuel, 1661, 1662, 1664; Actes cap., B.N. MS. fr. 16856, fols. 159, 208, 221; MS. fr. 16857, fols. 126, 313; contracts, e.g., A.N., M.C., Etude CX, 200 (16 mai 1661). Cf. similar long-term rentes of the manse abbatiale, A.N. H5 3700.

41. Omer Talon, *Premier Avocat Général* of Parlement, constituted two loans, one of 4,000 and another of 13,000 livres, A.N., M.C., Etude CX, 97 (26 oct. 1652—2 contracts). His family was still collecting interest in 1663, Comptes, A.N. H5 4274.

42. See vol. 3 of Newton's "Port-Royal and Jansenism," pp. 385–564, in which he discusses the "société de Port-Royal."

43. Grosjean, loans noted in Comptes, A.N. H5 4275; gift in Actes cap., B.N. MS. fr. 16856, fol. 280; burial in Séniorat, B.N. MS. fr. 18819, fol. 325 (15 déc. 1667).

money on a rente viagère to St. Germain des Prés, and was buried there together with his wife and daughter.[44]

Among institutional investors St. Germain des Prés also had appeal. The Hôtel Dieu, the Faculty of Canon Law of the University of Paris, and various religious communities entrusted their funds to the Parisian abbey. In 1648 and 1652 the monks repaid loans to the Carmelite nuns of Chartres and Pontoise; in the first case the nuns had complained that the interest payments were irregular, but they received full return of their principal.[45] Two communities of Dames de la Charité located within the seigneurial jurisdiction of the abbey sought paternal protection for a modest 2,280 livres of capital, as did a group of Religieuses de la Miséricorde with 4,000 livres.[46]

The transactions with the Hôtel Dieu, involving large sums borrowed for others, illuminate the role of St. Germain as a guarantor of other monasteries and the Congregation of St. Maur. Prosperous Parisians gladly offered their money to St. Germain des Prés because they saw the excellent security promised by the abbey's lands in the Parisian region. At the same time, monasteries in the provinces received a distinctly cooler reception in the capital market. Le Bec, St. Ouen de Rouen, St. Martin de Sées, Jumièges, and other famous Benedictine houses had difficulty borrowing at Paris. They, and the poorer Parisian houses of St. Martin des Champs and Notre Dame des Blancsmanteaux, could obtain credit only through the support of St. Germain des Prés. The congregation itself in 1638, St. Savin de Poitou in 1659, St. Ouen in 1660, Le Bec in 1662—all had to admit that they could not borrow any money at Paris without the guarantee.[47] But once the lenders had received the written assurance of St. Germain, they even reduced the interest rate. In 1654, for example, St. Martin de Sées and St. Colombe saw the rate fall one-half a point.[48] As the Maurist movement spread through France, the newly acquired monasteries and the congregation frequently needed financial support. To obtain control of claustral offices and priories from unreformed monks, the Maurists had to promise them guaranteed pensions. The loan guarantees of St. Germain des Prés thus insured the success of the reform in France as a whole. From 1638 to 1645, St. Germain co-signed 104,144 livres of borrowing by others; from

44. Séniorat, B.N. MS. fr. 18819, fols. 132v, 134; Registre des Mortuaires, B.N. MS. fr. 18818, fol. 356.

45. Actes cap., B.N., MS. fr. 16855, fols. 59, 133; Pontoise, Contract, A.N., M.C., Etude CX, 97 (7 juin 1652).

46. Actes cap., B.N. MS. fr. 16857, fols. 196, 264 (Charité): Contract, A.N., M.C., Etude CX, 97 (1 déc. 1656—Miséricorde).

47. Actes cap., B.N. MS. fr. 16852, fols. 166–67; MS. fr. 16856, fols. 131, 150, 175.

48. Actes cap., B.N. MS. fr. 16855, fol. 159.

1646 to 1650, 73,500; and from 1651 to 1655, when the Parisian house itself had so little money, its guarantees nevertheless rose to 209,800 livres. In 1656 the Congregation of St. Maur and five abbeys of the former Congregation of Chezal-Benoît had to pay 24,000 livres for papal bulls of union and annates. They asked St. Germain for a borrowing guarantee which the chapter granted reluctantly, "in view of the present much-encumbered condition of the monastery. . . ."[49] Yet the monks must have decided that they had not exceeded the limits of prudence, for in the rest of the year they gave guarantees of 56,000 livres, and in the next two years they supported over 100,000 livres of borrowing by others. The procedure was as follows: those institutions needing money would first seek a willing lender and then ask for the guarantee of the chapter of St. Germain. Thus, when the Congregation of St. Maur wanted to borrow 33,000 livres to buy houses for a new monastery at Orleans in 1654, the superiors obtained a tentative commitment from the Hôtel Dieu, which advanced the money on St. Germain's guarantee.[50] In 1659, when the abbey was ready to repay a rente of 12,600 livres, outstanding since 1636 to Catherine Aubery de l'Esdon, widow of an advocate, the congregation borrowed 20,000 livres from another lender and proposed to combine this sum with the money for l'Esdon to repay the Hôtel Dieu. The monks of St. Germain agreed, and transferred their rente to the congregation with the appropriate guarantee.[51] To Madame de l'Esdon and other lenders, a loan guaranteed by St. Germain des Prés was as secure as a direct obligation of the abbey; to the monks, their fraternal support through loan guarantees represented a practical application of monastic ideals. Using their special advantages in the money market, calling upon their wealthy constituency, the community of St. Germain des Prés borrowed wisely and well. The mutual support of the Benedictine monasteries rescued more than one house from financial crisis; at the end of the century those so rescued included a hard-pressed St. Germain des Prés itself.

49. "Vu l'état présent du monastère déjà beaucoup endetté. . . ." Actes cap., B.N. MS. fr. 16855, fol. 235.

50. Actes cap., B.N. MS. fr. 16855, fol. 178.

51. Actes cap., B.N. MS. fr. 16856, fols. 105, 129, 130; the loan had originally been set at 5.5% interest, but it was reduced to 4.5% in 1653, A.N., M.C., Etude CX, 97 (5 sept. 1653); the reimbursement is recorded in CX, 200 (1 mars 1660).

5

Financial Difficulties

So much has been written about crisis in the seventeenth century that the difficulties of St. Germain des Prés may appear minor by comparison. Secure in their possession of vast landed wealth, able to borrow on demand, favored by their political and social position, the monks were well insulated against the storms of their age. Only gross mismanagement could have produced financial difficulties internally, yet this seems unlikely in view of the monks' careful handling of property and loans. The only external forces strong enough to buffet this powerful abbey were those affectting the French economy as a whole: poor harvests, taxes, plagues, and wars. In the Middle Ages the abbey had known the impact of Viking raids, aristocratic plunder, black death, and the Hundred Years' War; more recently, in the Wars of Religion of the sixteenth century, St. Germain des Prés again risked alienation and destruction of its rural property. The monks had survived those trials, losing little of the abbey's patrimony and compensating handsomely for their losses through new acquisitions afterwards.[1] In this context, the threatening nature of the seventeenth-century problems must be made clear.

Several times the meetings of the chapter discussed the need for money. These discussions often occurred when French agriculture as a whole suffered great difficulties: during the Fronde, for example, and also during the crisis years of the 1660s and 1690s. Borrowing was the monks' perennial solution to these temporary problems, whose traces could be obliterated by prosperity, donations, and self-extinguishing annuities. Two of these periods, however, deserve more careful attention because extraordinary means were required to solve them. Twice, in 1653 and in 1690, the burden of debt became so heavy that the abbey asked for help from the Congregation of St. Maur. In both cases external catastrophes forced the monks to look for outside solutions.

1. Jacquart, *La Crise rurale*, p. 729

The first request for subsidy from the congregation was presented at the annual diet of 1653. It showed an accumulated debt of 278,843 livres, of which 80% was funded in rentes; the rest represented unpaid bills.[2] Cracks had appeared in the pyramid of debt, too, with requests for refunds indicating the creditors' own discomfiture. For two years previously many tenants in the Parisian region had not paid their rents; reports of devastation from the Fronde agree that the harvest year 1652–53 was the worst, with some villages losing a third of their population.[3] The buildings and lands of the abbey required 80,000 livres for repairs and maintenance, and the coffers stood empty.[4] St. Germain des Prés therefore requested permission to borrow 30,000 livres, to accelerate payments from other monasteries, and to postpone settlement of the congregation's claims on the abbey. Massive turnover of abbey loans followed, and in the next year St. Germain des Prés was still in arrears on the pensions of the unreformed monks and on its general obligations.[5] Yet the reader may hold doubts about the gravity of this crisis, for 85% of the newly borrowed capital went to refund older loans. The abbey continued to guarantee the loans of others, and by 1658 the chapter thought the situation stable enough to solicit fresh life annuities, initially more burdensome obligations carrying higher rates of interest.[6] Still it is significant that the Parisian monks took this unusual course, setting a noteworthy precedent for the future.

The financial crisis of the 1690s, which followed this precedent, nonetheless differed because it was not primarily caused by bad agricultural conditions. Instead, seigneurial responsibilities and taxes played larger roles. The new parish church of St. Sulpice, an imposing baroque structure located in St. Germain's neighborhood only a hundred yards from the abbey, cost much more than expected. When the revenues of the parish itself did not suffice, the obligations fell upon its spiritual lords, the abbot and monks of St. Germain des Prés. From their point of view, this responsibility was particularly unfair because they had lost control of St. Sulpice in 1668, following a hard contest with the archbishop of Paris.[7] Now, twenty years later, the abbey found itself saddled with the extravagance of its builders, 88,000 livres of bills payable immediately, over and above the normal assessment of property in the parish.[8] While two-thirds of the total

2. Actes cap., B.N., MS. fr. 16855, fol. 146; Séniorat, B.N. MS. fr. 18819, fol. 39.
3. Jacquart, La Crise rurale, pp. 583–84.
4. Actes cap., B.N. MS. fr. 16855, fol. 134.
5. Actes cap., B.N. MS. fr. 16855, fol. 168.
6. Actes cap., B.N. MS. fr. 16856, fol. 101.
7. See part 5, Spiritual Life and Politics.
8. Choses mém., B.N. MS. fr. 18816, fol. 151; Actes cap., B.N. MS. fr. 16857, f. 286.

was charged to the abbot, the remainder, or 29,000 livres, had to be paid by the monks.

A second cause of financial problems for the abbey was the continuing warfare of Louis XIV, which led the king to impose confiscatory taxes. When St. Germain des Prés and other religious communities (*gens de mortmain*) purchased property from private individuals, the king and other lords could no longer collect the usual mutation fees, for it was assumed that the property would stay permanently in the possession of the institution. As compensation, the seigneur could demand a lump-sum settlement (*amortissement*), but he could also waive this payment. Through political influence Louis XIV, the ultimate seigneur, had often been persuaded to waive payments from religious houses that bought property. A royal declaration of July 5, 1689, however, cancelled all exemptions granted since 1641.[9] By revoking exemptions going back more than half a century, Louis brought about "a true St. Bartholomew's massacre of the clergy."[10] St. Germain des Prés, a large buyer of property, was hit hard. Many of its purchases were only replacements for other properties it was practically forced to sell. For the expansion of the park of Versailles, for example, the king had taken woodlands belonging to the abbey, and part of his payment was exemption from amortissements incurred by the purchase of replacement properties, the seigneuries of Berny and Fresnes, acquired at a cost of over 400,000 livres.[11] Similar circumstances attended sales of land to the royal ministers Colbert and Louvois, who had used their influence to obtain exemptions for the abbey's replacement lands. The old regime, with its insistence on privilege and compensation, lacked a general system of refunds on amortissements, or even tax credits, to religious institutions that sold their property to assessable persons. Each sale was therefore a special case and required royal letters of exemption. When Louis XIV withdrew all of these letters at one fell swoop, the monks of St. Germain had to pay 69,000 livres in amortissements, and their abbot, Cardinal Fürstemberg, was liable for 107,000 livres for his portion of the abbey's lands.[12]

Since ordinary revenues, magnificent as they were, could not meet these payments, a special borrowing program was needed. The monks were able to find 29,000 livres in a short time.[13] Cardinal Fürstemberg asked for and received their borrowing guarantees for loans totaling 103,000 livres from eight persons. It is instructive to note who had money to lend in difficult times—royal officials, particularly agents of the financial

9. Declaration, B.N. Imp. 4° F 23614/610.
10. Marion, *Dictionnaire*, p. 19.
11. Choses mém., B.N. MS. fr. 18816, fol. 151v.
12. Actes cap., B.N. MS. fr. 16857, fols. 260, 286.
13. Actes cap., B.N. MS. fr. 16857, fol. 256.

administration, appeared again on the lists of lenders. A maître des requêtes, a *maître de la chambre aux deniers*, and a *président conseiller au Parlement* figure prominently. The lone military officer, a colonel in the royal regiment of Roussillon, appears out of place, but his participation was arranged in his absence by his agent, a président of the Court of Currency. Three widows on the list had been married to men of similar backgrounds: another master of requests, an intendant of Alsace, and a treasurer of France and receiver-general from Tours.[14]

Louis XIV, like his sixteenth-century predecessors, had pressured his clergy to do his borrowing for him, although he promised nothing in return. The money came from royal officials charged with the collection of taxes, administration of expenditures, and justice; for them the security of the clergy was better than that of state loans. An indirect consequence of the wars, more directly related to spending, taxation, and borrowing, was an increase in the rate of interest. Now, in 1690, the loans had to be made at 5.0%, considerably less palatable to the abbey than the voluntary borrowings made at 3.8% only three years before.[15]

The superior general of the Congregation of St. Maur, "touched with compassion by the pitiful state" of St. Germain des Prés, proposed that other Benedictine houses each offer to borrow 3,000 to 5,000 livres in their own names and agree to pay the interest for ten years. At the end of that time St. Germain would take over the loans. Twelve monasteries immediately accepted this scheme; a number of them had previously benefited from the borrowing guarantees of their Parisian brothers, and now, returning the favor, they raised 35,000 livres.[16] Two other monasteries, St. André of Avignon and St. Sulpice of Bourges, reported that they could not find money in the provinces, but they gave guarantees to help St. Germain borrow 7,000 livres in Paris.[17]

Earlier the stream of borrowed money had flowed from Paris to the provinces, but now the direction was reversed. The community of St. Nicaise in Reims actively sought money for St. Germain des Prés in their area. In 1684, the Parisians had borrowed 30,000 livres at Reims under favorable conditions—4.0% or lower interest.[18] Thanks to the intermediary work of Dom Pierre Sauveaumare, procureur, and Dom Pierre de la

14. Comptes, Manse abbatiale, A.N. H5 3700; Carnot, notaire (12 juil. 1690).

15. Actes cap., B.N. MS. fr. 16857, fols. 233–34.

16. Participants and amounts: Bonne Nouvelle de Rouen, 2,000 livres; St. Ouen, 3,000; St. Georges, 1,000; Le Bec, 3,000; Jumièges, 3,000; Fécamp, 3,000; Tyron, 3,000; St. Vandrille, 4,000; St. Père de Chartres, 2,000; St. Pierre de Conches, 3,000; St. Martin de Sées, 4,000; St. Nicaise de Reims, 4,000. Actes cap., B.N. MS. fr. 16857, fols. 268–70.

17. Actes cap., B.N. MS. fr. 16857, fol. 276.

18. Actes cap., B.N. MS. fr. 16857, fol. 185.

Croix, cellerier of the house at Reims, St. Germain obtained three loans amounting to 9,500 livres in 1691. Later in the decade, Reims became the principal source of the Parisian abbey's borrowed money. More than 57,000 livres flowed from there to St. Germain in 1697 and 1698. The lenders included two widows (one of a tax judge, the other of a merchant), two canons of St. Symphorien, two other priests and doctors of theology, one physician, and two parish churches. The interest on these loans was 4.2% or less, falling to 3.8% again in some cases.[19] Despite their financial difficulties, the monks could return to their traditional practice of reimbursing old loans with new ones at lower rates.

The finances of St. Germain des Prés remained turbulent into the first years of the eighteenth century, with bad harvests, new assessments, and more taxes. In 1709 it was even necessary to borrow 17,000 livres to buy wheat for seeding the lands.[20] The War of Spanish Succession went badly for France, and the winter was so cold that wine froze in the glasses on the dinner tables at Versailles. The next year the king extracted 24 million livres from the clergy, which in general had to pay an exorbitant 8.3% on its borrowing; but St. Germain des Prés obtained its share of 18,000 livres at 5.0%.[21] From Reims came additional funds, and by 1714, with the return of peace, the interest rate there had fallen to 3.5%.[22] Still, the restoration of financial equilibrium at the abbey had to await the time of cheap money under John Law's scheme. At least 41,000 livres of borrowing was then reimbursed in 1719 as lenders offered consistently lower rates; by 1720 the monastery could borrow at zero interest.[23]

The abbey's response in times of trouble further illuminates its favored position in the money market. The vicissitudes of its temporal situ-

19. Loans at 4.2%, all in 1697: Marguerite Bachelier, veuve de M. l'Espagnol, élu de Reims, 6,000; Louis Dutemps, chanoine de St. Symphorien, 3,000; Fabrique St. Symphorien, 4,000; Fabrique St. Jacques, 3,000; Actes cap., B.N. MS. fr. 16857, fol. 317. Loans at 4.0%, 1691: François de Forest, prêtre, 4,000; Nicaise Oudinet, prêtre, chanoine, 2,500; M. Bachelier, 3,000. Actes cap., B.N. MS. fr. 16857, fols. 270, 276, 281. Loans at 3.8%: 1697, unspecified; 1698, 25,000, "une personne à Reims." MS. fr. 16857, fols. 318, 320.

20. Actes cap., B.N. MS. fr. 16857, fol. 444.

21. Actes cap., B.N. MS. fr. 16857, fol. 450.

22. From Dame Antoinette le Clerc, widow of Etienne Coquebert, Sieur de Montfort, Lieutenant particulier au présidial de Reims, 22,000 livres; from Remy Joseph Coquebert, son of the preceding, conseiller au Parlement de Metz, 6,000 livres. Actes cap., B.N. MS. fr. 16857, fol. 481. These loans were repaid in part, 7,000 and 3,000 livres respectively, when Louis Dutemps, chanoine de St. Symphorien, offered to reduce the interest rate on 13,000 livres. Five other lenders were repaid 20,000 livres; 5,600 was borrowed at 3.5%; and 3,000 livres was received interest-free for two years. Actes cap., B.N. MS. fr. 16857, fol. 482.

23. According to marginal notes on the preceding loans. See also Actes cap., B.N. MS. fr. 16857, fol. 543.

ation are apparent. Laden with heavy responsibilities, both to their own community and to the congregation of which their house was the head, the monastic managers did well. They kept detailed accounts and records of their deliberations; their decisions to grant leases, to purchase land, and to accept and reimburse loans show prudence. In all of these actions the monks collectively acted as directors of a secular institution; their commitment to the religious life, too easily misunderstood as a retreat from the world, included an obligation to administer the abbey's worldly resources. When unforeseen external circumstances brought the abbey into financial difficulty, the monastic officers, working together with the congregation, found remedial measures. Concern for spiritual well-being also required concern for material well-being; that the monks applied sound business practices shows their necessary secular bent. In managing their revenues, as in managing their population, the monks had to contend with outside social forces. The distribution of their expenditures naturally complements the management of their revenues, and forms the next part of this study.

PART 3

Monastic Expenditures

6

General Budget and Physical Plant

Like the revenues, the expenditures of St. Germain des Prés were subject to agricultural, economic, and fiscal conditions. Expenditures, however, may be more indicative of the monastic view of the world. To uphold the position of the abbey in Paris, to maintain the community, and to achieve its spiritual purposes, choices had to be made when the money was spent. The monks' spending cannot easily be divided into necessities and amenities, for at St. Germain des Prés, the royal Benedictine abbey in Paris, a center for scholarship and the headquarters of the reformed congregation, monastic life required a certain standard of dignity.

The Maurist leadership adhered to established Benedictine tradition when it rejected extreme austerity. Excessive mortification, misguided zeal, and abstinence for the sake of appearances could all be found elsewhere in seventeenth-century France.[1] If, by contrast, the account books of St. Germain suggest less spiritual enthusiasm and too much concern for material well-being, it may be because St. Germain des Prés was not allowed to be a typical monastery. The festive days of patron saints, French military victories, the birth of royal children, and the death of persons of quality, all called forth public celebrations led by the monks as spiritual authorities in their neighborhood. Grand ceremonies, though they may have called into question monastic modesty and simplicity, were accepted as an obligation. The high social standing of St. Germain des Prés demanded commensurate celebrations and the expense they involved. In the Maurist scheme of priorities, the material aspects of the monastery were prerequisites to good observance and sound scholarship. The literary and spiritual goals of St. Germain des Prés required well-maintained physical structures and a prosperous community, as well as religious services themselves. These three

---

1. Cuthbert Butler, *Benedictine Monachism*, pp. 301–03; also consult Orest Ranum, "A Generation of Saints," *Paris in the Age of Absolutism*, pp. 109–31; and A. J. Krailsheimer, *Armand-Jean de Rancé*.

broad areas of expenditure—the material, the communal, and the spiritual—testify in ascending order to the values of the Maurist view of the
world.

As the documentation for this view, detailed expenditure books exist
for the years 1660–63, 1679–84, and 1691–99.[2] To supplement their
serial data we have indications of expenditure in the revenue books,[3] the
deliberations of the council,[4] and the minutes of the chapter.[5] Extraordinary items can make simple annual comparisons misleading, but the
monks tried to separate unusual payments from ordinary operating expenses. They divided their accounts into the following broad categories:
food; non-food supplies; clothing; medical expenses; church; alms;
charges, interest, wages; repairs; travel and legal expenses; property; extraordinary items; debts from previous years. The largest four categories were
charges, debts, food, and property; together they accounted for over half
of the total. The two spiritually important categories of church and alms
received less than 5% of the budget in most years. To summarize—about
two-thirds of the expenditure went to the physical plant of the abbey and
its dependencies, one-fourth to the needs of the community, and the rest
to spiritual purposes and extraordinary expenses. The chart shows the distribution by categories in a typical year, 1679.

How much free choice was there in expenditures? The monks were
certainly limited by the burden of fixed expenses, particularly in debt service and maintenance. Financial charges alone amounted to one-third of
the budget. These continuing expenses included taxes, debt service, and
seigneurial obligations. The first of these, taxes, occupied a relatively minor
position in the accounts of St. Germain des Prés because the abbey was
exempt from the *taille*, the general royal tax on persons and property. To
capture at least some of the wealth of the church, the government had
persuaded the clergy to contribute "voluntarily" to the treasury. Although
the Assembly of the Clergy ostensibly met every five years to decide the
amount of the contribution, by the early seventeenth century this gift had
come to resemble an ordinary tax. Certainly it was a forced exaction, and
the clergy's refusal to grant the full amount requested by the king was met
with threats and bargaining.[6] Beginning with the sixteenth-century Wars
of Religion the clergy had borrowed money on behalf of the crown; the

2. Comptes généraux des mises, A.N. H5 4274, H5 4276, H5 4277, H5 4278.
3. A.N. H5 4275, H5 4279.
4. Séniorat, B.N. MS. fr. 18819 (1649–1723).
5. Actes cap., B.N. MSS. fr. 16852, 16854–16857.
6. See the standard works by Pierre Blet, *Le Clergé de France et la monarchie: étude
sur les assemblées générales du clergé de 1615 à 1666*, 2 vols. (Rome, 1959); and *Les
Assemblées du clergé et Louis XIV de 1670 à 1693* (Rome, 1972).

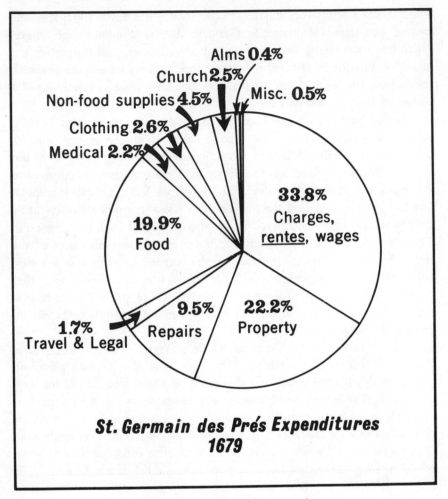

Alms **0.4%**
Church **2.5%**
Non-food supplies **4.5%**   Misc. **0.5%**
Clothing **2.6%**
Medical **2.2%**

33.8%
Charges,
<u>rentes</u>, wages

19.9%
Food

9.5%   **22.2%**
Repairs   Property

1.7%
Travel & Legal

St. Germain des Prés Expenditures
1679

GRAPH 10   Expenditures, 1679

décimes, direct taxes on ecclesiastical income, were used to pay the interest on these debts and the forced contribution. Since the décimes were levied on benefices, the collectors assessed St. Germain only on part of its income, the priories it held for the community. These taxes were not particularly onerous, but they were predictable and regular. In the diocese of Meaux, for example, the abbey annually paid 137 livres 18 sous for the priory of St. Germain lès Coully. In 1660 an additional fifty livres in *décimes extraordinaires* was levied to help pay for the Assembly of the Clergy. Décimes were often paid several months after they were assessed: those for October 1660, for example, were paid in January 1661. The abbey was more prompt in paying membership taxes to the Congregation of St. Maur, which levied 1,800 livres annually in the 1660s, and 2,500 livres annually twenty years later. Of course, St. Germain also contributed to the congregation by guaranteeing the borrowing of other houses, and supporting the superiors. Finally, local taxes for streets and lanterns were quite nominal, and indeed, the total of regular taxation took only about 3,000 livres of a budget of over 97,000 in 1679.

Debts, particularly the rentes of the abbey, weighed more heavily. St. Germain des Prés enjoyed a good credit rating because it paid its obligations regularly. Delays of more than one or two quarters were uncommon, and even these were relatively brief postponements compared to the delayed payments on rentes of the Hôtel de Ville. Official manipulation had already impaired the usefulness of these instruments of credit by the 1630s, and later contributed to the discontent that found expression in the Fronde.[7] As for the presumably more secure general rentes of the clergy, repeated delays meant that interest accrued in 1673 was not paid until 1710![8] At such times the unlucky bondholders could only wait: they might sell their rentes, propose revised schedules of payments, or request return of their capital, but they could never make demands or expect interest on the arrears.

The Maurists of St. Germain des Prés may have been more sympathetic to problems of their lenders, because some of them had placed all their capital with the abbey and depended on regular payments for their livelihood. The unreformed monks, for example, were always paid as promptly as possible, even if further borrowing was required to meet the obligations.[9] Other creditors had to accept delays, but were eventually paid. Damoiselle Anne Casaulx had been in poor health for some time in 1683, when she offered to sell a house in Paris to the abbey at a reduced price in rentes.[10] For the first few years, payments on these rentes were made on schedule, but in the 1690s, the time of great financial difficulty at St. Germain des Prés, Damoiselle Casaulx was neglected. In 1693 the payments had slowed to a trickle and were five years in arrears. By 1697 Casaulx was willing to remit the accumulated arrears and to convert her rentes to a life annuity at 5%, "provided that it be paid exactly on time for the rest of her life," and that after her death, the monks would say 1,000 masses

7. On these *rentes*, see Julian Dent, *Crisis in Finance: Crown, Financiers and Society in Seventeenth Century France* (Newton Abbot, 1973), esp. pp. 46–54.

8. Marion, *Dictionnaire*, p. 104.

9. Actes cap., B.N. MS. fr. 16852, fol. 225, 25 jan. 1641, fol. 247, 21 nov. 1641; B.N. MS. fr. 16855, fol. 134, 24 juil. 1652; fol. 147, 21 mai 1653; fol. 168, 13 juil. 1654.

10. Actes cap., B.N. MS. fr. 16857, fol. 180, 18 oct. 1683; Séniorat, B.N. MS. fr. 18819, fol. 131, 20 nov. 1683. The initial payments appear in Comptes, A.N. H5 4276.

for her soul.[11] In this way she abandoned hopes of collecting back interest and recovering capital, in exchange for assured income and spiritual relief. If some creditors of St. Germain des Prés, an abbey with enormous wealth, were reduced to these expedients, those who lent money to weaker religious institutions must have been expressing even greater faith and support: transactions that began as loans might well become donations.

When rentes occasionally did go unpaid, they were likely to appear in the following year's budget as "debts from previous years." The monks also used this category to record ordinary payments on account to the suppliers of the abbey, with difficulties caused by poor harvests and wartime taxes reflected in its columns. In 1661 and 1662 they show delayed payment of rentes as well as merchants' bills, so that in 1663 back interest accounted for nearly a third of the debts paid, which in turn came to a similar proportion of the total budget. Still, seven of the fifteen payments of interest represented January settlements of notes that came due in December: only one rente had been in arrears as long as three years, while the rest were three to six months overdue. At least St. Germain des Prés made the payments within a reasonable time, and during periods of prosperity it was even able to make payments in advance or return the capital to anxious *rentiers*.

Unlike the crown, St. Germain des Prés caught up with its rentes. In 1684 there were 30 individuals and 2 institutions who received interest from the abbey. Only 6 rentes were in arrears, and these were brought up to date.[12] Complex relationships existed between the abbey and its rentiers, as well as among the rentiers themselves. One example will illustrate: Antoine Milot, sieur de Villecourt, had lent 54,000 livres to the abbey in 1682, when the money was needed to buy Berny, a seigneurie destined to replace land taken by the king for his park at Versailles. This loan was arranged at 4.17%, for an annual interest of 2,250 livres; the first payment, for two years' interest, was made in 1684.[13] At the same time Milot's son-in-law, Bernard Martineau, *hérault des armes des ordres du roi*, was collecting interest on 14,400 livres that he had lent at the same rate. Two years later Martineau requested return of the capital, and offered to pay the notaries' fees for replacing his money with an equivalent sum from persons at Meaux.[14] In 1687 the abbey found means to refinance part of the rente at a lower rate of interest—3.85%.[15] In 1688, after Antoine

11. Séniorat, B.N. MS. fr. 18819, fol. 153, 25 mai 1697.
12. Comptes, A.N. H5 4276.
13. Comptes, A.N. H5 4276; Actes cap., B.N. MS. fr. 16857, fol. 238, 20 fév. 1688.
14. Comptes, A.N. H5 4276; Actes cap., B.N. MS. fr. 16857, fol. 217, 20 mai 1686.
15. Actes cap., B.N. MS. fr. 16857, fol. 234, 22 août 1687.

Milot had died, the remaining debt was transferred from his two daughters, Marie (the wife of Martineau) and Anne (the wife of Pierre Duqui,
sieur de Meudon), to Christophe Milot, sieur de Croissy.[16] Marie Milot
Martineau, however, still held a rente that paid 1,200 livres interest annually in the early 1690s. Although the interest for 1691 was delayed, by
April of 1692 the scribe could record "parfait paiement."[17] Despite the
heavy burden of assessments for St. Sulpice and amortissements, St. Germain des Prés met its long-standing obligations and went even further to
satisfy lenders and their heirs who wanted their money back.

Informal loans also played an important role in the organization of
expenditures. The monks frequently obtained short-term credit by defer-
ring payment to tradesmen. Sales on open account were common, and no
interest was charged on unpaid balances. Consequently, patience was a
requisite for all merchants who did business with the Parisian abbey. At
the end of 1661, a summary showed 30,245 livres 14 sols of debts outstanding, including 5,614 livres 3 s. to M. Le Laboureur, grocer; 2,861
livres to M. Gerant, cloth merchant; 800 livres to the butcher, and 700
livres to fish merchants.[18] While awaiting payment the merchants continued to supply the abbey with its needs. At the beginning of 1661, for
example, M. Gerant was owed 2,168 livres 4 s. for cloth delivered in
1660, yet in February and April of 1661 he supplied additional white
serge costing 207 livres 15 s. That year the abbey paid him 495 livres in
April, and 470 livres in July, but their account balance had risen to 2,861
livres by the end of the year because of purchases in August, September,
and November. In 1662 payments exceeded purchases, and the balance
outstanding declined to 1,941 livres. The next year, 1663, saw more purchases and substantial payments of back debts—Gerant received 1,114
livres 3 s. So it went: purchase, postponement, payment, and purchase
again. During bad years the regular suppliers of the abbey had to share its
financial crises: although the abbey's needs and orders remained about the
same, its payments extended over a longer time. Normally, this system of
informal credit functioned well, as an integral part of the abbey's financial
management, which sought to balance revenues and expenditures over
time.

Inside its enclosing walls St. Germain des Prés was a miniature
service-oriented society. While the monks served God through the holy
office and scholarship, their servants attended to daily household chores.
The abbey employed at least twenty full-time servants, not counting the

16. Actes cap., B.N. MS. fr. 16857, fol. 238, 20 fév. 1688.
17. Comptes, A.N. H5 4277.
18. Sommaire des Dettes, Comptes, A.N. H5 4274.

boys who worked as personal servants for the monks. There were two cooks, a baker, a laundryman, stablekeepers, gardeners, a tailor, a porter, and numerous boys. The abbey church had its own organist, choirmaster, bellringer, and sexton. A carpenter, glazier, and roofer found regular employment, while other skilled construction workers were called as they were needed for specific jobs.[19] The abbey also appointed a consulting doctor and surgeon with annual salaries. By contrast, the notary and various lawyers were paid according to the services rendered. Some servants requested permanent affiliation with the monastery: after a probationary period they received the status of *serviteur perpetuel, commis,* or *frère convers* (lay brother). Although they could not aspire to the rank of choir monks or priests, they obtained a promise of life tenure from their employers. The majority of the servants, however, were subject to immediate dismissal if their work was unsatisfactory.

How well did the monks treat their servants? Their fatherly interest is shown by carefully structured wages and fringe benefits. Wages depended first upon services rendered. The laundryman was the highest paid (400–500 livres per year, 1660s to 1680s), followed by the organist (200 livres) and the tailor (165 livres). The baker and the stablekeeper were paid 120 livres per year, while a cook received only 46 livres and a pair of shoes. Ordinary servants also had living quarters in the abbey, and those who worked faithfully and well received more paternal assistance from the monks. Nicolas Bruslé, the laundryman, once asked their help in collecting rent from a vineyard that he owned within their jurisdiction.[20] Jean Brugerin, who had worked at the abbey for three and a half years, was taught a useful trade.[21] Pierre Le Mesle l'Iroquois, a former servant, wanted to open a shop in the courtyard of the abbey: he and his brother offered to share in the cost of construction. Once the work was finished, the brothers promised to keep children from playing and making noise there, and to prevent passersby from befouling the area. These worthy objectives met with enthusiastic approval in the council.[22] In another instance showing special friendship, the community decided to give the surgeon, Mathurin Mesnard, *une demie queue* (133 liters) of wine in addition to his salary of 100 livres, "but without making any obligation to him, and on the condition that he take care to serve us well."[23]

Servants could involve the abbey in legal difficulties, too. When

19. Cf. Corinne Beutler, "Bâtiment et salaires: un chantier à St. Germain des Prés de 1644 à 1646," *Annales, E.S.C.* 26:2 (1971): 484–517.

20. Séniorat, B.N. MS. fr. 18819, fol. 54, 5 nov. 1654.

21. Séniorat, B.N. MS. fr. 18819, fol. 130v, 4 nov. 1683.

22. Séniorat, B.N. MS. fr. 18819, fol. 141, 27 fév. 1694.

23. Séniorat, B.N. MS. fr. 18819, fol. 50, 24 août 1654. In 1661 M. Varrice, *avocat*

Pierrot, a forest warden, injured a woman in the woods belonging to the abbey, the community agreed to pay 50 livres compensation on his behalf.[24] But lay brother Pierre Damide, who had without permission hired gardeners "on very disadvantageous conditions," was disavowed and sued. The contracts he made were broken, and new hiring was done.[25] Sometimes disputes between servants required forceful resolution. In 1648 two men were employed as guards in the church. The first worked every morning and received wages and food for his family, while the second, employed only on holidays and Sundays, received wages and a ceremonial uniform, colored violet like those of the sextons of Notre Dame, and emblazoned with a silver coat of arms of the monastery. When jealousy erupted, the monks found both men lacking in fidelity and discharged them.[26]

The abbey's patronage of artisans and members of the legal profession was quite valuable. The carving and installation of new choir stalls in the later 1650s resulted in several extra payments to Fermery, the woodworker.[27] Ornate sculpture and decoration in the church required craftsmen of talent. And an indication of the importance of legal business at the abbey appeared in 1676, when notary Philippe Lemoine retired—he sold the St. Germain des Prés practice separately to his successor for 4,000 livres.[28] From the monastic point of view, notarial fees, legal fees, and the wages of servants were fixed expenses; in seventeenth-century France they were necessities that could not be cut without risking deterioration of the status, privileges, and physical plant of the abbey.

Seigneurial obligations also represented fixed charges against the budget from the lands of the abbey. The most important of these related to religious services—the collection of the *dîme* (tithe) and payment of the *portion congrue* (priest's salary). The dîme was originally collected by parish priests themselves, but in many areas the right of collection had passed to the seigneurs, who then paid an allowance (portion congrue) to the actual priest or vicar.[29] How this arrangement came about can be seen in an agreement between the abbey and the curé of Selles, signed in 1655.

---

de la communauté, received 400 *bottes de foin*, B.N. MS. fr. 18819, fol. 101v, 1 avril 1661.

24. Séniorat, B.N. MS. fr. 18819, fol. 59, 31 jan. 1655.

25. Séniorat, B.N. MS. fr. 18819, fol. 121v, 5 mai 1674.

26. Sacristie, B.N. MS. fr. 18818, fols. 150–51. Similarly, two unruly organists were threatened with dismissal, Séniorat, B.N. MS. fr. 18819, fol. 115v, 24 juil. 1670.

27. Séniorat, B.N. MS. fr. 18819, fol. 64, 7 mai 1655; fol. 81, 8 jan. 1657.

28. Séniorat, B.N. MS. fr. 18819, fol. 126v, 21 oct. 1676.

29. E. Le Roy Ladurie and Joseph Goy, *Les Fluctuations du produit de la dîme* (Paris, 1972): M. Marion, *Dictionnaire*, p. 176.

In exchange for a portion congrue of 200 livres per year, the priest ceded to the abbey the rights to one-half of the dîme accruing to his office. In this case the dîme was not sufficient to support a priest, and the monks who guaranteed his income regarded the transaction as an act of charity. Indeed, although it is not mentioned in the formal agreement, they also decided to give the priest 50 livres from their own funds in addition to the 200 livres.[30]

Because the dîme was stated as a fixed portion of the crop, seigneurs who collected it stood to make profits in good years by selling the grain and giving the priest only a small cash income; in bad years they would have to supplement the proceeds. But at St. Germain des Prés the dîmes were affected by urban growth as well as by agricultural conditions. When new houses and streets replaced fields of grain between the Faubourg St. Germain and the Invalides, the owners refused to pay dîmes, arguing that they were exempt. Rather than risk losing the case in court, the abbey sought accommodation with the most important landowner, the Hôpital des Incurables.[31] Every year the abbey had to pay allowances to parish priests in its jurisdiction. These sums ranged from 50 livres to 425 livres; the latter figure went to the curé of Antony, while priests at Issy and Suresnes received 400 and 325 livres, respectively. The curé of Epinay, who collected only 60 livres from the abbey, probably had support from other seigneurs as well. In another example of overlapping boundaries, dîmes from three seigneuries—Courdevoie, Suresnes, and Puteaux—made up the 72 livres paid by the abbey to the parish priest of Colombe. Where there was no resident priest, the abbey paid for mass said for the country population by a visitor. The payments appear to have been made regularly in most years: only in the 1690s do they occur under "debts from previous years." That the parish priests had to wait six months, a year, or longer, for their salaries is another indication of the severity of the abbey's financial crisis during this period.

Seigneurial obligations were not the only expenses associated with the lands of the abbey; the operation and maintenance of the seigneuries themselves figured significantly in the budget. As has been noted in the discussion of revenues, these lands were generally managed by fermiers, chief tenants who took responsibility for ordinary operations and paid rent to the abbey. In spite of occasional bad experiences with incompetent or bankrupt fermiers, the monks found this arrangement less troublesome than working or managing the land themselves. Thus many seigneurial expenses had already been deducted from the revenues.

30. Actes cap., B.N. MS. fr. 16855, fol. 255, 11 déc. 1655.
31. Actes cap., B.N. MS. fr. 16857, fol. 226, 20 jan. 1687.

Although the primary responsibility for working the land belonged to the tenants, the abbey did itself employ agricultural laborers during the harvest, when the monks supervised the collection of the dîme and the production of wine. For the former only a few days of occasional, probably unskilled labor was needed, but the latter gave rise to a large expedition. Every year during the *vendanges*, the time of grape harvest and wine making, delegations of monks went into the countryside, hired workers, and watched over the gathering and pressing of grapes, the barreling and transport of wine. A festive atmosphere ruled the work, with so much crudity and horseplay that the monks had to prohibit "any person, no matter who he is, from swearing and blaspheming, causing and doing any action that may scandalize, under penalty of imprisonment and fine."[32] For the grape harvest at the seigneurie of Suresnes in 1661, for example, several kinds of workers were hired. The grape pickers, the most numerous workers, received the lowest wages: 10 sous or even 8 sous per day. The workers who carried the wicker baskets full of grapes were paid twice as much, as were the operators of the wine press. Once the wine had been put in barrels and loaded on carriages, the drivers took the production of 12 *muids* (3,218 liters, or 850 U.S. gallons) from Suresnes, northwest of Paris, to the abbey. The costs of the operation were as given in table 6. To these expenses must be added the cost of food for the monks while they were away from the abbey, and the import duty of 20 livres per muid, which had to be paid to bring the wine into Paris. In 1660 the total of these duties amounted to 3,795 livres, suggesting a production of 189.75 muids (50,893 liters or 13,446 gallons). At the beginning of the eighteenth century the amount St. Germain des Prés brought into the city had fallen to 155 muids, still a considerable amount, but only 1/2,200 of the total taxable wine brought into Paris.[33]

TABLE 6   Expenses of the Vendanges at Suresnes, 1661

Man-Days	Rate	Group	Total
19	15 s.	Drivers	20 l. 5 s.
89	20 s.	Press Operators	89 l.
209	10 s.	Grape Pickers	101 l.
4	8 s.	Grape Pickers	1 l. 12 s.
35	21+ s.	Basket Carriers	37 l. 10 s.
		Guards	14 l. 10 s.
		Transport Costs	30 l.
		Total	293 l. 17 s.

32. Quoted by Jacquart, *La Crise rurale*, p. 311.
33. Comptes, A.N. H5 4274. "Entrées de Paris," in Papiers des Contrôleurs-Généraux,

All during the year the abbey appropriated funds for garden supplies, repairs, and improvements to its properties. Fertilizer, lime, straw, chicken feed, barrels, and wine-making equipment are mentioned. General maintenance included gifts to the parish churches: ornaments and hymnals, robes for the priests.[34] To indicate the jurisdiction of St. Germain des Prés, the monks decided to erect signposts bearing the coat of arms of the monastery.[35] These actions, and the charitable giving to be discussed later, further illustrate the paternal and protective attitude of the monks as seigneurs. They preferred to let the fermiers take the initiative in making improvements, though they did approve the purchase and sale of land, and the construction or remodeling of buildings on the seigneuries. Whether the proposed building was a barn or a parish church at Bailly, a house at St. Placide, a stable at Suresnes, or the seigneurial baking oven at Varenne, any major project was certain to involve expenditure by the abbey. These were substantial projects: the design and building of the parish church came to 2,500 livres, while the oven required more than 1,000 livres for carpentry and masonry.[36]

The Maurist century at St. Germain des Prés was an age of restoration and building—in the church, the quarters of the monks, and the supporting structures. From the beginning of the reform, construction at the abbey drew heavily on the budget. Between 1631 and 1710 the monks spent more than 200,000 livres on rebuilding the church, the interior structures of the monastery, and the enclosing walls.[37] Prior to 1644, when the reconstruction of the church began, the ceiling was in decay, and the roof of simple tile. The pillars lacked ornamental sculptures, the stained glass windows were "toutes simples et sans embellissement," the walls were rough and blackened, and the floor was badly paved.[38] By 1656, when new choir stalls were placed, all of these faults had been corrected. New ceiling work and slate on the roof, ornamental pillars, new stained glass windows, and new paving stones had been installed.[39] The choir stalls, given by a sympathetic *ancien religieux*, were made from lumber that had been bought as standing timber at Palaiseau, south of Paris near the abbey's seigneurie of Antony.[40] Practically the entire cost of these improvements was borne by the monastery itself, even though the coat of arms of

---

A.N. G7 1182, published by A. de Boislisle, *Mémoires des Intendants, Généralité de Paris* (Paris, 1881), p. 502.

34. Séniorat, B.N. MS. fr. 18819, fols. 83–83 v, 3 août 1657.
35. Séniorat, B.N. MS. fr. 18819, fol. 78, 9 nov. 1656.
36. Comptes, A.N. H5 4274.
37. Biens de l'Abbaye, B.N. MS. fr. 16864, fol. 54.
38. Sacristie, B.N. MS. fr. 18818, fol. 126.
39. Sacristie, B.N. MS. fr. 18818, fol. 127.
40. Séniorat, B.N. MS. fr. 18819, fol. 54, 5 nov. 1654.

Marguerite de Lorraine, duchess of Orleans, was placed on the rebuilt and enlarged chapel of Ste. Marguerite. The duchess laid the cornerstone, as the sacristan tartly noted, "but she gave nothing to put the following ones in place."[41]

Striking improvements were also made in the buildings where the monks lived. The first problem following the reform was the need for walls: the garden of the abbey, which had faced open fields, now encountered the expanding neighborhoods of Paris. In 1640 the monks decided to sell land on the outer edge of the garden, with the proviso that only houses with no windows facing the abbey might be built, Thus the community was spared the expense of constructing its own walls, and monastic closure, a point of spiritual life, was strengthened by hiding the view of the secular world. The funds realized from this sale were used for paving and sewer construction.[42] For the comfort of the monks who walked in the garden during the heat of summer, three rows of trees were planted: elms on the first walk, near the refectory; pears in the middle of the garden; and figs on the last walk, next to the great walls.[43] Before 1657, running water had been available only at a fountain by the abbot's lodge, but then it was brought to the monks' quarters.[44] The dormitory received renovation also. Owing to the small size of the windows, the upper cells of the building became too hot during the summertime. In 1675, as a first corrective measure, sliding vents were installed in the doors. When this did not provide sufficient relief, the monks sought bids for adding larger windows. In 1679 a contractor offered to do the job for 12,000 livres, an attractive price because it required no borrowing on the part of the abbey; in the face of other projects, however, the monks could not take action on the proposal.[45]

The 1684 chapter general of the Congregation of St. Maur ordered the construction of an entirely new building to house the hierarchy and visiting monks who stayed at St. Germain des Prés. Fifty thousand livres was appropriated for the project. Initially, a building running all the way from the church to the Rue St. Benoît was proposed, but the chapter felt that such a structure, containing a library as well, would be too large and give no advantage to St. Germain des Prés. The prior of the abbey, Dom Claude Bretagne, suggested another design: a building forming one side of the

41. Sacristie, B.N. MS. fr. 18818, fol. 127.

42. Actes cap., B.N. MS. fr. 16852, fol. 207, 19 déc. 1639; fol. 214, 20 avril 1640; fol. 230, 3 avril 1640.

43. Séniorat, B.N. MS. fr. 18819, fol. 54, 14 nov. 1654.

44. Actes cap., B.N. MS. fr. 16856, fol. 29, 12 fév. 1657. Choses mém., B.N. MS. fr. 18816, fol. 126v, 19 sept. 1672.

45. Séniorat, B.N. MS. fr. 18819, fol. 123v, 7 août 1675; fol. 129v, 15 mai 1679.

cloister and going from the refectory to the church. He also proposed a building with rooms for women who came to visit the monastery; the present system of monks speaking with women in the church or under the doorway was "une chose indécente."[46] At first the other superiors rejected this design because they feared that it would cost over 100,000 livres. But when St. Germain des Prés offered to pay the excess over 50,000 livres, they agreed to the plan. In fact, the officers of the monastery had examined the design and believed that 50,000 livres would be more than sufficient; to be sure the chapter of the abbey agreed to spend an additional 20,000 livres if necessary.[47] Construction began in September 1684 and had reached the cornices before November 1. Although the first frost caused some stones to crack, work continued during the winter on the pressing rooms, cellar, bakery, and storerooms, all of which were ready by spring 1685. The rest of the building was largely completed by the fall of 1686. Because of problems in the construction, the congregation had to provide an additional 12,000 livres; supervision on the site was lax, and various faults appeared. One chronicler thought the entrance to the monastery "trop superbe," not in keeping with monastic simplicity. However, he conceded that all designs and work had been approved by the superior general; the finished structure, much grander than previous projects at the abbey, had to be accepted.[48]

In their building the monks did not neglect the supporting structures of their microcosm. They built a new porter's lodge in the courtyard of the abbey, and they spent a thousand livres or more on a new laundry.[49] While Cardinal Fürstemberg carried out a great building program on the properties of the manse abbatiale, both at the monastery and at the Château of Berny, the monks cleared the courtyard of the old houses of the *anciens*, making room for new boutiques.[50] Fire at a house next to the monastery on the Rue St. Benoît in 1694 caused alarm, but quick response by the monks, the servants, the neighbors, and the priests of St. Sulpice prevented the blaze from spreading; together they put it out in two hours. Upon reflection the monks decided to move their *chaufoir* from the passageway between the dormitory and the library, where a fire might burn for some hours before being noticed, to a room between the dormitory and the infirmary. By the end of 1694 improvements in its financial condition gave the monastery an opportunity to make these changes.[51]

46. Choses mém., B.N. MS. fr. 18816, fol. 141v.
47. Actes cap., B.N. MS. fr. 15847, fol. 190, 4 sept. 1684.
48. Choses mém., B.N. MS. fr. 18816, fol. 141v.–144.
49. Séniorat, B.N. MS. fr. 18819, fol. 64, 12 juin 1655; fol. 110, 11 sept. 1667.
50. Choses mém., B.N. MS. fr. 18816, fol. 154v, fol. 176.
51. Choses mém., B.N. MS. fr. 18816, fols. 199–200, 1694.

It would be surprising if a corporation as large as St. Germain des Prés had gone through a century of business transactions without entering litigation. Indeed, the abbey was involved in its share of legal disputes. To evict tenants or confiscate their property, the abbey could rely upon its own officers. More serious problems arose, however, when powerful persons differed with St. Germain des Prés over jurisdiction and seigneurial rights. The two greatest disputes turned on political jurisdiction. These were the abbey's exemption from the spiritual authority of the archbishop of Paris and its independence from the royal justice of the Châtelet. In each case the abbey had created its own competing unit of administration: the prior and bailliage of the abbey. Against the greater political power of its opponents, whose attempts to suppress particular jurisdictions accorded with the centralizing tendency of absolutism, the abbey decided not to wage costly legal battles for its rights. After pamphlet warfare, negotiations led to agreements with the archbishop in 1668 and the king in 1674: as will be noted later, principles gave way to necessity and authority.[52]

Most of the disputes for which expenses are recorded under the heading "procès et voyages" dealt with seigneurial rights. The monks had the right to collect mutation fees every time property in their jurisdiction changed hands. The fees were an important source of income for the abbey, but this income was lost in perpetuity when other religious houses bought property within the jurisdiction. These houses and their protectors often sought reductions in the standard compensation to the seigneur. While the abbey had a right to demand full compensation, it wished to avoid displeasing powerful persons. Signs of political pressure are unmistakable. When a group of Benedictine nuns bought a house and land at Issy in 1645, they asked St. Germain des Prés to remit the mutation fees. On January 2, 1646, the request was denied, and the abbey demanded payment of 6,000 livres compensation. But on April 30, the monks were forced to recognize the pressure that "quelques personnes de qualité" were exerting on behalf of the nuns. Although the amount of 6,000 livres already represented a reduction of 500 livres, the monks agreed to accept 5,000 livres, or, "à toute rigeur," 4,500 livres.[53] By August 23, 1646, when a final settlement was made, the nuns struck a bargain at 3,700 livres, much less than their lords originally expected to collect.[54] With M. Olier, the dependent curé of St. Sulpice who founded the famous seminary, the

---

52. Agreement with the Archbishop, reported in Sacristie. B.N. MS. fr. 18818, fol. 220, 1668; agreement with the king on justice, Choses mém., B.N. MS. fr. 18816, fol. 130v, 1674. See part 5, Spiritual Life and Politics.

53. Actes cap., B.N. MS. fr. 16855, fols. 5 and 10–11.

54. Actes cap., B.N. MS. fr. 16855, fol. 14.

abbey had more success: in 1648 St. Germain remained firm in its demand for compensation, albeit reduced by one-third.[55] But the abbey's greatest loss was the struggle against the establishment of the Collège Mazarin. From its inception the new institution threatened the jurisdiction of the monks. In 1662 they protested and began lawsuits to protect their rights. Nevertheless, the king had the Tour de Nesle demolished and construction began on property within the jurisdiction of the abbey, "sans qu'on lui en ait rien payé."[56] In 1677 the protests were reiterated, but to no avail; the dispute was still alive in 1691, when the abbey chronicler wrote, "There are no means nor chicaneries that the business managers of the college and the controller general of the domain have not invented in order to deprive the abbey of its rights."[57] Other institutions could also be troublesome: the parish of St. André des Arts, with the support of its wealthy inhabitants, attempted to assert that the Collège Mazarin and several nearby streets were not part of the parish of St. Sulpice, the principal church of the Faubourg St. Germain and a dependency of the abbey. This was a scheme to evade the St. Sulpice building tax, whose heavy burden helped cause the abbey's financial crisis of the early 1690s. Fortunately for the abbey, St. Sulpice won its suit on a precedent of 1210, and St. André des Arts stood condemned of a "félonie spirituelle."[58]

Powerful individuals were no less insistent when seeking to reduce or evade obligations to the abbey. In 1651 Etienne d'Aligre, *conseiller d'état*, bought 48,000 livres worth of land in the abbey's seigneurial jurisdiction of Issy. Instead of a payment of *lods et ventes*, the monastery agreed to accept an exchange of land and a "reasonable present" to the church.[59] M. de Faverolle, who invested 36,000 livres at Issy in 1655, offered the abbey 1,000 livres compensation; acceptable, as the séniorat noted, although "at the standard rate we could demand more."[60] In 1678 when the minister Jean-Baptiste Colbert wished to purchase Châtillon, an alienated holding of St. Germain des Prés, he first asked the monks' permission and supporting documents. Since the chapter decided that repurchase would not be advantageous for themselves, they gave him their help and assurances of approval.[61] Five years later the same Colbert required the

55. Actes cap., B.N. MS. fr. 16855, fol. 60.

56. Choses mém., B. N. MS. fr. 18816, fol. 101; Actes cap., B.N. MS. fr. 16856, fol. 186, 7 oct. 1662.

57. Choses mém., B.N. MS. fr. 18816, fol. 154v. Earlier protests, Actes cap., B.N. MS. fr. 16857, fol. 93, 28 juin 1677.

58. Choses mém., B.N. MS. fr. 18816, fol. 195, 7 août 1694.

59. Séniorat, B.N. MS. fr. 18819, fol. 22, 22 mars 1651.

60. Perhaps three times as much—Marion, *Dictionnaire*, fol. 39; Séniorat, B.N. MS. fr. 18819, fol. 67, 25 sept. 1655.

61. Actes cap., B.N. MS. fr. 16857, fol. 106, 17 juin 1678; fol. 21, 6 déc. 1678.

abbey to render fealty and homage for a tract of woods acquired when the seigneuries of Berny and Fresnes were purchased.[62] Like the king at Versailles, Colbert was in the habit of simply enclosing land he wanted for his park at Sceaux; not until ten years after his death did his son, the Marquis de Seignelay, come to an agreement with St. Germain des Prés for the rights and dîmes of the confiscated property.[63] Seignelay's agreement, of course, did not mean that he would pay immediate compensation; actually, his heirs made the final settlement in 1699. They granted the abbey a *rente foncière* of 104 livres, seigneurial jurisdiction over 15 *arpents* at Berny, 5 arpents of arable land and vineyards at Antony, and the lods et ventes on a house at Bourg-la-Reine.[64]

Struggles with institutions and grandees were protracted, risky, and expensive. It took ten years for the abbey to obtain a favorable ruling on seigneurial rights against M. d'Effiat, sieur de Massy, in 1679. Even then the monks chose to compromise, since there was a chance that their opponent would win on appeal to the Parlement. The cost of such an appeal was figured at 35,000 livres; in view of the risk of defeat, a settlement of 12,000 livres cash, rights of justice, and a silver bowl every twenty years seemed preferable.[65] Ultimate victory in a lawsuit of long standing was an occasion worthy of record in the *Book of Memorable Events*, and perhaps a memorial object in the church. To give thanks for their victory over the Marquise de Palaiseau in 1684 the monks had a silver lamp made and set it in front of the eucharist.[66]

Even when the abbey was certain of the justice of its cause, it could not be sure that a favorable settlement would result, or that if it did, that the legal fees of a lengthy struggle would not exceed the settlement itself. Fortunes were made and lost in the *procès*, and only officers of the courts could relish prolonged suits. Consequently, the abbey had to find less expensive ways of joining suits and paying its legal advisors. In 1649 the monks were able to join M. du Plessis in a suit against the Comte de Maran; the fee for participation was 300 livres per year until the matter was settled.[67] By 1653 du Plessis had recovered a portion of the money that Maran owed him, and this he offered to share with the abbey. Although the monks collected only one-quarter of the obligation, they decided to accept this settlement as the best possible: "one does not always

---

62. Actes cap., B.N. MS. fr. 16857, fol. 178, 1 fév. 1683.
63. Actes cap., B.N. MS. fr. 16857, fol. 286, 18 sept. 1693.
64. Actes cap., B.N. MS. fr. 16857, fol. 330, 27 avril 1699.
65. Actes cap., B.N. MS. fr. 16857, fol. 133, 19 juin 1679.
66. Choses mém., B.N. MS. fr. 18816, fol. 146v, 30 sept. 1684.
67. Séniorat, B.N. MS. fr. 18819, fol. 2, 20 jan. 1649.

have the liberty of vigorously pursuing powerful persons."[68] M. Dacolle, the abbey's procureur in Parlement, requested payment of 2,945 livres for his fees in 1657, but indicated his willingness to accept 500 livres in cash and assignment of a debt of 2,915 livres owed to the abbey by Sieur de Ste. Marie. After considering the great difficulty of extracting money from Ste. Marie and the long time that Dacolle had been waiting for payment, the council agreed to his terms.[69]

Legal costs were unpredictable and fluctuated considerably from year to year. At the end of 1661 the abbey owed 8,000 livres to procureur Dacolle. The following year the monks paid 1,058 livres to a new procureur, de Linon, in part for his services in a suit against his predecessor. Dacolle won that suit in 1663, collecting 12,000 livres from the abbey for back wages and his own legal expenses.[70] Minor legal costs continued even when the decisions were favorable: copies of documents, clerk's fees, and printed opinions of the courts were always needed at the abbey. Consultations with legal advisors were, after judgments, the largest item in the legal services budget. These sums were not spent with enthusiasm, but rather out of necessity. Typical legal costs ranged from several hundred to two thousand livres per year.

These expenses of the physical plant constituted the major portion of the budget. Within the context of overlapping privileges, obligations, and jurisdictions that constituted the *ancien régime*, these expenditures were regarded as unalterable, as permanent as the agrarian society itself. The monks' attitudes toward their property showed no changes in the course of the century: the same techniques of management of revenues and organization of expenditures appear during the whole period. Short-term credit was used to balance the budgets in years of fluctuating income, and there is no indication of reduced spending on maintenance. Community and observance, the social group and the absolute goal, also required expenditures; these are the subjects of the next two chapters.

68. Séniorat, B.N. MS. fr. 18819, fol. 41, 23 juil. 1653.
69. Séniorat, B.N. MS. fr. 18819, fol. 87, 4 oct. 1657.
70. Comptes, A.N. H5 4274.

ILLUSTRATIONS

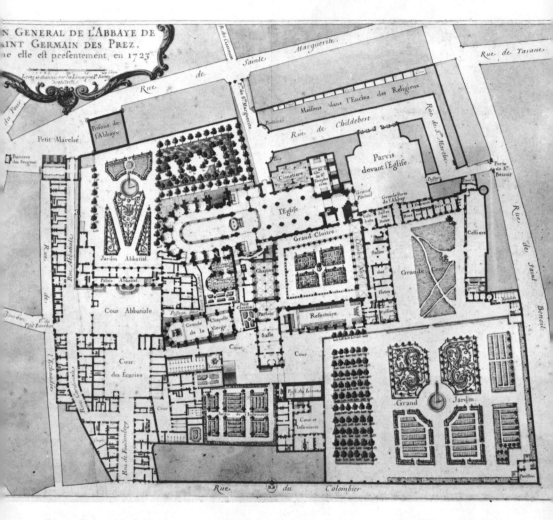

1. Plan of the abbey in 1723, surrounded by the Faubourg St. Germain. (Source: B.N., Estampes, 73 C 60581)

HENRY DE BOVRBON EVESQVE DE METZ.
*Prince du Sainct Empire Abbé de sainct germain des prez
fescamp et autres, Marquis de Verneuil et Conte de Boisgency.*
Balt Moncornet ex.

2. Henry of Verneuil, commendatory abbot of St. Germain des Prés, 1623–68. (Source: B.N., Estampes, 75 B 68996)

3. Jean Casimir, erstwhile Jesuit, cardinal, king of Poland, and commendatory abbot of St. Germain des Prés, 1669–72. Tomb sculpture in the Church of St. Germain des Pres. (Source: Parish Church of St. Germain des Pres)

Paul Pelisson
Maistre des Requestes et de l'Academie francoise.

4. Paul Pelisson, royal administrator of the abbey, 1672–90. (Source: B.N., Estampes, 75 B 70021)

5. Guillaume Egon Cardinal Prince de Fürstemberg, commendatory abbot of St. Germain des Prés, 1690–1704. (Source: B.N., Estampes, 65 C 26340)

Guillaume Egon Prince de Furstenberg, Cardinal, Euesque de Strasbourg.

Cet air simple, et modeste, ou rien n'est affecté,
J'offre de MABILLON l'exacte ressemblance;
Et dans un tresor de science,
Un prodige d'humilité.

6. Jean Mabillon (1631–1707), greatest of the monastic scholars at St. Germain des Prés. (Source: B.N., Estampes, 50 A 3534)

D. BERN. DE MONTFAUCON, R. DE LA CONG. DE St MAUR.

7. Bernard de Montfaucon (1655–1741), monk of St. Germain des Prés, expert on antiquity, prominent in the republic of letters. (Source: B.N., Estampes, 52 B 11195)

8. Decorations in the abbey church for the memorial service for Queen Marie-Thérèse, September 15, 1683. (Source: B.N., Estampes, 56 C 11352)

9. Chapel of Ste. Marguerite, showing women coming to receive blessings. The coat of arms of St. Germain des Prés is in the upper corners, and a suggested prayer appears below. (Source: B.N., Estampes, 76 C 78200)

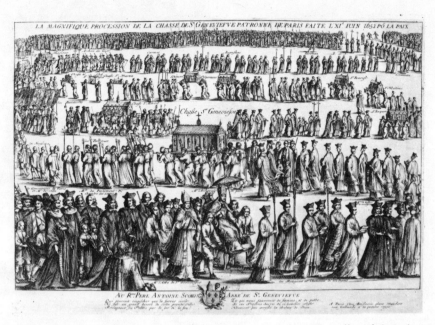

10. Procession of Ste. Geneviève, patroness of Paris, June 11, 1652. The relics of the saint appear in the center of the picture, along with religious communities and legal officers carrying their own banners, signs of rank, and lesser relics. Note the prominent presence of the archbishop of Paris. (Source: B.N., Estampes, 76 C 78201)

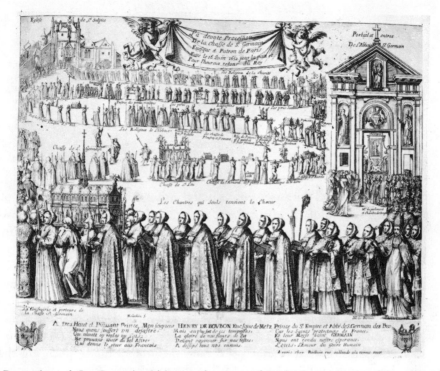

11. Procession of St. Germain, bishop and patron of Paris, June 16, 1652. The relics of the saint appear in the left foreground, and are followed by chanting monks of St. Germain des Prés. Here too the artist has depicted and labeled religious communities and their relics, as well as officers of Parlement and the Chambre des Comptes. Note the presence of the papal nuncio at lower right. (Source: B.N., Estampes, 70 C 41546)

7

Feeding the Community

With fifty monks, thirty servants, guests, visiting scholars, and officers of the Congregation of St. Maur, the community of St. Germain des Prés had to prepare large quantities of food. Some food, notably grain and dairy products, came from the lands of the abbey, but much had to be bought in the markets. On the average, food costs took 14.3% of the budget, about 9,000 to 12,000 livres per year for fish, eggs, cooking fats, fruits, and vegetables. Of course, food is "not only a collection of products," but also a "system of communication, a body of images, an etiquette of usage, situations, and conduct."[1] Food is inseparable from the sociology of consumption, the historical, anthropological, and medical factors influencing the decision to eat particular foods. What the monks ate depended on what was available, and on what they were allowed to eat by their religious rules.

For most people in early modern Europe, cereal grains provided 60% or more of the calories in their diet: as Fernand Braudel has written, "to eat was to consume bread, and more bread, or porridge, all through life."[2] Peasants were condemned to a monotonous diet, seldom including meat and then only pork or tripe. Spices were scarce and expensive, and when sugar was still a luxury, honey served as a sweetener.[3] Wine was also too expensive for the poor, and brewing beer meant giving up part of the precious grain harvest. The poorest people did not even eat bread because of the seigneurial charges for milling and baking; they simply boiled their grain to make porridge. In the cities, workers spent half their income on

1. Roland Barthes, "Pour une psycho-sociologie de l'alimentation contemporaine," *Annales, E.S.C.* 16 (1961): 977–86. Reprinted in *Pour une histoire de l'alimentation* (*PHA*), J. J. Hémardinquer, ed., Cahiers des Annales, 28 (Paris, 1970).

2. Fernand Braudel, *Civilisation matérielle et capitalisme*, (Paris, 1967), vol. 1, p. 97.

3. Marc Bloch, "Les Aliments de l'ancienne France," *PHA*, pp. 231–35.

bread for themselves and their families. As late as 1789, the average Parisian consumed only 2,000 calories per day (if we can use general calculations); when so many people were eating the subsistence diet, shortages of bread and consequent public disorders were constant concerns of French governments.[4]

For those with money, however, the variety and quantity of food could be much greater. Cereals furnished a smaller proportion of their total calories because meat, fish, eggs, and fats were more important. The absence of central heating, the vigorous exercise of horseback riding, and even the general heaviness of seventeenth-century clothing, furniture, tools, and weapons may have pushed caloric requirements to high levels. But whether or not they worked hard, in wealthy households and institutions throughout Europe, people ate 5,000, 6,000, or even 8,000 calories per day—staggering totals by modern standards![5] The monks of St. Germain des Prés, whose social origins were generally in the prosperous groups, consumed less, but still must be ranged among the well-fed.

The rule of St. Benedict contains explicit references to food. The founder expected his monks to work, and understood that they would need a reasonable diet. St. Benedict did not intend strict vegetarianism: his earliest commentators agreed that eggs and fish, milk, butter, and cheese should be part of a monk's ordinary meals.[6] A pound of bread and a "measure" of wine were also prescribed. The rule proposed two cooked foods at daily refection, with salad or fresh vegetables when available. Only "the flesh of quadrupeds" was forbidden to all except the sick. Some authorities did go so far as to prohibit the eating of fowl as well, but opinion was divided on this point.[7] The close association of fish and fowl in the biblical account of the creation may have influenced the medieval monks to eat birds—large orders of fowl "seem to point in this direction, though the sick and guests must always be remembered."[8] Benedict's original schedule of meals was designed for the Italian climate and temperament:

4. Braudel, *Civilisation*, p. 97; cf. minimum requirements in E. W. McHenry, *Basic Nutrition* (Philadelphia, 1957), p. 35. Government interest in the grain supply has been studied by Steven L. Kaplan, *Bread, Politics and Political Economy in the Reign of Louis XV*, 2 vols. (The Hague, 1976).

5. Pierre Couperie, "Régimes alimentaires dans la France du XVIIe siècle," *Annales, E.S.C.* 18 (1963): 1,133–41; Frank Spooner, "Régimes alimentaires d'autrefois: proportions et calcul en calories," *Annales, E.S.C.* 16 (1961): 568–74, also in *PHA*, pp. 35–42.

6. Dom Cuthbert Butler, *Benedictine Monachism*, pp. 44, 287.

7. Sister M. A. Schroll, *Benedictine Monasticism as Reflected in the Warnefrid–Hildemar Commentaries on the Rule* (New York, 1941), p. 33.

8. Dom David Knowles, *The Monastic Order in England, 940–1216*, p. 460, n. 1.

St. Benedict's Meal Schedule

13 September to begin Lent	1 meal at 2:30 or 3:00 P.M.
Lent	1 meal at 4:30 or 5:00 P.M.
Easter to Pentecost	2 meals: 1 at midday, 1 at 5:00 P.M. or 5:30 P.M.
Pentecost to 13 September	2 meals, as above, but only one early meal on Wednesday and Friday

The rationale for this schedule is clear—monks would eat more while doing agricultural work in the summer, and less in other seasons, particularly in Lent. During the middle ages in northern Europe, the schedule was modified to include a second meal in winter. As a consequence, monks had two cooked meals on most days of the year.[9]

Benedictine tradition limited diet at St. Germain des Prés, yet at first glance the records do not suggest austerity. The Maurists had both dinner and supper except on Wednesdays and Fridays that were not holidays. Fish and eggs, butter and cheese, bread and wine were their staples, served in quantity every day. Only meat was conspicuously absent; all other foods, including seafood, vegetables, and fruits in season came from the farms of the abbey and the markets of Paris.

Nowhere is the variety and luxury of monastic diet better illustrated than in the thirty kinds of fish that appeared on the menu. Fresh-water fish such as carp and pike came from the Seine, from nearby ponds, and sometimes from the seigneuries. Salt-water varieties such as sole and cod were brought from the Atlantic coast by special relays.[10] Judging from the accounts, carp and sole were the favorite fish, served roughly twice a week, while cod and eel, less expensive per portion, appeared once a week. Less frequently mackerel, herring, pike, salmon, and even oysters were eaten. Scoters, a kind of sea duck, were not regarded as meat and therefore met the dietary requirements; their fishy taste made them good monastic food.

Parisian fish prices show remarkable stability over the years. Although the accounts of St. Germain des Pres do testify to seasonal variations, relative and absolute annual prices remained constant, illustrating the "majestic stability" of prices in the later reign of Louis XIV.[11] Like other foods rich in protein, fish were luxuries whose prices reacted slowly to fluctuations in the grain market. Patterns of migration, weather, and trans-

9. Ibid., pp. 456–57.

10. On the transport service, the *chasse-marée*, see Leon Bernard, *The Emerging City: Paris in the Age of Louis XIV* (Durham, N.C., 1970), pp. 246–48.

11. Pierre Couperie, "Les Marchés de pourvoirie: viandes et poissons chez les Grands au XVIIe siècle," *Annales, E.S.C.* 19 (1964): 467–77. Reprinted in *PHA*, pp. 241–53.

port affected the supply of fish, but the average cost of a portion sufficient to feed the community varied little. The monks bought fish regularly, and a typical price for carp was 18 livres. Other varieties were generally within 10% of this price; cod, at 12 livres per portion, was an exception. But price does not seem to have influenced the lay brother who went early to market every day to choose the dinner. The monastery's fish bills easily ran to 300 or 400 livres per month, and more if important guests were expected: then the cooks made special delicacies such as crayfish, oysters, and salmon garnished with lemons and oranges from Portugal.[12]

Eggs were another source of high-quality protein in the monastic diet. The community bought eggs by the thousands every month except during Lent, when only sick monks were allowed to eat them. Every three or four days the monks received market eggs in lots of ten to twenty dozen, while larger quantities came from the egg merchant. In 1681, for example, the accounts record 50,132 eggs bought at a cost of 1,259 livres 8 s. 6 d. If this figure is converted to a monthly average, based on ten and one-half months of consumption per year, it appears that the monks were eating close to 4,800 eggs per month at a time when the community numbered about 50. In fact egg consumption was much higher, on the order of 7,500 eggs per month or more. During some months the community's purchases on the open market alone exceeded this figure;[13] in addition, the year-end settlements with tenant farmers for eggs and dairy products supplied from the seigneuries often ran into hundreds of livres. In view of the frequent purchases and primitive methods of preserving eggs, all of them were probably consumed soon afterwards. A communal total of 7,500 per month would allow 5 eggs per day to each of the 50 monks; even if 30 servants are added to the group, average individual consumption remains over 3 eggs per day.

The price of eggs, like the price of fish, remained the same over the years. From 1659 to 1711, the contracted price for suppliers to the king was 40 livres per thousand.[14] But this price, reviewed only once every six years, does not show seasonal variations, which can be seen in the purchases of St. Germain des Prés. The abbey bought eggs at prices ranging from 20 livres per thousand in summer to 48.5 livres per thousand during the crisis winter of 1693–94. Note that the royal price was pegged at a high level; the monthly average price generally moved in cycles, with higher prices in winter and lower prices in summer. While monks did not

---

12. "Diner de Messieurs les Intéressés" (Spring 1679), Comptes, A.N. H5 4276.
. 13. E.g., in 1682 there were five months when eggs bought totaled 7,500 or more. Comptes, A.N. H5 4276.
14. Couperie, "Les Marchés de pourvoirie."

starve in times of poor harvests, their budget was certainly affected by extremely bad years.

Butter and cheese were monastic staples also. The most complete records suggest that the community ate about 450 livres-weight, or 220 kg., of butter every month. This is equivalent to 147 grams (5.2 ounces) per person daily for 50 people, or 92 grams (3.2 ounces) per person for 80 people. The figures may strike us as high, but we should remember that butter was used on bread and in cooking: the cuisine of northern France is renowned for the heavy omnipresence of melted butter and butter sauces. Generally, the abbey paid between 6 s. and 8 s. per livre-weight in the 1690s, when the royal contract price was 10 s.[15] Prices had been higher in the 1660s and 1680s, but the contract prices do not reflect the decline. Like butter, cheese was brought to the abbey from its farms, though there were market purchases of Dutch cheese, "petits fromages," Brie, and Pont l'Evêque.

From St. Benedict's rule, the exact quantities of bread and wine are difficult to determine, but it is unlikely that the monks of St. Germain received smaller rations than the nuns of Marcigny, a convent in the Charolais. A document from 1631 gives a detailed description of their meals: in addition to nearly 600 grams of meat every day, the nuns ate 980 grams of bread.[16] St. Germain des Prés had its own bakers, who used flour milled from grain grown on the farms. In normal times, this grain was sufficient to assure the abbey's independence of the volatile grain markets. Occasionally, however, the monks had to buy more grain from their fermiers or from other institutions like the Abbey of St. Denis; in the early 1690s, St. Germain des Prés bought additional grain every year, paying the curé of Bailly a high price of 30 livres per *sétier* in March, 1694.[17] Once grain was available, the major expenses in making bread were milling and transport, which might come to 200 or 300 livres per year. As we have noted previously, the abbey also produced its own wine. Each monk received 0.61 liters of wine per meal, almost a full modern bottle.[18] With two meals a day, consumption of 1.2 liters per person would have been more than the 0.75 liter of the nuns, but still less than the generous 2 liters per day allowed to the monks of Cluny.[19]

Finally, we should note the variety of fruits and vegetables. In January, chestnuts, raisins, and leeks were bought; by April, spinach, asparagus,

15. Ibid.
16. Couperie, "Régimes alimentaires," pp. 1135–36.
17. Comptes, A.N. H5 4276, H5 4277.
18. Actes cap., B.N. MS. fr. 16855, fol. 198, 8 juin 1655.
19. Couperie, "Régimes alimentaires," p. 1,138.

lettuce, and turnips appear. Peas, either fresh or dried, were available all year round. In midsummer, cherries were especially popular, sometimes being served every other day. Raspberries, apricots, and thousands of apples enter the accounts. But the amount of money spent on fruits and vegetables was small in comparison with the cost of fish.

With a list of products and quantities, it is possible to figure out food values in the monastic diet. The undefined fish present a problem, since food values vary widely, but it seems reasonable to figure fish as 300 calories. Green peas are the vegetables used here, and (following a note in the council minutes) we have reckoned on white bread.[20]

The total of 4,575 calories far exceeds our recommended daily allowances, but it is quite conservative, for it does not include cheese, fruit, or cooking fats other than butter. Our estimates of eggs and butter consumed are also restrained. Even so, the monks of St. Germain des Prés ate extremely well: more than the 4,280 calories consumed on ordinary days by the meat-eating nuns of Marcigny, for the absence of meat at the Parisian abbey was counterbalanced by fish, butter, and eggs.[21] Both of these totals may seem unhealthy and excessive by modern standards, but they were not high in comparison with other well-to-do seventeenth-century diets. To eat well meant to eat less grain and more fat and protein.[22] Then as now, a

TABLE 7   Daily Diet at St. Germain des Prés

	Quantity	Calories	Protein	Fat	Carbohydrate
Fish	x	300	24 g.	24 g.	0 g.
Eggs	4	300	27	22	0
Butter	120 g.	890	.6	98	.5
Vegetables	100 g.	100	21	1.5	47
Bread	980 g.	2235	80.4	11.8	450.8
Wine	1.2 l.	750	0	0	(150)
Total		4575	153.0	157.3	648.3

20. Séniorat, B.N. MS. fr. 18819, fol. 83, 23 juin 1657. The caloric equivalents and chemical composition are taken from Couperie's articles and from *De Grote Winkler-Prins* (6e druk, 1954).

21. The chemical composition of the nuns' diet was similar: 20.2% proteins, 18.8% fats, 60.9% carbohydrates; compared to 15.3% proteins, 17.0% fats, 67.7% carbohydrates for the monks. Couperie, "Régimes alimentaires," pp. 1,135–36.

22. Frank Sponner's calculations limit beverages to 10% of the caloric total and show the cereal proportion as 60–80% in many organizations. At St. Germain des Prés, that proportion is 53%; only the heavy meat diet of Cardinal Mazarin's servants shows a lower figure. Spooner, "Régimes alimentaires," pp. 39–41; Couperie, "Régimes alimentaires," p. 1,137. Relative costs of energy units in the eighteenth century appear in R. Philippe, "Une Opération pilote, l'étude du ravitaillement de Paris," *Annales, E.S.C.* 16 (1961): 564–68.

diet of high quality was expensive—the cost of calories in fish, eggs, and cheese was two to seven times as much as in grain. Consequently, the abbey's yearly expenditure on food per person (110–240 livres) easily exceeded the annual income of an urban worker, rural peasant, or vicar. Such were the social divisions of old regime France.

The next three areas of expenditure were as necessary to the community as food, but not as important in the total budget. Under *autres usages que la bouche* the monks listed non-food supplies—tools and kitchen implements; wood, coal, and oil; writing paper and pens, ink and wax. Occasionally the abbey bought new pens, knives, and porcelain; more regularly, it needed sand for scouring purposes and wood for the cooking fires and ovens. At times St. Germain des Prés paid the market price for wood, although supplies from the seigneuries also reached the abbey. As we might expect in a center of scholarship, reams of paper were purchased, as well as books, but the accounts do not give detailed descriptions. The median expenditure on all of these items was 4.5% of the total budget.

Clothing took only 1.8% of total expenditure, but this figure is understated because large payments to cloth merchants were deferred. To make monastic robes, St. Germain des Prés employed a tailor. Certain ready-made articles such as shoes, stockings, and hats accounted for a smaller part of the clothing costs. It was also necessary to pay for the robes of monks who came to the abbey from other monasteries. When monks of the Congregation of St. Maur went from one house to another, they took their robes with them, and the receiving house had to pay compensation, typically twenty-five livres. On the sending monastery fell the cost of traveling, which naturally varied with the distance and type of conveyance. A healthy monk who walked from St. Germain to St. Denis, on the northern side of Paris, might spend no more than one livre, but a sick one who required a horse or coach and servant all the way to Soissons could spend fifteen times as much.[23]

Medical expenses, the upkeep of the infirmary, included the wages of the doctor and surgeon. But these were quite overshadowed by the cost of meat for the sick: for red meat alone, communally consumed between Easter 1660 and Mardi Gras 1661, the abbey paid 1,000 livres. During a ten-months period in 1678–79, meat ran to 667 livres 8 s. Poultry was believed to have special restorative powers, and the tender meat of pigeons, chickens, and turkeys no doubt went into broth for weaker monks. Lemons, sugar, and donkey milk were also among the special foods of the sick. During a single two-year period over 1,000 livres was spent on *drogues*: one

23. Three were sent to St. Denis for 3 livres in July 1663; Dom François Duvivier sent to St. Medard de Soissons in January 1661. Comptes, A.N. H5 4274.

monk served as apothecary and prepared these raw materials as medications for his colleagues. Another sort of shared expense, put in the same category, was the cost of registration letters for those taking holy orders, but these sums were nominal, amounting to 53 s. each in 1679. In only five of nineteen years did the percentage of the budget for *malades et frais communs* exceed 3%; the more typical median figure is 1.9%.

To summarize, food was the largest expense of maintaining the monastic community. The monks' diet was limited by the foods available at Paris in the seventeenth cenutry and by the restrictions of the Benedictine tradition. Within these limits the monks ate well: fish and eggs, butter, cheese, and vegetables were regularly consumed at St. Germain des Prés. The prices of most foods purchased by the abbey, though subject to seasonal variations, remained stable over a long time. Because of the low proportion of caloric intake furnished by cereals, the St. Germain diet must be regarded as one of comfort, if not luxury, in its time. The other categories of communal expenses—non-food supplies, clothings, and medical costs —were relatively minor in importance.

8

Spiritual Spending

Of the three categories of expenses described at the beginning of this part, spiritual spending was the smallest. Nevertheless, there is reason to assert that it was the most important. The monks took vows of stability, obedience, and conversion of morals as means to the end of divine service. Likewise, all the revenue of the abbey, whether spent for the maintenance of the physical plant or the community, had no other stated purpose. If the actual amounts expended for spiritual costs were slight, it was because the very existence of the abbey worked toward and simultaneously embodied spiritual purposes. By building a glorious church, the monks called attention to God's splendor; by living in accord with the principles of the rule, the monks brought themselves and the rest of society closer to God. Still, there were two direct financial expressions of spiritual purpose: alms and church maintenance.

Very little of the income of St. Germain des Prés was given away as alms to the poor. Only in years of exceptional severity did the total rise much above one percent of the budget. This may appear surprising. Were not all early modern Christians, and especially beneficed clergy, strictly obliged to give alms? Sermons and tracts urged the clergy to avoid personal luxury and distribute their money instead. Beautiful churches were very good, but as St. John Chrysostom asked, "What advantage does Christ receive from having a table set with golden chalices, while he is dying of hunger in the person of the poor?"[1] The Counter-Reformation shines with examples of Catholic reformers who restored discipline while helping the poor; ought not the Maurists to have followed St. Charles Borromeo and St. Francis de Sales? Certainly the monks provided spiritual support to the poor through religious services and prayers; their small material gifts were both general and specific to needs as they perceived them.

Living in cloistered regularity, with assuredly adequate income, the

1. Cited by Jean-Baptiste Thiers, *L'Avocat des pauvres* (Paris, 1676), p. 291.

monks of St. Germain des Prés could have seemed oblivious to the suffering world. But in their youth they all had lived outside the protective walls; they travelled to the abbey's lands during the harvest season, and from one monastery to another; last but not least, as holders of wealth, seigneurs, and priests, they constantly received supplications. In response, the monastery gave to the poor both in cash and in kind. The porters of the abbey distributed 30 to 40 livres per month to the parade of misery passing at the door. They gave more in the harsh winter months of February and March, less as agricultural produce became more plentiful and more affordable in late spring and summer. Two distributions of food were also made by the monastery. In 1656, when the government attempted to lock up the vagrant poor in the Hôpital Général, Parisian corporations that had previously given their own poor relief were persuaded to give to the new institution on a regular basis.[2] For its contribution, the council of St. Germain des Prés decided to offer 144 livres-weight (70.4 kg.) of bread per week, "as bread itself as well as in the soup."[3] Although the amount of bread was about half of that given independently by the abbey before, the monks declared that now they would give the poor their own more expensive white bread, with the resultant cost being the same. They also contended that their soup, supplied every Friday and Saturday, was better than that given to the poor before the Hôpital was built. Later, in the deliberations of the council for 1675, another charity is mentioned: "the praiseworthy custom of this monastery" of giving thirty loaves of bread per week to poor families and students.[4] The recipients' names were listed in a catalogue used by the porter who made the distribution. Once a year the prior examined this list and made appropriate additions and deletions.

Special cases for charity were discussed by the council, and generally fell into three groups: first, friends and relatives of the monks; second, other religious communities and those whose spiritual condition made them deserving; and third, people working on lands under the jurisdiction of the monastery. Charity, perhaps once seen as a general Christian obligation, was translated into a specific claim on the abbey's resources by persons related to it, dependent on it, or bound to it by similar religious ideals. For these souls, poverty always represented a temporary condition, never a necessity of social structure. Those most worthy of the abbey's help could ordinarily help themselves, and only came into difficulty through uncontrollable external circumstances.

2. Emmanuel S. Chill, "Religion and Mendicity in Seventeenth Century France," *International Review for Social History* 7 (1962): 400–25; Bernard, *The Emerging City*, p. 147, citing M. Félibien, vol. 3, p. 1,481.

3. Séniorat, B.N. MS. fr. 18819, fol. 83, 23 juin 1657.

4. Ibid.. fol. 126v, 3 oct. 1676.

Thus we can understand the grants made to friends and relatives to help place them in society. To the nephew of Brother Sébastien Varembault the abbey gave four silver écus, "to help him learn an honest trade that will allow him to make a living."[5] The sister of another monk received money to enter a convent, and the mother of Dom Gilles Henriau obtained help to return to Vendôme, her native area.[6] The idea of helping family members overcome temporary difficulty found a parallel in grants to other monasteries. Not only did St. Germain des Prés guarantee their borrowings, but it also gave them money and wine, as in 1698, when the Blancs-manteaux of Paris received a carriage-load from the vineyards of Thiais.[7] The principle of mutual assistance among monasteries proved the salvation of St. Germain des Prés itself in the troubled 1690s.

Four communities of nuns also shared in the generosity of the abbey. The nuns of the Holy Sacrament, who came to the Faubourg St. Germain in 1650, enjoyed and appreciated the kindness of their spiritual lords. The monks supported their efforts to restore a special medieval devotion at the convent, and took seriously their legal responsibility to the new house.[8] In 1661 the nuns lent the abbey 5,700 livres to be used for reconstruction of the church at the seigneurie of Bailly.[9] Good relations continued, with loans, repayments, and gifts: in 1691 the nuns gave St. Germain des Prés a set of damask linens, and the monks showed their gratitude by sending to the convent a load of wine for the sick.[10] One of the poorest convents in Paris, the English Benedictines of the Faubourg St. Antoine, appeared repeatedly in the minutes of the council. These nuns received gifts of wheat, wine, and wood for several years running from 1679 to 1683. As they themselves stated, their lack of money and need for all things made them seek help from St. Germain des Prés, known for its "charité si prompte et si généreuse."[11]

The monks were more inclined to give alms to other religious communities when they saw the spiritual worthiness of the recipients. A similar motive inspired their grants to persons recently converted to Catholicism, and to those who suffered persecution on the distant frontiers of Christianity. Abjurations of Protestantism were important events in the

5. Ibid., fol. 127v, 7 jan. 1677.

6. Ibid., fol. 132, 2 sept. 1685; fol. 115v, 14 juin 1670.

7. Ibid., fol. 155v, 5 nov. 1698; cf. their gift to St. Josse sur Mer, fol. 120, 30 oct. 1673.

8. Jean Leclercq, "St. Germain et les Bénédictines de Paris," *Mémorial*, pp. 223–30.

9. Recette du casuel, Comptes, A.N. H5 4275.

10. Séniorat, B.N. MS. fr. 18819, fol. 136v, 20 déc. 1691. Note also that Madeleine Robinet, the doorkeeper of this convent, had lent St. Germain des Prés 3,000 livres. Actes cap., B.N. MS. fr. 16857, fol. 126, 20 jan. 1679.

11. Séniorat, B.N. MS. fr. 18819, fol. 130, 27 fév. 1680.

religious life of the abbey, and those who made them did not go unre-
warded. A Danish Lutheran won to the Catholic faith left with one *pistole*,
while a newly converted *pauvre gentilhomme* recommended by Cardinal
de Bouillon received two.[12] Eastern Christians also visited Paris on their
fund-raising tours, and St. Germain participated nobly; in 1667 and 1668
the abbey gave to help ransom Hungarian canons from the Turks, to assist
Armenian Jacobins in paying tribute to the Persians, and to send volunteers
to rescue besieged Christians in Crete.[13]

The monastic minutes give the impression that the abbey, as a good
seigneur, exercised paternal supervision over the peasants who worked its
lands. When the monks went out to collect to the seigneurial dues and
rents, they took along money to distribute to the poor.[14] The officers noted
cases of extreme hardship. In April of 1662, when the scarcity of grain
was so severe that the peasants were in danger of dying from hunger, the
monastery decided to borrow 4,000 livres for relief. With the borrowed
money the abbey bought bread and meat to make soup for the poor.[15]
About the same time the royal government distributed foreign grain in
Paris; as a consequence, the price of one livre-weight of bread fell from
8 s. to 2 s. 6 d.[16] Further references to aid to the seigneuries abound. Of
course, the most common kind of aid to the distressed on the farms was the
postponement or forgiveness of their financial obligations to the monastery. Reductions were granted frequently to farmers during the Fronde
and afterwards, in the early 1660s, and in later years when the harvests
were not successful. Under the leasing system the abbey had little direct
contact with the tillers of the fields, but the tenants who received reductions
in their rents did not forget those working under them. On the suggestion
of the tenant at Aurainvillers in 1664, the monks gave the poor on their
land two sétiers (312 liters) of barley, one *boisseau* (13 liters) of peas,
and two boisseaux (26 liters) of beans to sow crops for the next season.[17]
Here charity went hand in hand with self-interest. When a mission to the
parish of Antony in 1671 revealed seven or eight persons in need, several
boisseaux of grain were sent.[18] Noting the severe winter weather in Janu-

12. Séniorat, B.N. MS. fr. 18819, fol. 122, 5 nov. 1674; fol. 121, 12 avril 1674.

13. Séniorat, B.N. MS. fr. 18819, fol. 109, 12 avril 1667; fol. 109v, 24 avril 1667;
fol. 113v, 21 août 1668.

14. Eg., "A divers passants et pauvres de Suresnes, Thiais, et Antony pendant les
vendanges des dits lieux, 4 livres 10 s." Comptes, A.N. H5 4274, oct. 1661. "Donné par
le R. P. Procureur étant aux champs, 6 s." Ibid., jan. 1663.

15. Actes cap., B.N. MS. fr. 16856, fol. 180, 4 avril 1662. Wheat and bread bought
from July to Nov. 1662—1,007 liv. 16 s. Also, 129 liv. for soup meat. A.N. H5 4274.

16. N. Delamare, *Traité de la Police*, (Amsterdam, 1729), vol. 2, pp. 862–65, cites
documents relating to the royal intervention.

17. Séniorat, B.N. MS. fr. 18819, fol. 105, 4 avril 1664.

18. Ibid., fol. 117v, 3 juin 1671.

ary 1677, the council sent the cellerier and the procureur to the villages, in order that they might study the condition of the poor and give grain or money to them.[19] Two years later winter relief was dispatched to the inhabitants of Suresnes.[20] At the end of the century it appeared that aid to the seigneuries might be needed for several years in a row: then, in December of 1698, grain and flour for making soup were allocated to the farms. When the misery continued the following winter, the council extended the program of relief.[21]

The high points of expenditure on alms were reached in the years 1662 and 1694, by general agreement among the worst of the century. In these years 3.1% and 4.1% of the respective total budgets went to poor relief. In the light of these figures, St. Germain des Prés cannot be described as very generous. Alms for the poor never involved personal sacrifice for the monks. But at least their gifts were not accompanied by that punitive attitude of the secular Parisian "devout" party, who saw poverty "in the setting of debased 'nature' rather than as concrete expression of a specific social and political order."[22] There is no suggestion of harsh conditions attached to the abbey's help. The monks accepted the permanence of a certain amount of "honest" urban poverty, as shown by their general distributions of money and bread. In addition, the specific and temporary poverty of relatives, religious brothers and sisters, and legal dependents called forth specific temporary help. If the amounts given were modest, they were nevertheless thought to be commensurate with the abbey's responsibilities. When these responsibilities suddenly grew larger than the available funds, borrowing made up the difference. Probably the fairest conclusion for a modern mind struck by the slightness of the alms is that St. Germain des Prés always maintained a correct, Christian attitude toward the poor.

Religious practice itself made only modest demands on the budget. Certainly the abbey had to assure a supply of sacramental bread and wine, candles and incense, altarware and altar cloths. These were the elements and implements necessary for the celebration of mass. Every Catholic church had and still has these needs: if St. Germain des Prés differed from the ordinary parish church it was probably in the quantity of the supplies used. Besides the mandatory round of daily offices, mass was said at least six times a day, and more often on the religious holidays. Each ordained priest in the community had an obligation to say mass daily. While this

19. Ibid., fol. 127v, 7 jan. 1677.
20. Ibid., fol. 129, 8 jan. 1679.
21. Ibid., B.N. MS. fr. 18819, fol. 156, 11 déc. 1698; fol. 160, 14 jan. 1700.
22. Chill, "Religion and Mendicity." This view has recently been challenged by Mary Anglim, "The Hôpital Général of Paris," unpublished paper, University of Michigan.

obligation could be fulfilled through communal celebration, there were many masses that had to be said separately. According to the terms of perpetual foundations, at least one mass per day was said for the benefactors and friends of the abbey; four more masses were said each week to fulfill the conditions of gifts.[23] High masses were celebrated yearly or more often in memory of prominent deceased persons. The rhythm of observance had in some cases gone on for hundreds of years: for example, Blanche, daughter of St. Louis IX, king of France, was remembered with three high masses per year—on the Thursday after Pentecost, during the week following the celebration of the Birth of the Virgin Mary (September 8), and, on the twenty-second of October, a requiem.[24] If the Revolution of 1789 had not placed final punctuation on monastic life at St. Germain des Prés, these masses might still be said now and onward into perpetuity.

A charitable foundation imposed a duty on the monastery. When St. Germain des Prés accepted the money it had to be sure that a suitable investment for the capital was found, and that there were enough priests to meet the obligations. Claude l'Huillier, bourgeois de Paris and *banquier expéditionnaire en cour de Rome*, created such a foundation in 1645. He desired to have mass said daily after his death, and to have a high mass once a year, as well as extra masses for his family. In return he gave the monastery 6,000 livres cash and the full remission of a rente of 1,000 livres principal that had been outstanding since 1613.[25] Claude l'Huillier died in 1646, but one condition of his gift to the abbey was not satisfied until 1663, when a painting of his namesake, St. Claude, archbishop of Besançon, and St. Guillaume, archbishop of Bourges, was placed in the abbey church. This painting, commissioned by the monks, cost 120 livres.[26]

The great number of masses required by the foundations, increasing from time to time as more donors approached the abbey, led the monks to take on the "great and very onerous" expense of four choirboys during the 1640s. The boys received complete support from the monastery because they would give responses to all the masses. However, the great number of priests in the community made this impossible; more children of bourgeois in the neighborhood had to be accepted as day students. The resident choirboys soon became lazy and troublesome, and the monks decided to disengage themselves "honnêtement" from the matter by sending the boys away to boarding school.[27]

By October of 1654 the large group of day students had also become

23. Livre des fondations, B.N. MS. fr. 18816, fol. 229. See also part 5, Spiritual Life and Politics.
24. Livre des fondations, B.N. MS. fr. 18816, fol. 230.
25. Livre des fondations, B.N. MS. fr. 18816, fol. 229.
26. Comptes, A.N. H5 4274; Sacristie, B.N. MS. fr. 18818, fol. 202, 5 mai 1663.
27. Sacristie, B.N. MS. fr. 18818, fol. 154.

unmanageable. In spite of the care and education they received from the monks, the boys fell to quarreling, and disturbances occurred daily in the church. It was found that a small number of well-chosen boys would suffice; four was too few if the monks kept up their other duties, but six was adequate, and two substitutes were chosen as well. The upkeep of this little group was not inconsequential—violet serge robes, a special fire in the sacristy that they might warm their hands on cold days, dinner, and finally, a master to teach the boys "les rudiments et humanités, et l'écriture."[28] The master received 100 livres yearly in installments, paid quarterly.

Simultaneously the abbey hired a new full-time servant for the church and specified his duties, which before this time had been done by the concierge, or porter of the monastery. The new servant came to work before 6 A.M. to open the doors of the church, and stayed there all day except for a fifteen-minute break to go home to eat. He had an obligation to keep watch over the altars, to guide the priests, to light candles, "and principally to keep the very numerous poor from begging there, and to stop them at the door."[29] But with the opening of the Hôpital Général, the poor temporarily disappeared from the streets.[30] The sacristan could give the servant other work: cleaning the floors, walls, tapestries, and courtyards, and chasing away children. As compensation the servant received housing next to the great doorway of the abbey, a salary of 40 silver écus, dinner on days when he had to sound the bells, leftover wine, and various privileges in the church, including rights to sell candles, to let chairs, to dig graves, and to collect a fee of 10 s. when services were held in Flemish.

This chapter on expenses for spiritual purposes has focused on two of the smallest categories in the budget. Charity at St. Germain was both general and particular, but the strongest support was given to those who were already tied to the abbey. For these persons poverty was only a temporary state, while alms were the means of regaining their places in society. The abbey's expenses for religious services included traditional church supplies, and were increased by special requirements—endowed masses, urban pressures, local cults, and memorial services. Devotion, honor, and self-interest converged in these expenditures. The monastic practice of religion raises questions of spiritual life and politics that can be answered for the individual monk and the community as a whole.

In distributing their expenditures in general, the monks of St. Germain des Prés saw their freedom circumscribed by fixed obligations that

28. Sacristie, B.N. MS. fr. 18818, fol. 159.
29. Ibid., fol. 162.
30. "On ne voit plus de pauvres à l'occasion de l'Hôpital Général nouvellement établi. . . ." Sacristie, B.N. MS. fr. 18818, fol. 162.

consumed a major portion of their budget. To fulfill the spiritual purposes of the abbey, the monastic properties and community had to be maintained. Taxes, debt service, wages, and seigneurial obligations represented commitments of long standing: if St. Germain occasionally fell into arrears on its payments, it nevertheless recognized its obligations and made efforts to return to prompt payment schedules. Merchants who sold to the abbey, as well as persons who bought its annuities or worked as its servants, could expect the monks to make good their commitments. Agricultural production, when carried out under the direct supervision of the monks themselves, meant expense as well as income; building maintenance and legal fees were also essential to the abbey's continued well-being.

Monastic expenditure for food illustrates several aspects of monastic life. First, the monks' diet was restricted by religious rules and the availability of food. While other seventeenth-century diets were high in calories and cereals, if fair comparisons can be made the monks' diet was generous and of above-average quality, despite the absence of meat. At St. Germain the diet did not vary with general economic conditions; again the monks were a favored population. They ate well, by modern standards and by those of their own century: their expenditure on food confirms the generally stable prices that have been found by other studies. Non-food supplies, as necessary for the monks, took only a small part of the budget.

Spiritual expenses of the monastery demonstrate the monks' attitudes toward charity and public celebration, attitudes that can be likened to those of the world outside the cloister and again illustrate the bonds between the abbey and society in general. The concept of general medieval charity had largely given way to particular charity for those who were most deserving—who were already identified with the monks in family or spirit, or who worked on the lands that provided the abbey's sustenance. Help to those in need was designed to help them return to independence: to give more, or to expect less, would have been out of tune with the times. Religious practices included necessary masses and celebrations—necessary to remain true to the foundations, however distant in the past; necessary also to uphold the abbey's ceremonial rank and to win the favor of persons in power.

The monks exercised conscious choices when they spent money, but the point should be clear that many of these choices were determined by legal, moral, spiritual, and traditional obligations. These obligations had their basis in the principles of French society, among them lordship and ownership of land, sanctity of contract, Christian charity, and monarchical splendor; life in the monastery required the monks to express their continuing social participation.

PART 4

The Monk as Steward

9

Claude Coton

"A Benedictine community is primarily a body of men devoted to a life of prayer; and the daily round of liturgical offices in the choir of the abbey church is apt to leave few traces in the records."[1] Monks choose to live a restricted life; as much as possible, time and place become constants for them. Confined to a cloister, living according to a set schedule for every hour of the day and every day of the year, the monk limits his physical experiences in order to deepen his spiritual understanding. Stability and obedience, two of the three vows, are prerequisites to the third, reformation of life, "the rooting out of vices and the planting of virtues."[2] Only the exceptional monk writes, and then usually impersonally. The oral and confessional traditions of the monastery probably have a negative influence on writing for personal expression. The monks of St. Germain des Prés, seeking to minimize the personal element in writing, often worked in teams and published some books anonymously.

It is therefore remarkable that some monks did leave behind autobiographical fragments. For the light that they shed on thoughts, feelings, and daily life of cloisters past, these fragments merit special attention. At St. Germain des Prés, scholarly projects often involved correspondence with learned men all over Europe, and these letters can be read both for their literary value and for fine points of knowledge. Yet there is only one carefully and continuously kept private journal from St. Germain des Prés: that of Claude Coton. His journal begins with the arrival of the reform in 1631 and extends to 1660, thereby providing an inside view of the first thirty years of Maurist activity at the abbey.

In the first three parts of this study, our subject was the corporation, its recruitment, revenues, and expenditures—the collective way of life. In

1. H. P. R. Finberg, *Tavistock Abbey*, p. v.
2. Cuthbert Butler, *Benedictine Monachism*, p. 131; interpreting chapter 58 of the Rule of St. Benedict.

this part, using Father Coton's journal, we turn to the life of an individual. This sincere monk, religiously simple but financially shrewd, served his monastery well. As steward of vast possessions, he observed much that refines the general picture of monastic life. Quite apart from antiquarian interest in Coton, then, this chapter examines questions of recruitment, revenues, and expenditures through his eyes. If statistics, the bones of history, have depersonalized the monks of St. Germain des Prés for the reader, this account seeks to restore to him their flesh and blood.

Claude Coton was born on September 8, 1588, the feast of the nativity of the Virgin Mary; every year for the last five years of his life he recorded the day and his age precisely.[3] His few references to his family suggest that they were comfortable Parisians from the legal profession. Coton had at least one sister, also named Claude; she married a Pierre Baudoin. Their daughter Marie was married to Michel Martin, a procureur of the Châtelet.[4] This indicates family prosperity, for a woman marrying a procureur would have brought a dowry of 6,000 to 12,000 livres in the mid-seventeenth century.[5] In 1639, Martin became an officer of the abbey at the seigneurie of Antony; his wife's uncle, the monk Coton, no doubt influenced the appointment, because he had held the post himself for five years previously.[6] Claude Coton also referred twice to his great-nephew Pierre Martin, son of Michel: in 1655 he sent Pierre three livres in cash as a New Year's gift, and two and a half years later, at the death of Marie Baudoin Martin, Claude mentioned Pierre as an avocat.[7] From this information, we can understand that Claude Coton had some financial means to enter the unreformed Abbey of St. Germain des Prés during the reign of Henry IV.

An active partisan of the reform, Claude Coton nevertheless remained true to his original vows and did not take a second novitiate in the Congregation of St. Maur. Perhaps he felt too old to begin anew: when the reformers came to St. Germain, Coton was already forty-two. He had been striving for better observance for some time, and the Maurists were most

3. Journal of Claude Coton, B.N. MS. fr. 18822, fol. 47. Nécrologe, in Jacques Bouillart, *Histoire de l'Abbaye Royale de St. Germain des Prés* (Paris, 1724), Pièces Justificatives, no. 124.

4. Journal, B.N. MS. fr. 18822, fol. 39. Martin appears on the 1649 list of procureurs, and the first indication of a successor to his post is in 1671. Listes des procureurs, A.N. Y 6611, no. 114.

5. A. Furetière, *Le Roman bourgeois 1666*, ed. F. Tulov (Paris, 1919), pp. 33–34; cited by Julian Dent, *Crisis in Finance*, p. 180.

6. Actes cap., B.N. MS. fr. 16854, fol. 9; another source notes Coton's appointment in 1635: A.N. L 1126, fol. 280, cited by Dom Anger, *Les Dépendances de l'Abbaye de St. Germain des Prés*, vol. 2, p. 278.

7. Journal, B.N. M.S. fr. 18822, fols. 25, 39.

grateful for the role he played in winning St. Germain des Prés for their movement. In 1627 Coton had pushed the chapter general of the older Congregation of Chezal-Benoît to make stricter rules; two years later, when disorders continued, the leaders of this congregation made Dom Coton prior of the abbey. As the Maurists saw it, "the promotion of Father Coton was the work of the hand of God."[8] The new prior applied the rules strictly, but when he saw that his good work could quickly be undone by corrupt superiors, he resolved to work for the introduction of the Maurists. With the help of Dom Adrien Barisel, an older monk who had sought reform in 1615, Coton persuaded the commendatory abbot Henry of Verneuil to support the plan. In February of 1630 secret agreements were prepared, but the disgrace of Michel de Marillac, royal Keeper of the Seals and leader of the devout party, prevented their taking effect.[9] In December a second agreement was made with Verneuil. While the new Keeper of the Seals Châteauneuf studied the papers, Prior Coton sought to win the consent of the monks one by one. Coton knew that an open session of the chapter would have led to stormy discussion and jeopardized his chances of success; he therefore held it only after many private conversations. Finally, 27 of the 33 monks gave their consent at the chapter meeting, 2 agreed shortly afterwards, and only 4 opposed the reform.[10]

Dom Cyprien Leclerc, a former monk of St. Germain who had joined the Maurists, came with eight reformers to take possession of the abbey on February 12, 1631. Dom Coton welcomed them at the church for the singing of the *Veni Creator*, and later led them around the monastery to the refectory for the evening meal.[11] Coton's journal entry, specially signed on this day, noted his prayer to the Lord "que laditte introduction soit à sa gloire, et au salut tant dudit Coton que de tous ses confrères."[12]

But the reform of St. Germain des Prés was not to be accomplished so easily, even though the strength of the reformers soon rose to fifteen. Their opponents appealed to the Parlement of Paris, which issued an injunction against the reformers on the very day of their introduction. A month later the court sent two commissioners to conduct an investigation at the abbey. They asked Prior Coton why he had defied the court order, and he replied that reform was a necessity: "That this necessity was not unknown to him

8. Edmond Martène, *Histoire de la Congrégation de St. Maur*, vol. 32, p. 15.

9. Marillac was not disgraced until after the Day of the Dupes in November 1630. Another reason for delays in royal business over the summer was the king's illness and absence from Paris. G. Pagès, "Autour du grand orage: Richelieu et Marillac, deux politiques," *Revue historique* 179 (1937): 63–97.

10. Martène, *Histoire*, vol. 32, p. 18.

11. Ibid., pp. 18–19.

12. Journal, B.N. MS. fr. 16853, fol. 28.

[Coton], after all the orders on this subject issued by the court since 1612, that Pope Paul V and the Most Christian King had ordered it, and that the Most Serene Prince, their abbot, wished it thus.[13] The royal letters authorizing the reform were safely with the *grand conseil*, where the cases of the congregation were heard. The commissioners accepted this response and went on to question the supporters of the reform. The opponents asked for and were given rooms in the dormitory and guest lodgings, but they were not released from their obligation to obey Prior Coton.

By the summer of 1631, the would-be reformer Coton was certainly out of favor with the other superiors of the Congregation of Chezal-Benoît, who believed that he had betrayed their interests. He was replaced as prior by one of the opponents, and this appointment was recognized by the grand conseil. On September 9, it appeared that the cause of the reformers was lost, for another order would have expelled them within twenty-four hours. While the Maurists slept peacefully, their less temperate supporters among the anciens set about building barricades. The main door of the abbey was blocked when the commissioners arrived with armed men the next morning, but they gained entry by the abbot's palace. Although moved by the sight of the devout reformers in prayer, the commissioners did not spare their criticism of Dom Coton as "léger, imprudent et précipité."[14] At these words Dom Barisel spoke up in defense of the prior, whose responsibility was certainly limited in view of the years of preparation for the reform and the consent of all the responsible authorities. At last, however, the reformed monks submitted to the order by sending five of their number to the nearby monastery of Notre Dame des Blancsmanteaux and by promising to have the rest leave St. Germain des Prés within five days.

The final settlement in favor of the Maurists was due to the personal intervention of the great. Two monks went to Compiègne to secure the support of Châteauneuf, by then firmly established in his office. With the help of Marshal Schomberg and Cardinal Richelieu, Châteauneuf persuaded the king to interfere in favor of the reform.[15] Soon the religious practice of the newcomers justified Coton's confidence. When, on May 28, 1632, Dom Quentin de Varannes became the first Maurist to die at St. Germain,[16] Dom Coton praised his calmness during the disturbances associated with the reform. For all the reformed monks Coton had respectful awe: "It is true that I do not know of any monk of the said congregation who is

13. Martène, *Histoire*, vol. 32, p. 20.
14. Ibid., p. 22.
15. Ibid., p. 24.
16. Vanel, *Nécrologe*.

not a very good monk, and to explain myself I say that they are all the best, each and every one. I pray to God that they may persevere."[17]

Yet Claude Coton had not given up his responsibilties. The Maurists chose him as procureur général of the community in May of 1631.[18] In this post Dom Coton received money from the tenants of the abbey, and represented St. Germain des Prés in controversies with other institutions, as in a dispute with the Abbey of St. Geneviève over seigneurial dues.[19] Repairs on the seigneuries and transactions with village priests were all handled by the procureur.[20] Every three months he would pay over the receipts to the reformed monk serving as cellerier, and together they would check the accounts and sign the books.

Under the terms of contracts between the anciens and the Maurists, the former gave up all control over the monastery in exchange for guaranteed annual pensions. In April of 1632 Cotton's pension was set at 600 livres per year, plus an allowance for food consumed in the refectory or outside the abbey.[21] About eighteen months later, however, Coton accepted an assigned income from a seigneurie instead of a fixed pension. His revenue from the farm of Monteclin, the land and its accompanying rights, was set by lease at 600 livres per year.[22]

Monteclin was located fifteen kilometers south of Paris in the modern commune of Bièvres.[23] When Coton took it over, it contained more wasteland than arable surface. The dwelling was "tout en ruine"—so dilapidated that Coton found it necessary to remove the whole roof and put up a completely new framework, new rafters, and tiles. The ceilings of the stable and the granary also required repair and extra supports. In 1634 Coton spent 339 livres on improvements: included in this total were iron grates for the windows, tiles, lath, plaster, and 126 man-days of labor.[24] The following years saw the monk purchase odd lots of land and repay various rentes owed by the estate. Throughout there is no suggestion that his goal was the reconstitution of an ancient seigneurie; rather, he sought to reduce the obligations of the farm in order to concentrate his efforts on profitable cultivation of the land. His acquisitions may be considered genuine agri-

17. Journal, B.N. MS. fr. 16853, fol. 41.
18. Actes cap., B.N. MS. fr. 16852, fol. 93.
19. Journal, B.N. MS. fr. 16853, fol. 34v.
20. Repairs at Suresnes, 25 nov. 1632, Actes cap., B.N. MS. fr. 16852, fol. 103. Transaction with Louis Abelly, curé de Longuesse, 27 mars 1636, Manse conventuelle, A.N., LL 1126, fol. 298.
21. Journal, B.N. MS. fr. 16853, fol. 156.
22. Ibid., Registre d'Actes, A.N., LL 1058.
23. Anger, Les Dépendances, vol. 2, p. 240.
24. Journal, B.N. MS. fr. 16853, fols. 46–49v.

cultural improvements, since they included putting wastelands into production. Trees were planted, pieces of land exchanged, and annual payments to nearby parish churches were ended with lump-sum settlements.
All of this took money, and Coton did not hesitate to put his own funds
back into the land. Undoubtedly his willingness to make the investment
contributed to his success in raising the revenue, from 600 to 1,000 livres
in seven years.

In 1637, while continuing to draw the revenue from Monteclin and
fulfilling the office of procureur, Claude Coton reported to the Maurist
community on the repurchase of the barony of Cordoux, the greatest financial project since the coming of the reform.[25] Cordoux had been alienated
by the manse abbatiale of St. Germain des Prés during the wars of religion
in the sixteenth century, when special taxes were levied on religious institutions. This alienation was effected with the privilege of repurchase reserved by the abbey as the original owner. In 1592 the Parlement of Paris
had even ordered the abbey to buy back Cordoux, but neither the abbots
nor the new owners of the land showed enthusiasm for the proposal.[26]
This is understandable: for the former, repurchase was out of the question without substantial borrowing and perhaps sacrifice of current income; for the latter, the fruits of possession of a "bargain seigneurie"
were sweet. Perhaps this is why Coton was able to arrange the transfer of
the empty right of repurchase from the manse abbatiale to the manse conventuelle.[27]

The cost of buying back the barony was estimated at 70,000 livres.
Coton feared that the land would not return enough revenue to pay the
costs of borrowing. Two monks, Romain Rodoyer (the cellerier) and
René Viot, went to Cordoux to inspect the property. When they presented
their report a month later, they pointed out that much could be done to
increase the income from the estate.[28] With this in mind, the community
then decided to ask the superior general of the congregation for permission
to borrow the necessary funds.

In fact most of the money for the repurchase came from the sale of
three arpents of garden near the Hôpital de la Charité in Paris. This sale
produced 50,000 livres, and was to set the pattern for future sales of urban
property.[29] The monks had discovered that the capital invested in urban

25. Actes cap., B.N. MS. fr. 16852, fol. 130.
26. Anger, Les Dépendances, vol. 1, p. 203.
27. Manse conventuelle, A.N., LL 1130, fol. 191; Anger, Les Dépendances, vol. 1, p.
203.
28. Actes cap., B.N. MS. fr. 16852, fols. 131–32.
29. Biens acquis ou retirés par les religieux, B.N. MS. fr. 16864, fol. 54+; Anger,
Les Dépendances, vol. 3, p. 201. Actes cap., B.N. MS. fr. 16852, fol. 135.

properties would produce a greater return if it were placed in agricultural lands. In January of 1638 an additional 11,000 livres was borrowed at 5.55%: two-thirds of this money came from the Parisian Président Duvelot, and the rest from a priest at the Collège de Lisieux.[30] The formal repossession of the barony of Cordoux took place on the twenty-seventh, when 57,376 livres 4 s. was paid to the descendants (and their creditors) of Marshal Artus de Cossé, *conseiller du roi et surintendant des finances*, who had bought the seigneurie in 1562. Although the price had been fixed at 67,535 livres 18 s., deductions of 5,135 livres for repairs and 5,034 livres 14 s. for sales and alienations were made. At the same time, the abbey bought back another six arpents of land at Cordoux for 721 livres.[31]

Dom Anger located Cordoux in the modern commune of Courpalay, near Rozay-en-Brie.[32] The barony would then have fallen within the *élection* of Rozay, a royal fiscal jurisdiction on the eastern edge of the *généralité* of Paris. For military purposes, however, the area belonged to the *gouvernement* of Champagne. Cordoux is about sixty kilometers southeast of Paris, farther than Melun, but not as far as Provins. Coton, a seventeenth-century traveler on horseback, usually broke the trip from the metropolis to the seigneurie over two days. His overnight stopping place was Brie-Comte-Robert, about halfway.[33]

What sort of domain did the monks possess at Cordoux? A contemporary description made by the previous owner, Charles, Comte de l'Hospital, certainly gives the impression of "une magnifique dépendance":

> Château and seigneurial seat of Cordoux, consisting of a large, high lodge with several rooms, kitchen, servants' rooms, cellars, storerooms, and galleries—the whole being nine spans long, covered with tile. A gallery at the end, made of pillars and arcades, containing seven spans, with a cellar at the end; above the gallery, there are grain storerooms and promenades; above those, an attic covered with slate.
>
> Another lodge in the form of a hall, kitchen, and stables covered with tiles, five spans long, with four towers, with a portal on the front of the said castle, and the whole enclosed by a moat with a drawbridge.
>
> In front of this lodge there is a spacious farmyard, at the end of which there is a slate-covered gateway. In this farmyard,

30. Actes cap., B.N., MS. fr. 16852, fol. 140.
31. Biens acquis, B.N. MS. fr. 16854, fol. 54+.
32. Anger, *Les Dépendances*, vol. 1, p. 190.
33. Journal, B.N. MS. fr. 18822, fol. 21.

directly facing the drawbridge and the front of the castle, there
is a ruined chapel in honor of the Virgin Mary; because it is
important to the place, it has been rebuilt on the square of Cordoux. In this chapel the deans, canon, and chapter of Courpalay
are required by a foundation of a seigneur of Cordoux to sing
or to have sung, said, and celebrated the following masses and
offices: all Sundays and holy days, those of Notre Dame, the
apostles, also three times per week and also all the days of Lent
and holy week.

Pigeon coop, garden, second farmyard with lodgings for
the tenants, large stables, pond with fountain and willow grove;
below that, a mill and fish ponds. Behind the château, a wooded
rabbit warren with several lanes.[34]

Four villages, various farms, fishing rights, justice and seigneurial dues
were all included in the barony. It was an immense domain, covering hundreds of acres of fields, meadows, and woodlands. But its resources were
not being used in the most efficient way, and its revenues were less than
they could have been with better management. From the moment that the
monks repurchased the barony extensive repairs were necessary. In 1638
the community borrowed 15,000 livres for general agricultural improvements: at Cordoux alone 5,125 livres was spent in five years.[35]

Until January of 1640 Claude Coton stayed at St. Germain des Prés
and continued to take his meals in the refectory with the reformed monks.
In order to compensate them for the meals consumed by his serving boy,
Coton regularly returned his 200 livres allowance for food.[36] But, at the
end of December 1639, the ancien monk gave up his servant and his
residence at the abbey. With the approval of the community, he went to
live at Cordoux. His successful management of Monteclin recommended
him for the larger estate, and about a year later he agreed with the chapter
to become the tenant of the basse-cour at Cordoux.[37]

The basse-cour had been leased at 1,200 livres per year, but Coton
estimated the annual yield of the land to himself at 1,600 livres. In exchange for this income, he offered the monastery the greatly improved
seigneurie of Monteclin along with a package of rentes and provisions
totaling 1,620 livres. For the Maurists, the increase of 420 livres in total

34. Extrait de l'adveu et dénombrement de la terre et baronie de Cordoux. . . , A.N.
LL 1126, fols. 198–200, in Anger, Les Dépendances, vol. 1, p. 204.
35. Actes cap., B.N. MS. fr. 16852, fol. 158. Biens acquis, B.N. MS. fr. 16864, fol.
54+; Anger, Les Dépendances, vol. 3, p. 201.
36. Journal, B.N. MS. fr. 16853, fol. 158.
37. Actes cap., B.N. MS. fr. 16852, fols. 227–28; acte, fol. 229.

annual income was further augmented the following year, when Coton's former farm at Monteclin was let at 1,050 livres instead of 1,000 livres.[38]

For Coton the barony of Cordoux proved even more profitable than the seigneurie of Monteclin. The basse-cour contained 180 arpents of arable land, 8 arpents of meadow, and 18 arpents of woodland.[39] Coton managed its resources so well that within four years he was able to repurchase rentes and offer the Maurists capital sums of 5,400 livres.[40]

Not only was Coton's landed income flowing back to the monastery in donations but it was also used to improve the land. Near the end of 1646 the enterprising monk prepared to accept even more responsibility. Besides the basse-cour at 1,600 livres, he agreed to manage eight other farms and all the seigneurial rights of the barony for the abbey. It was a tremendous expansion of his stewardship, and he took it only on special conditions. The worn-out land needed to be fertilized, and to this end Coton proposed *marnage*—marling, the spreading of chalky clay over the acidic soil. Ordinarily marling was carried out over all the arable land on an estate at once; the high cost was borne by the proprietor, since a tenant could not hope to recover the investment during the term of a nine-year lease.[41] Thus Coton proposed marling at his own expense only if he were guaranteed a lifelong lease at 2,700 livres per year, plus up to 20 livres of mutation fees. After Coton's death, his friend Brother Antoine Lopinot was to have his pension increased by 10% of the cost of agricultural improvements. The chapter accepted these conditions on November 11, 1646.[42]

The Maurists entrusted Cordoux to Dom Coton as fermier, an independent operator of the farms, entitled to take the profits as well as required to suffer the losses. Yet his special tie to the abbey meant that he was no ordinary tenant. When the chapter decided in 1650, for example, to sell or exchange six arpents of land bought back at the same time as Cordoux, Claude Coton received their power of attorney.[43] Coton also helped the abbey by watching for opportunities to exercise the seigneurial jurisdiction of Cordoux. If private persons wanted to sell land in this

38. Actes cap., B.N. MS. fr. 16854, fol. 61.

39. Anger, *Les Dépendances*, vol. 1, p. 209.

40. Repurchase of liferent of 88 livres with 1,000 livres principal, Actes cap., B.N., MS. fr. 16854, fol. 90, 10 juin 1644; 2,200 livres donation to raise Antoine Lopinot's pension by 200 livres, ibid., fol. 96, 9 sept. 1644; 2,200 livres donation to cover allowance for food, ibid., fol. 104, 11 fév. 1645.

41. "Marnage," *Encyclopédie, ou dictionnaire raisonné* (Geneva, 1777+), vol. 21, p. 135.

42. Actes cap., B.N. MS. fr. 16855, fol. 18.

43. The land was bought by Nicolas Fouquet, later the ill-fated superintendent of finance of Louis XIV. He paid 1,000 livres for what had cost the monks 721 livres fourteen years before. Actes cap., B.N. MS. fr. 16855, fols. 94, 112.

jurisdiction, the abbey could consider using its seigneurial rights to make the purchase itself. Coton notified the abbey on such occasions.[44]

We have already referred to 1653 as one of the low points in the financial history of the abbey. While many fermiers of lands nearer to Paris asked St. Germain des Prés to reduce rents following the devastation of the Fronde, Claude Coton met his obligations in full and even had money to spare to lend to the abbey. He put at their disposal 4,600 livres, his savings of twenty years. Again, the terms were generous: in exchange for his capital, Coton received a life annuity of 400 livres and remembrance in the prayers of the monastery after his death. The monastery used the money to repurchase perpetual rentes: since Coton had already reached age sixty-five, his life rent promised to be more advantageous to the community.[45]

By November of 1654 Dom Coton had been at Cordoux for nearly fifteen years. He was sixty-six years old, and his declining health interfered with active administration of the land. Consequently, he wished to give up his post of fermier and retire to the abbey. During his management of Cordoux, the annual revenue increased from 4,310 livres to 6,750 livres in constant money. This increase of 57% was certainly due to improvements and purchases: Dom Claude and Brother Antoine had repaired and built new lodgings, storehouses, courtyards, gardens, pigeon coops, ditches, and a rabbit warren. Brother Antoine now took over the farms, while Dom Claude received rights to "déjeuner, dîner et souper" from the kitchen of the abbey, as well as an annual pension of 1,600 livres and 400 livres interest on his loans. Lopinot was then drawing 900 livres per year from the abbey: 500 livres as pension and the rest from annuities that Coton had constituted in his favor.[46]

Although Coton showed considerable entrepreneurial talent, he had no desire to accumulate money in excess of his personal needs. From his term at Cordoux the subtenants still owed him 10,310 livres in secure obligations; but instead of trying to collect from them, he decided to donate the money to the abbey. Only 310 livres was withheld for repairs to the windmill; the 10,000 livres became testimony of his affection for the monastery and his desire to participate in its good works. These proposals were accepted gratefully by the community. Coton returned to Paris, and his days of active service were over.

What picture of Claude Coton's private life emerges from his journal?

44. Purchase of 15 arpents of land in 1651: Actes cap., B.N. MS. fr. 16855, fol. 122.

45. A.N., M.C., Etude CX, 97 (4 sept. 1653): Actes cap., B.N. MS. fr. 16855, fol. 153.

46. A.N., M.C., Etude CX, 97 (11 nov. 1654); Actes cap., B.N. MS. fr. 16855, fol. 180.

Because Coton received his food and lodging from the reformed community, his journal gives more details of his personal spending, about 200 livres per year. This was enough for a modest but respectable style of life. Necessities such as clothing, candles, firewood, and medical care were supplemented by books, paper, and a full-time servant. Although he was more comfortable than some other monks, Coton was surely not living in luxury: his independence from the Maurists meant that he made personal choices to live modestly and to work hard. Finally, Coton was responsible only to his conscience for observance of the Benedictine Rule.

As Coton got older, he continued to wear simple monastic robes and to attend religious services as his health permitted. But he bought fewer candles and books, and it is reasonable to suppose that he was reading less. Although he could have used the magnificent library of St. Germain des Prés, he had tended to buy books for himself, at Paris as well as at Cordoux. Most of the titles are not unexpected—the Bible, the Rule of St. Benedict, lives of the saints, and other works of religious devotion. Acting as spiritual leader of the seigneurie, he had bought catechisms by the dozen "to give to the children" of Cordoux.[47] But Coton also purchased books on Canada and China, a history of Paris, and pamphlets printed during the Fronde. Unlike his Maurist brothers, he did not seem to have great interest in the classics. His book buying revealed a more practical bent, as when he bought an arithemetic book for Brother Antoine and three medical books for himself.[48] Their counsel must have stood him in good stead, for in the next five years his medical bills were slight.

During his long term of service to the monastery, Claude Coton displayed remarkably good health. This may well have shaped his positive, improving attitudes toward farm management. In good times he needed only an occasional tooth pulled and a few drugs to improve his digestion. While managing Cordoux, he suffered only two serious illnesses. From September of 1644 to June of 1645, he struggled with a fever so serious that he had to be carried from Cordoux to the abbey. Enemas, bleedings, changes of diet, and medications cost him nearly 450 livres, more than one-quarter of his annual income. His life was spared on this occasion, and he enjoyed generally good health for the next nine years. Yet in 1654 he cited his age and poor health as reasons for giving up his post; he felt the need to prepare himself for death.[49] Coton's view of these compelling necessities may have been formed in the month immediately preceding his great transaction with the community, when he suffered his most serious illness in

47. Journal, B.N. MS. fr. 18822, fol. 16.
48. Ibid., fols. 20v, 11v.
49. ". . . désirant se retirer en ladite abbaye de St. Germain des Prés pour se mieux

years. It began on October 12, during a routine trip to Paris: "Arriving in the evening from Cordoux at the St. Maur bridge, I was seized by a powerful fever that did not go down at all; arriving at St. Germain the next day, I was put to bed, and the fever did not go away until Tuesday, the 27th. . . ."[50] Though this illness, treated by the painful medical procedures of the time, lasted only two weeks, Coton knew that this journey to the abbey should be his last: "I left Cordoux to come to live, if it please God, the rest of my days at St. Germain."[51]

The conjunction of illnesses and journeys is revealing. The trek between St. Germain des Prés and Cordoux normally took a day and a half, but in bad weather it could last as long as three days. Usually Coton made three round trips per year, traveling in winter as well as in summer. Though he might spend as much as two months of the year at the monastery, Coton seems to have preferred Cordoux. He made no special effort to be present at the abbey for Christmas or other great holidays, yet he sometimes stayed a bit longer than business demanded. Whether he traveled on horseback or on foot, Coton was always exposed to the dangers of the road—flooded paths, washed-out bridges, and highwaymen. It was no consolation that the robbers were often royal soldiers: money, hats, robes, and shoes were lost just the same. Even when the journey was not troubled by these annoyances, it still meant great effort, fatigue, and a costly overnight stop at Brie-Comte-Robert. One understands why few early modern people traveled unless they had to, and why the Maurist congregation was all the more remarkable for ordering its monks from one house to another.

Coton had a genuine fatherly interest in the welfare of his servants, young boys aged about fourteen who took this short-term work before entering careers. Dom Claude paid tutors to teach them how to read and write, and encouraged those who wished to learn a trade, join the army, or get married. To the energetic servant Coton could be warm and generous: when in 1639 Louis Margat enlisted in a cavalry company, his master gave him 10 livres as a going-away present after four and a half years of service. Another servant, Louis Nicolas Delicourt, decided to marry in 1651; Coton gave him shirts and cloth as wedding presents. Etienne Legendre, who worked only fourteen months for Coton before going into apprenticeship as a carpenter's helper, continued to receive alms from Coton for four

---

préparer à la mort. . . ." Contract, A.N., M.C., Etude CX, 97 (5 nov. 1654); Actes cap., B.N. MS. fr. 16855, fol. 180.

50. Journal, B.N. MS. fr. 18822, fol. 12.

51. "Voyages," in Journal, B.N. MS. fr. 18822, fol. 23.

years.[52] On the other hand, servants who were too young, too lazy, or too weak to work were quickly discharged; at times, it was difficult to keep good servants in the countryside.

Coton paid his serving boys 30 to 36 livres per year, plus clothing, room, and board. Shortly after he returned to the abbey in 1654, however, he felt that he needed an adult servant instead of a boy. As the secretary of the chapter noted, "His infirmities multiply from day to day."[53] Coton's new servant, Mahiet Valeran, was at least forty-two years old and had been tailor of the monastery. His salary was 50 livres per year, along with wine at dinner and supper. To fulfill this stipulation, his master bought a measuring cup and offered 1,000 livres capital to the Maurists for the wine.[54] In this planning, and in Coton's later payments of servant's wages in advance, do we detect intimations of mortality? Coton, fearing his own imminent death, wished to make certain that he had met all of his financial obligations.

The vision of impending death is reflected clearly in the journal. In December of 1654, just one month after the illness that forced his retirement, Coton granted Brother Antoine the rights to a small wood at Cordoux—two years in advance. Coton knew that the trees would not be cut until the end of 1656, "if I live that long, for if God calls me before then it will come to nothing."[55] Coton also changed his method of accounting: instead of separating expenses into categories, he kept only a running account of cash spent. This new casualness about finances was accompanied by a shift in his patterns of spending. Gifts appeared more often. To his former servant Louis Delicourt, now a married farmworker at Cordoux, he sent 63 livres; to an unidentified man from a good but ruined family, he gave 30 livres; to yet another, 10 gold pieces worth 11 livres each.[56] Coton gave freely to his fellow monks as well. He offered to pay for new choir stalls in the abbey church. The Maurist superior general praised this pious plan, by which Coton contributed more than 4,200 livres toward beautifying the abbey.[57] Dom Claude's liberality extended also to purchasing books for the abbey library, and to paying a copyist to help Dom Robert Quatre-

52. Journal, B.N. MS. fr. 18822, fols. 17v, 18v. Legendre received Coton's help from 1655 to 1659.

53. ". . . il a été contraint de prendre un homme. . . ." Actes cap., B.N. MS. fr. 16855, fol. 198.

54. Ibid., also in Journal, B.N., MS. fr. 18822, fol. 17.

55. Journal, B.N. MS. fr. 18822, fol. 24v.

56. Ibid., fols. 25, 37v, 43. He also gave another ancien 100 livres for medical expenses, fol. 30.

57. Séniorat, B.N. MS. fr. 18819, fols. 59, 61; Journal, B.N. MS. fr. 18822, fols. 25, 26v, 29v, 31, 32, 33v.

maires defend the privileges of St. Germain des Prés.[58] These gifts were
much larger than the ordinary alms of the monastic community as a whole,
but Coton felt that his end was near.

It is apparent that his health was declining. In September of 1655
Coton reported that he had been advised to eat meat, "because of my age
and necessity."[59] The regular monastic diet, hearty though it was, did not
give him enough strength in times of illness. One "fluxion" was caused, in
Coton's opinion, by the odor of grapes and new wine next to his lodgings,
where the work of the vintage took place. Fortunately, he was able to move
to another room.[60] Lesser digestive complaints continued nevertheless, and
by his next birthday, his sixty-eighth, Coton began to express longings for
a good death: "I pray that God will give me the grace to die well."[61]
Colds and coughs, fluxions and fevers: an agonizing series of illnesses
marked Coton's last three years. In February 1659 a sudden attack that left
him weak and sweating appeared as an unambiguous warning. On each
birthday, he wrote more fervent prayers for death in his journal; his
seventy-first, the last he would live to celebrate, was an occasion for particularly somber reflection.

> I pray God to show me the grace of death as a true Chris-
> tian. The last six months of my seventy-first year have been very
> painful to me because of the attacks of colic, gas, and stones that
> I have suffered. Let God be praised in everything.[62]

Did Coton fear death? Probably not, but with his years of religious experience, he was more anxious that his inevitable death be a good one,
fitting the patterns of the saints' lives and monastic necrologies that he
knew so well. All his life he had been preparing for death.

Events occurring around Coton were continually increasing his per-
ception of the pervasiveness of death. François Toutin, an old bourgeois
servant in the abbey to whom Coton had lent money, fell deathly ill and
asked Dom Claude to accept all of his possessions, to pray for his soul, and
to give alms to the poor. The abbey's notary Philippe Lemoine formally
recorded Toutin's will on April 1, 1659, the day of his death.[63] In the

---

58. Journal, B.N. MS. fr. 1882, fols. 37, 36v. The dispute was over the abbey's jurisdiction, discussed below in part 5.

59. Ibid., fol. 29v.

60. Séniorat, B.N. MS. fr. 18822, fol. 86.

61. Journal, B.N. MS. fr. 18822, fol. 34.

62. Ibid., f. 46.

63. Will, A.N., M.C., Etude CX, 137 (1 avril 1659). Coton saw that Toutin's few
possessions would barely cover his debts to the abbey; he therefore asked the Maurists to
help him carry out Toutin's last wishes. Inventory, A.N., M.C., Etude CX, 199 (2 avril

previous eighteen months, no one had died at St. Germain des Prés, and aside from a memorial service for Gaston de Foix, nephew of the commendatory abbot, the abbey had been free from funereal concerns for some time. The last death of a monk of the choir of St. Germain occurred in 1653, six years before. The mid-sixteen-fifties were certainly a sunnier period than the Fronde; when dark clouds of increasing deaths again appeared on the horizon in 1659, the psychological effect on the monks, particularly the older ones like Claude Coton, may have been much greater.[64]

Death perceived by Coton himself, enduring the daily pains of what he prayed might be his last illness, included the passing away of priests and monks, servants and famous persons who constituted the visible, experienced world of St. Germain des Prés. Only a month after François Toutin's death, Siméon Hay, a priest from Brittany, underwent surgery for the removal of two large stones. Although the operation was successful, the patient suffered fatal complications. Before he died, Hay was granted his last wish: to be clothed in the robes of a reformed monk.[65] In August, Dom Etienne de Pradines, a reformed monk of Parisian origin, died aged fifty-four; Coton described him in the journal as "très bon religieux."[66] In September and October, the surgeon's wife and a carter serving the abbey died there; in November, Coton noted the demises of Dom René Viot, another victim of surgery, and "le sieur Charron, très docte avocat et plus homme de bien."[67]

With all these deaths around him, Coton wisely planned for his own. The financial future of Brother Antoine was assured, the servant had been paid in advance, and his family seems to have had no need for his support. Yet he still had substantial sums to give away. His fellow unreformed monks like Dom Guillaume de Flandre had already benefited from help with medical expenses and outright gifts, but Coton wanted to make more lasting provisions for them. Flandre and Laurent Lestourcelle, whose pensions were "insufficient to live respectably [honnêtement]," each received liferents on the abbey.[68] These were the last great acts of charity, but be-

1659); Journal, B.N., MS. fr. 18822, fol. 44. Burial, Registre des Mortuaires, B.N., MS. fr. 18818, fol. 322.

64. The moratility figures for five-year periods show the low points at St. Germain and in the Congregation as a whole: 1649–53—1.2 and 20.2 deaths per year; 1654–58—0.0 and 14.6; 1659–63—1.0 and 35.0. (from Matricula and Nécrologe).

65. Vanel, Nécrologe; Journal, B.N., MS. fr. 18822, fol. 44v.

66. Journal, B.N. MS. fr. 18822, fol. 45v.

67. Registre des mortuaires, B.N. MS. fr. 18818, fol. 323; Journal, B.N. MS. fr. 18822, fol. 46.

68. Journal, B.N. MS. fr. 18822, fol. 47; contracts for 1,200 livres each at 10 percent, A.N., M.C., Etude CX, 199 (7 jan. 10 jan. 1660).

fore his death Coton had opportunities to pass out New Year's gifts to the servants and firewood to a poor family for the winter.

On February 2, 1660, the illness of the great conspirator Gaston d'Orléans proved fatal, and, as befitted the uncle of Louis XIV, he received an unemotional obituary in our monk's journal.[69] Three weeks later, Coton's last entry noted the hopeful celebration of the Peace of the Pyrenees with Spain. After the great masses in the abbey church and in Notre Dame, fireworks, fountains flowing with wine, and public festivities were not beyond Coton's admiration. In another hand is written what follows:

> Dom Claude Coton, who wrote this journal, died this year 1660 on March 16. May God reward him for his good works and give him eternal peace. Amen.[70]

We can only hope that Coton was given his wish of dying well. What he may have had in mind, following the "ritual organized by the dying person himself who presided over it and knew its protocol,"[71] can be seen in monastic necrologies and official histories. In 1623 when Dom Didier de la Cour died, "his face became so beautiful and so radiant that the monks as well as the seculars were inspired." More than fifty persons declared that they had seen a star shining over the church where his body was on display.[72] The last words of Brother Mathieu Bardoult, "Adieu, mes chers frères," were "so edifying that all of his colleagues were given the desire to have a similar death."[73] Dom Grégoire Tarisse, superior general of the congregation, set an excellent example: when he was found to have bladder stones in 1646, he chose painful, lingering death through deterioration instead of chancy surgery.[74] From the beginning of his journal, Coton had admired monks who lived and died well. Of one Maurist, he wrote, "It was easy to see that the spirit of God was with him"; of another, "he lived in a very praiseworthy manner in accord with his vows."[75]

For Coton a good death came as the conclusion of a good life, and he had personal models. Dom Athanase de Mongin, a reformed prior who died in 1633, exercised great influence on him. Mongin, who was born about the same time as Coton, urged him to change his life, but by his own regretful admission, Coton did not pay much heed to this advice. Years after Mongin's death, however, Coton repeatedly felt signs of his affection:

69. Journal, B.N. MS. fr. 18822, fol. 47.
70. Ibid., feb. 47.
71. Philippe Ariès, *Western Attitudes toward Death* (Baltimore, 1974), p. 11.
72. Dom Edmond Martène, *Histoire*, vol. 31, p. 169.
73. Ibid., vol. 31, p. 190.
74. Dom Bernard Audebert, *Mémoires*, vol. 11, pp. 52–53, 93.
75. Journal, B.N. MS. fr. 16853, fols. 41, 43v.

"While praying over his grave or thinking about him in our room, I felt myself instantly surrounded and perfumed by a very pleasant fragrance."[76] This sensation occurred "more than a hundred times," and particularly on October 17, 1656, while Coton was on his knees at Mongin's grave. He prayed for Mongin's help to obtain God's grace, in order to correct his faults, "above all to obtain a spark of true humility." At the mention of the word *humility*, Dom Claude sensed the pleasant fragrance again.

Coton's desire for a good death reminds us that he was first and foremost a professed monk. His involvement in seigneurial administration did not exempt him from the strict dictates of a monastic conscience. His prayers over the grave of Dom Athanase de Mongin, twenty-three years after Mongin's death, show voluntary devotion that went well beyond the obligatory presence at services. Coton was there, too; arising at 1:30 A.M. at the sound of the bell, participating in the divine offices—vespers, compline, matins, regular mass, and the rest of the hours, every day of the year. There were additional services on the feasts of the church, which he described in great detail, giving the nature of the celebration, the celebrants, and the names of notables from the outside world who attended. Coton and other monks gloried in ceremony. On St. Benedict's Day, March 21, 1656, for example, matins began at 1:30 A.M., with the superior general as celebrant. Meditation was held at 5:15 A.M., followed by prayer. There was tierce, procession, and display of the sacrament; then, at 8:15, bells sounded for the grand mass. After the mass, the office of sext was said. "If time had permitted, there would have been an interval between the said grand mass and vespers, but it being already late, sext, nones, and then vespers were said." At 3:30 P.M. the bishop of Montauban preached the sermon; afterwards came compline, the litany of the Virgin, and hymns for serving the eucharist. On the same day, mass was also said at the altar by Cardinal Antoine Barberini, nephew of the late Pope Urban VIII. The cardinal, the archbishop of Bourges, and three other bishops stayed for dinner.[77] Coton showed great deference to ecclesiastical dignitaries. When on Assumption Day, 1656, he found himself on the same side of the chancel with three bishops, he handled the situation tactfully: "I, Brother Claude Coton, who was next to them, left two empty stalls between the said lords and me, for respect."[78]

Coton officially belonged to a shrinking unreformed community. Most of their privileges had been given to the Maurists, but the unreformed monks still met once every three years to elect a prior and a dean. On

76. Journal, B.N. MS. fr. 18822, fol. 34v.
77. Ibid., fol. 31v.
78. Ibid., fol. 34.

these occasions two notaries and two Maurists were also present. After sprinkling blessed water but before the grand mass, the monks got down on their knees and said the *Veni Creator*. Voting was done by written Latin ballot, and following the count the notaries certified the election.[79] The death of an unreformed monk also required a meeting for the division of his property among the survivors. In these circumstances it is not surprising that the spiritual vitality of this group was weak. The more zealous members did not succeed in an effort to require attendance at all services where their prior officiated. "It was decided by general agreement that no one should be forced. . . ."[80] This casualness exemplifies a community on the decline: forbidden to accept novices, removed from control of the abbey, the unreformed group could only see their numbers diminish and their vitality decrease with time. They were like other communities whose spiritual growth was restricted—dying out slowly. A quarter of a century after the reform, eleven of the thirty-three anciens were still alive; the last survivor, Dom Jacques Douceur, lived on until 1695.[81]

Coton's journal has provided much information about his personal life—his expenses, illnesses, travels, and participation in religious services. There will probably still be unanswered questions about Coton's spirituality—his views on Jansenist theology and Cyranist discipline—and his possible literary activities. No evidence suggests that Coton ever strayed from orthodoxy, or that he produced any writings apart from his remarkable journal. He began by keeping financial accounts; then, as he retired to prepare for death, he wrote more about what he saw and how he felt. He was curious enough about the world to record victories of the king, birthdays and deaths of famous persons, bad weather and agricultural conditions: all of these were traditional subjects for monastic chronicles, and all of them might require religious services to thank God or to implore his mercy.

Coton observed and understood his surroundings from a position of religious commitment. His life was more varied, more active than that of a stereotyped monk silently praying in a cloister. He was certainly atypical in keeping a journal, but his other activities were not unique. At least two other anciens made gifts to the reformed community in exchange for free meals in the refectory.[82] Three others were made administrators of seigneuries for the abbey, and at least six proposed repeated loans of 2,000 livres or more to the community.[83] All of these men participated in general

79. Ibid., fol. 27. Election report, A.N., M.C., Etude CX, 200 (8 mai 1661).
80. Journal, B.N. MS. fr. 18822, fol. 28.
81. Choses mém., B.N. MS. fr. 18816, fol. 217.
82. Actes cap., B.N. MS. fr. 16852, fols. 146, 149 (1638).
83. Actes cap., B.N. MS. fr. 16854, fol. 68 (1642, Hotton of Bagneaux); MS. fr.

society rather than fleeing from it. If the monks of Durham could respond with resilience to a troubled economy, and if those of Canterbury could become wardens of estates and agents of the king,[84] then those of St. Germain des Prés acted in accord with monastic tradition when they responded to social disorders in their time. For us Claude Coton's special merit lies in his straightforward reporting. Through his journal we have penetrated the walls of the abbey and seen the life within. Beyond the rules and calendars, Coton has shown the monk's life itself.

16855, fol. 51 (1648, Bullet of Longuesse); MS. fr. 16855, fol. 190 (1655), and A.N., M.C., Etude CX, 199 (4 jan. 1659) (Lopinot at Cordoux). The loans appear in account books cited in part 2, Monastic Revenues.

84. R. B. Dobson, *Durham Priory, 1400–1450*, p. 253, R. A. L. Smith, *Canterbury Cathedral Priory*, pp. 99, 101.

PART 5

Spiritual Life and Politics

10

Closed Community

Spiritual life, so central to the monastery's purpose, we have left to this last part. Population and finances were the measurable aspects of St. Germain des Prés that provided the material foundations; but spiritual life itself is a quality rather than a quantity. Religious attitudes and observances have always depended on general societal conditions. In the sixteenth century, monastic laxity had coincided with social disorder during the Wars of Religion, when abbeys were forced to alienate their lands and suffer the depredations of greedy commendatory abbots. The seventeenth-century Maurists understood that spiritual restoration required a sound material base; therefore they bought back lost lands, improved their management, and defended their privileges. What were the effects on their spiritual life? That quality cannot be judged merely by counting services held and tracts written. Instead, we must compare the principled intentions of monastic rules and regulations with the practice at St. Germain des Prés. The sources may be criticized as diffuse and impressionistic: for example, a contemporary history of Paris:

> Since the Congregation of St. Maur was introduced into St. Germain des Prés, one can say without flattery and without ostentation that this abbey has prospered. . . . The principal application of the authors of the new reform has been to purify the sanctuary by a serious life, penitent and filled with pious exercises.[1]

Or, a guidebook to the city:

> One can say that there is no other religious house in Europe from which idleness is more singularly absent, and where the rule is more exactly observed.[2]

1. Michel Félibien and Guy-Alexis Lobineau, *Histoire de la ville de Paris*, vol. 2, liv. 27, p. 1,353.
2. Germain Brice, *Guide des étrangers à Paris* (Paris, 1698), cited by H. Leclercq,

But as the journal and papers of Dom Claude Coton gave us insight into the individual monk, so the minutes of the chapter and notes of outside observers can illuminate the reformed community, suggesting the changes the Maurists wrought, the troubles they faced, the battles won and lost.

Rules and regulations indicate the goals set for the monks. From the earliest days of Christian monasticism, monastic rules were proposed and observed, even prior to St. Benedict in the sixth century.[3] Benedict's rule was not the most austere, for his opposition to extremes of self-mortification and his compromises with human weakness led him to a reasonable regime. The Maurists in the seventeenth century proposed sensible interpretations of this rule in their own regulations, in commentaries, and in polemical pamphlets. While others have described ascetic qualities of the Maurist constitutions,[4] it will be useful to supplement them with regulations made at the general chapters of the congregation, and to consider life at St. Germain within the context of these statements. Our information on monastic practice is taken from chronicles and registers, minutes of the council and chapter meetings, and personal observations.

First of all, at St. Germain des Prés the traditional conflict between monastic scholarship and divine service was not a serious problem. Thierry Ruinart, companion and biographer of Jean Mabillon, noted compliments on the monks' scholarly work, and then modestly added, "We should pray to God that we may deserve this praise, and that we may work still more on virtue than on science."[5] Criticism of Maurist studies came more from outside the congregation, principally from the Abbé Armand-Jean de Rancé, founder of the Trappists. Rancé believed that monks were more suited to lives of manual labor and penitence than study, which he thought opposed to the monastic spirit. Mabillon himself eloquently responded to Rancé in the *Treatise on Monastic Studies*, "the classic statement of the Benedictine attitude to scholarship."[6] At St. Germain des Prés the Maurists' great glory was scholarship, and they would maintain Mabillon's standards into the eighteenth century through the distinguished work of the next generation of learned monks, Bernard de Montfaucon and his colleagues.

"St. Germain des Prés," *Dictionnaire d'archéologie chrétienne et de liturgie*, vol. 6, pp. 1,102–50.

3. Maurus Wolter, *The Principles of Monasticism*.

4. P. Salmon, "Aux origines de la Congrégation de St. Maur: ascèse monastique et exercices spirituels dans les constitutions de 1646," *Mémorial*, pp. 101–23.

5. Choses mém., B.N. MS. fr. 18817, fol. 6v.

6. A. J. Krailsheimer, *Armand-Jean de Rancé*, p. 52, where the dispute is discussed on pp. 46–54. See also H. Leclercq, *Dom Mabillon*, vol. 2, pp. 503–74. In 1693 Rancé and Mabillon did eventually meet and were reconciled.

There were, however, two distinguishable views of religious obligation beyond scholarship at St. Germain des Prés. The first was closed communal order; the second, public ceremonial service. As at other monasteries,
regular religious life meant enforced withdrawal from the world, but the
location and prestige of the Parisian abbey made complete withdrawal impossible. These monks had an obligation to serve their neighborhood, an
obligation as important as stability within the cloister walls. The tension
between these views found expression in religious practice at the abbey,
where the monks carefully balanced their private and public lives.

Closure had first priority. St. Benedict himself had withdrawn from
the world and wished to strengthen the spirit of community by removing
his monks from worldly temptations. In 1635, soon after their arrival at
St. Germain des Prés, the Maurist reformers ordered the construction of
solid outer walls. The garden was enclosed with houses facing outward,
their walls at least two feet thick and twelve feet above the normal level.
Contracts specified that these houses have no doorways or windows on the
side of the abbey. Other French religious reformers of this period also re-
established strict closure, either dramatically, as when Mère Angélique
Arnauld shut the door on her family at Port-Royal in 1608, or gradually
with the reconstruction of exterior walls at St. Antoine des Champs.[7]

Closure reaffirmed the vow of stability. As part of that vow, members
of the Maurist community were forbidden to leave the cloister without
permission from their superiors, and efforts were made to keep their minds
on spiritual things. Guests of the monastery stayed apart from the monks,
who were not to ask questions about life outside. The monks were not
allowed to visit prisons, courts, markets, or fairs. Monks who did go out of
the cloister on business were required to leave and return by the main door,
where they registered their names and destinations on a noteboard.[8] Later
the general chapter urged monasteries to limit themselves to only one door,
but it appears that St. Germain des Prés was too large to adopt this regulation.[9] How strictly, then, were these regulations enforced? In a houseful of
scholars, whose work required correspondence and consultation with
others, travel to archives and private libraries, negotiation with publishers
and booksellers, strict closure would have been difficult anywhere; it was
certainly impractical in the wealthiest monastery in Paris. Administering
estates, exercising temporal and spiritual jurisdiction, even buying food in

7. Contracts with Christophe Gamart, the builder, B.N. MS. fr. 16863, fols. 104v.–18
(1 juil. 1635–10 fév. 1636). On this subject in general, see J. B. Thiers, *Traité de la
clôture des religieuses* (Paris, 1681).

8. Salmon, "Aux origines de la Congrégation," pp. 103–04.

9. Règlements confirmés, 1657, A.N. L 814.

the markets required some monks to have contacts with the world. Entry and exist were, nonetheless, tightly controlled. Every night the porter, accompanied by a monk, made the rounds of the monastery to make sure that all doors were locked. Even when fire broke out in 1694 in the attic of a house built into the outer wall, the monks allowed only people they knew to enter the enclosure and help—priests and seminarians from St. Sulpice, and servants of the abbot.[10] Of course, the fear of burglary as much as the desire to maintain closure may have inspired this restriction; besides keeping the monks inside, the outer walls kept out poverty and crime.[11] A monk who wanted to leave on business as well as older clergy and seculars who wanted to retire inside the enclosure had to ask permission and respect the principle: the monastery is separate from the world.[12]

Problems with closure could arise when distinguished visitors came to the abbey. On January 22, 1647, Anne of Austria, queen mother and regent, arrived on St. Vincent's Day. While the monks were saying the office in the choir of the church, several curious women who had come with the queen penetrated the closed interior of the abbey. Subsequently these women walked through the cloisters, dormitories, and garden—all normally reserved for monks. The monks had great difficulty persuading them to leave, for the intruders believed that the presence of the Queen authorized an open house. Of course these were extraordinary circumstances, but the sacristan thought that closure should still have been maintained.[13]

The Maurist habit of transferring monks from one monastery to another also posed risks to closure. In the constitutions the superiors were urged to move monks as seldom as possible,[14] but young monks regularly took their novitiates and studies at different locations. Courses in philosophy and theology were taught at St. Germain des Prés; once the monks had been educated, they were often assigned to various houses. This meant a steady stream of young men to and from the Parisian abbey. Most of these transfers took place within the congregation, but the superior general could authorize other departures as well. Only rarely did the superiors discharge monks for reasons of health.[15] As a result, leaving the Maurists permanently often meant going to a less rigorous order, if not complete apostasy.

Apostasy was regarded with horror: to violate closure, to run away

10. Choses mém., B.N. MS. fr. 18816, fol. 199.
11. In 1663 thieves had stolen two silver lamps from the church. Chosés mém., B.N. MS. fr. 18816, fol. 99; Sacristie, B.N. MS. fr. 18818, fols. 202–06.
12. E.g., Actes cap., B.N. MS. fr. 16857, fols. 304, 320.
13. Sacristie, B.N. MS. fr. 18818, fols. 147–48.
14. Salmon, "Aux origines de la Congrégation," p. 106.
15. E.g., Matricula, no. 3404, François Tronchet, "Extra, cum licent. ob infirm."

from the cloister, was to disobey and break solemn vows. Any traveling monk was required to take a companion or servant with him;[16] if he was not carrying written permission from his superior, there was good reason to suspect that he was apostate. When a monk left the cloister illicitly, his superior informed the provincial visitor and the superior general of the congregation, who organized the search. If a delinquent monk was captured within five days and still wearing his habit, forgiveness for a "faute grave" was possible; but if he had discarded his habit or stayed away more than five days, the Maurist constitutions required arrest, trial, and punishment.[17]

The rate of apostasy was low among founders of the reform, but it rose among monks who joined later. Dom Bernard Audebert, assistant to the superior general at St. Germain des Prés in the 1650s, recalled in his memoirs "the deplorable end of several apostates." Odon Cahier died of "hydropsie" at the Charity Hospital in the Faubourg St. Germain; Philibert Oudin went to the pitiful order of Hospitaliers of St. Augustin, and was left with "neither order, nor convent, nor community"; and Philippe Dey was imprisoned at St. Martin des Champs.[18] One youthful friend of Audebert was sent to La Daurade in Toulouse for his "libertinage," but he escaped with money belonging to the monastery. Later the superiors learned that he had changed his name, moved to Bordeaux and married a widow, spent the money, and died of plague in 1653.[19] Naturally the orthodox monks saw divine justice in the consequences of apostasy: misery, torment, and madness befell those who left the cloister.

The Maurists were prepared to forgive their wayward brothers and take them back into the fold—if not seven times, at least the three times ordered by St. Benedict.[20] The superiors made no remarks about fugitives in the printed registers; instead, they recorded measures taken against them on separate sheets of paper, which could be burned after their death.[21] This decision not to hang dirty linen in public allowed them to uphold the reputation of the individual monk and the congregation, and made it more likely that sinners would repent. The way back to obedience had to be as attractive as possible, or the Maurists would see their fugitives die unrepentant. Yet the Maurists could not do without prisons, remote

16. Règs. conf., 1657, A.N. L 814, no. 23.

17. Salmon, "Aux origines de la Congrégation," p. 103.

18. Audebert, *Mémoires*, p. 304.

19. Ibid., p. 311.

20. *St. Benedict's Rule for Monasteries*, trans. Leonard J. Doyle (Collegeville, Minn., 1948), chap. 29.

21. Audebert, *Mémoires*, p. 312.

priories, and the dungeons of Mont St. Michel, the Gothic fortress off the coast of Normandy.[22]

Jean Mabillon, the great scholar of St. Germain des Prés, was personally affected by the problem of apostates when one of his younger colleagues, Denis de la Campagne, fled the cloister. Dom Denis had professed vows in 1685; by 1690 he had commenced a series of escapes that brought progressively worse misery and harder punishment. In letters to relatives of Dom Denis at Laon, Mabillon spoke with regret of "this wayward child" [cet enfant dévoyé]:

> I love him, but I love him in a Christian manner, and I feel much more grief for the miserable and pitiful state of his soul than for the extreme necessity to which he is reduced. I know that he is in Paris, that he often passes entire days without having anything to eat. I also know that people have lent him almost two *pistoles*, but that won't go very far, if it hasn't been dissipated already. Finally, I know that he is not yet touched to the point that he should be, for [us] to hope for his speedy return.[23]

Brother Denis did return about six weeks later, and the kindly Mabillon worked for lenient treatment of his offense. But in 1691 Denis fled again, and when he was recaptured, his superiors sent him to Mont St. Michel for fifteen years in the dungeons and five years of confinement to the monastery afterwards. Mabillon was distressed at the harshness of this sentence: "Fifteen years of prison will hardly serve to facilitate the means of his [return to God]; rather, it will harden him."[24]

During the next three years, Mabillon continued to press the superiors to moderate Brother Denis's punishment. In 1694, however, Denis seems to have escaped again; at this time Mabillon wrote his "Réflexions sur les prisons des ordres religieux," a tract pleading for more sympathetic treatment of monastic offenders in general. "Justice, good order, and example" demanded that misbehaving monks be punished, but Mabillon saw the aims of secular and religious justice as different. Not only should judges seek to maintain order and inspire respect in the wrongdoer, but

22. Dom Yves Chaussy, "Le Mont St. Michel dans la Congrégation de St. Maur," *Millénaire monastique du Mont St. Michel* (Paris, 1966–71), vol. 1, p. 242.

23. Letter of 23 juin 1690, B.N. MS. fr. 19649, fol. 167; published by E. de Broglie, *Mabillon et la société de St. Germain des Prés*, vol. 1, pp. 248–50; in H. Leclercq, *Dom Mabillon*, vol. 2, pp. 580–81. The reference to *cet enfant dévoyé* is in an earlier letter of 4 juin 1690, B.N. MS. fr. 19649, fol. 105; in Broglie, vol. 1, pp. 246–47; in Leclercq, vol. 2, p. 580.

24. Mabillon's letter to relatives of Dom Denis, 31 mai 1691, B.N. MS. fr. 19649, fol. 141; pub. by Leclercq, *Dom Mabillon*, vol. 2, p. 584.

also they should consider the health of his soul. Consequently, with monks, Christian charity to inspire penitence was preferable to severity—punishment by humiliation rather than by pain, for example. Extremely severe punishments could only drive the guilty monk to insanity, obduracy, or despair. Mabillon's enlightened views did not, of course, reflect the practice of Maurist superiors; indeed, the tract only appeared in print with his posthumous works in 1724.[25]

More dangerous than individual apostasy was organized dissent within the congregation. Divine justice would suffice for an apostate who disappeared, but those who remained cloistered while continually questioning the authority of superiors threatened discipline and closure. An organized group of dissidents litigating in the royal and papal courts could annoy the superiors for years. In the 1640s an important faction was led by Dom Faron de Challus, who had taken vows at St. Faron de Meaux in 1623. As an early member of the reformed movement, Challus himself was chosen for superior posts at the general chapters of 1630, 1636, and 1639. During the rapid expansion he undoubtedly held visions of his own advancement, but he came to disagree with the regulations and was removed from office. In particular, he was dissatisfied with the continuing rule of Dom Grégoire Tarisse, superior general from 1630 to 1648. Tarisse's predecessors had served single terms of three years or less; while his longer term did much to establish scholarhip at St. Germain des Prés, his tight control of the congregation probably provoked dissenters.[26] In 1642 Dom Faron de Challus appealed to Rome; in October of 1643, when he received a memorandum from his representative to the Curia, he had it printed and distributed as a papal brief against the congregation. But the forged brief was soon exposed. Challus was arrested at Notre Dame des Blancsmanteaux and imprisoned at St. Germain des Prés. There he was tried before the bishop of Saintes, and after confessing his crime and asking forgiveness, he was placed on probation in the house of his profession.[27] But this was not the end of the matter, for in 1645 Faron de Challus gained a powerful supporter in Ildephonse Le Velain, administrator of Le Bec in Normandy and procureur of the congregation. Together they attempted to profit from the separation of Maurists and Cluniacs, two groups that had been briefly joined in accord with the wish of Cardinal

25. Jean Mabillon, "Réflexions sur les prisons des ordres religieux," *Opera Posthuma* (Paris, 1724), vol. 3, pp. 321–29.

26. See the second volume of Dom Edmond Martène's *Histoire de la Congrégation de St. Maur*, where the disputes are chronicled at length. The point is also considered by Terence L. Dosh, "Growth of the Congregation."

27. Audebert, *Mémoires*, pp. 10–14. Registre de Dom Faron de Challus, Résolution sur un faux bref, etc., A.N., LL 993, fols. 103–35.

Richelieu.[28] Using the income of a priory and funds allegedly embezzled by Le Velain, the rebels met at the Collège de Cluny and attempted to take over the Blancsmanteaux. Their movement to expel the loyal Maurists from this house found support among the unreformed monks, who saw their own opportunity to regain control. Only the resistance of the unreformed prior prevented the coup from succeeding. Defeated at the Blancsmanteaux, Faron de Challus then tried to capture his former monastery of St. Faron de Meaux; there the Maurist prior had to seek the aid of the civil authorities to put the rebels out. They finally retired to St. Martin des Champs, where Challus continued his agitation by writing pamphlets. By 1646, the Maurists wanted to press criminal charges in Parlement rather than in Rome: they thought this was the "quickest and most assured" means of gaining a victory.[29] Faron de Challus had already let tempers cool by going to live with his relatives in the province of Maine, while Le Velain retreated to his priory in Dauphiné.[30]

The Abbey of St. Germain des Prés suffered from these disorders, too. Dom Anselme Le Michel, a scholar and son of an illustrious Norman family, supported the insurgents from the Parisian abbey by spreading "the venom of his ill will toward the congregation."[31] Despite the kindness of his superiors, Le Michel continued his disruptive activities. When the superiors resolved to send him away to St. Faron de Meaux, he began to cry out violently. Finally the other monks locked him in a cell and proceeded with an investigation. They searched his papers, questioned him, confronted him with witnesses, and tried him before five of his colleagues. His schemes were discovered: letters to Rome, plots with Faron de Challus, and libelous pamphlets distributed outside as well as inside the congregation. The superiors regarded violations of closure as most serious crimes: not only had Anselme Le Michel disobeyed, but also he had broadcast his discontent by writing to persons outside the cloister. On September 9, 1647, he was exiled to distant Landevennec in Brittany, where he served four years of actual imprisonment followed by two years of confinement to the monastery. Even his diet was restricted in order to teach him humility. Although he did escape once from captivity, Le Michel was recap-

---

28. Dom Paul Denis, *Richelieu et la réforme des monastères bénédictins.* Cf. Martène's opinion of the Cardinal: "S'il avait été aussi zèle pour l'avancement de la réforme que ses flatteurs voulaient le faire croire, il lui était très facile de l'affermir en se faisant élire un coadjuteur religieux; ou en se démettant du titre d'Abbé avant sa mort. . . ." *Histoire,* vol. 32, p. 245. Statements such as these may explain why Martène did not get permission to publish this history.

29. Audebert, *Mémoires,* pp. 22–32.

30. Ibid., p. 61.

31. Ibid., p. 76. *Matricula,* no. 97; Tassin, *Histoire littéraire.*

tured and served his full sentence, following which he retired to a Cluniac abbey in Dordogne.[32]

On December 1, 1647, the Maurists learned with joy that the Congregation of Regulars in Rome had pronounced judgment against Faron de Challus and his followers. The vindicated Superior General Tarisse, suffering from painful bladder stones, could now relinquish his office and die in peace.[33] Yet at the same time other religious orders were caught in general crisis: "It is unbelievable how many troubles and trials the devil has inspired among the majority of the religious orders in France," wrote Dom Bernard Audebert.[34] Besides the Maurists, the Capuchins of Touraine and Burgundy, the third order of St. Francis, the Bernardins, the Premonstratensians, and the Jesuits were torn by struggles that fit the general pattern of insurrections against superiors. They occurred during the Fronde, while the government of young Louis XIV was in disarray. Princely armies roamed the countryside, and rebellions seized towns, provinces, and even Paris. High churchmen, Cardinals Mazarin and Retz, intrigued for political power; as in the sixteenth century, when aristocratic factions were openly at war, the climate favored disturbances in the Church as well.[35]

Religious order was inextricably bound to social order. The Congregation of St. Maur, established under royal protection, saw itself driven out of some monasteries and badly treated at others. From their headquarters at St. Germain, Dom Audebert and other superiors well perceived the connection between political and religious disturbances, particularly when the same persons or their relatives actively supported both. An unsuccessful attempt to found a new monastic congregation for literal observance of the Benedictine rule had been sponsored by the abbess of Remiremont in 1631. In 1651 the same project, with obvious prejudice toward the Maurists, was brought back to life by Marguerite de Lorraine, niece of the previous sponsor. One small priory of three monks and two lay brothers already favored the literal life; the Maurists feared that their members might become infected with mistaken enthusiasm and join the competing organization.[36] On a higher political plane, Marguerite de Lorraine represented the forces of disorder as wife of Gaston d'Orléans, the conspiratorial uncle of Louis

32. Audebert, *Mémoires*, p. 77.

33. Judgment, ibid., p. 80; Tarisse is mentioned on p. 93.

34. Ibid., p. 176.

35. A. Lloyd Moote, *The Revolt of the Judges* (Princeton, 1972); J. H. M. Salmon, *Cardinal de Retz, Anatomy of a Conspirator* (New York, 1972); E. H. Kossman, *La Fronde* (Leiden, 1954). Some historians have argued for a "religious Fronde" after 1652: Richard M. Golden, "The Godly Rebellion: Parisian *Curés* and the Religious *Fronde*, 1652–1662," Ph.D. diss., Johns Hopkins University, 1974.

36. Audebert, *Mémoires*, p. 198.

XIV. While his wife proposed a new Benedictine observance, Gaston again tried his hand at revolt. Neither succeeded, but it is significant that both were perceived as threats to the established order.

Other powerful enemies were also plotting against the congregation. The nobility in general sought places or at least pensions in the monasteries for their children, while bishops wanted to extend their jurisdiction to exempt abbeys in their dioceses.[37] Contacts between these rapacious outside enemies and the unruly dissenters inside the cloisters could seriously undermine good monastic order. Of course the monks had some allies among the great: the pious regent Anne of Austria; Mazarin, whose interest had been bought with commendatory abbeys; Mathieu Molé, Keeper of the Seals; and even the chameleon Retz, whose personal interest in support from St. Germain des Prés outweighed Parisian episcopal interest in reducing the abbey's privileges. While these protectors lived, the Maurists' position remained strong.

The abbey had to remain closed to the world outside, yet it could not ignore the society to which it belonged, and its members were susceptible to worldly social disorder. Particular grievances quickly became general, as in the case of Dom Philibert Oudin. A monk of Notre Dame des Blancs-manteaux at the time of the reform in 1618, he joined the Maurists and devoted his time to historical writing. When the superiors refused to support his activities, he fled to St. Fiacre in Meaux, where he became infected with the ideas of Faron de Challus. Oudin was then transferred to St. Germain des Prés. He wrote more histories and requested permission to publish them, but "it was judged inappropriate to grant it to him."[38] Enraged at the refusal, Oudin communicated with Challus; one day in Lent he left the monastery at noon, taking his frock, his manuscripts, and several books. Afterwards he offered to return if allowed to publish, but he threatened to print a manifesto of complaints if his terms were not met. The Maurists, who held the upper hand in Rome, did not bargain with him; following an unsuccessful appeal, Oudin had to join a poorer order.

Unauthorized publication was a recurring violation of closure. In a congregation devoted to scholarly production, controversial works reflected poorly on the group. Despite the superiors' efforts to keep the congregation free of the taint of partisan activity, monks did occasionally write and print embarrassing pamphlets, even long after the Fronde had ended and Louis XIV's government was firmly in control. Dom François de la Bretonnière wrote a satire against Charles-Maurice Le Tellier, archbishop of Reims, and entitled it "Le Cochon Mitré." For this offense the archbishop's

37. Ibid., pp. 195–96.
38. Ibid., p. 232.

brother, the royal minister Louvois, had the monk put in the Bastille and transported to Mont St. Michel in 1685.[39] In the 1690s Dom Denis de Sainte-Marthe, a scholar who later became the superior general of the congregation, printed anonymous letters "filled with salt and fire" attacking the Abbe de Rancé. He was removed from his superiorship and brought to St. Germain des Prés to serve as parish priest and librarian: there at least his superiors could watch him closely.[40]

It was inevitable that scholar-monks would know the world. Even if they observed closure at St. Germain, they were certain to experience the conflict of private and public goals, a conflict that touched the heart of ceremonial life—the office, or *Opus Dei*. "Let nothing be put before the work of God," wrote St. Benedict.[41] The Maurists thought the office so important that they refused to accept postulants who did not have an aptitude for the chant.[42] Monks were encouraged to join enthusiastically in the chant, to blend their voices so that each individual would be perfectly united with the group.[43] The office was a private monastic endeavor demanding faithful service: at the larger monasteries like St. Germain des Prés, following St. Benedict and the Psalmist, the rule was, "Seven times a day I praise you."[44] Matins, the first office, began at 2 A.M. on ordinary days, and even earlier on Sundays and holy days. The last office, compline, was held at 6 P.M. in winter, and at 7 P.M. in summer; forty-five minutes later the monks ended their long day.[45] It is understandable that monks found the office fatiguing: Jean Mabillon, while a young monk at Corbie, once sang so strongly that he suffered a hemorrhage of the temple.[46] At St. Germain des Prés the choirboys hired to sing responses to the mass tired easily, and one older monk marveled that he had been healthy enough to attend all three masses on Christmas Eve.[47]

From year to year the routine of set hours for services varied little. The community had obligations to donors as well: 27 high masses and over 2,600 low masses per year by the end of the century.[48] In addition,

39. Chaussy, "Le Mont St. Michel," p. 242.

40. Tassin, *Histoire littéraire*, p. 445.

41. *St. Benedict's Rule*, chap. 43.

42. Règlements confirmes, 1648, A.N., L 814.

43. Dom Dominique Catta, "Le Chant liturgique chez les Mauristes," *Mémorial*, p. 303, citing Dom Pierre Benoît de Jumilhac, *La Science et pratique du plain-chant* (Paris, 1673).

44. Psalm 119:164; *St. Benedict's Rule*, chap. 16; Wolter, *The Principles of Monasticism*, p. 112. Smaller communities had fewer obligations: see Catta, "La chant liturgique," on the constitutions of 1646, and the R.c. of 1657, A.N. L 814, no. 23.

45. Salmon, *Cardinal de Retz*, p. 108.

46. Catta, "Le Chant liturgique," p. 303, citing Martène, *La Vie des justes*.

47. Journal of Claude Coton, B.N. MS. fr. 18822, fol. 40.

48. Registre des fondations, B.N. MS. fr. 18816.

the monks were required to honor their deceased brothers: each day a combined mass for the dead was celebrated, and when news of deaths arrived
at the monastery, each priest was supposed to say another mass. As part of
the agreement with the unreformed monks, they gave and received the
same remembrances after death, and to accomplish this purpose exactly,
necrologies were kept.[49] Not all of the masses were memorial services: two
daily masses, for example, were for the conversion of sinners, while one
mass per week sought new recruits for the Benedictine order. In case of
necessity, some of these obligations could be combined, but the register
suggests that this was seldom done.[50]

At least forty major holy days were celebrated at St. Germain des
Prés each year. Alongside the general festivals of the church stood local
celebrations, occasions of most intense observance. On the festivals of
patrons of the abbey, St. Vincent and St. Germain, the unreformed prior
celebrated the high mass. The services in honor of St. Germain began on
the eve of May 28, at vespers, when the monks moved his reliquary from
the sacristy to a wooden table placed between the great altar and the screen
of the nave. While the community sat in their choir stalls, the celebrant,
four chanters and a candle-bearer conducted the ritual for displaying the
relics. The next day, prior to the mass, the monks held a procession within
the enclosure. The curé and seminary of St. Sulpice, numbering forty or
more priests and seminarians, attended on command as spiritual dependents
of the abbey. After the procession, the monks passed through two lines of
visitors. At vespers one of the reformed monks preached to the assembled
people, and at the end of compline the relics were again covered and returned to their resting place. St. Vincent's Day was celebrated in similar
fashion, with a procession of unreformed monks and seminarians, and a
sermon by a Maurist.[51]

For the more important festivals, the reformed prior generally officiated in place of the celebrant of the day. On the holidays of St. Benedict
and St. Maur, however, the superior general of the congregation took
charge. Who attended all these services? Although St. Germain was not a
parish church for people living outside the enclosure, the monks did encourage everyone in the neighborhood to attend. Monastic processions invited public participation, and sent the message to a wider audience. Here

49. Rules for saying masses: R.c., 1651, 1654, A.N. L 814, no. 12. Necrologies, R.c.,
1648, A.N. L 814, no. 12. See also Vanel, Nécrologe; Bouillart, Histoire; and the volumes from St. Denis, B.N. MS. fr. 8599–8600.

50. Registre des fondations, B.N. MS. fr. 18816, fol. 230; R.c., 1657, A.N. L. 814,
no. 23.

51. A composite account taken from four records of St. Germain's Day (1655–
58) in Claude Coton's Journal, B.N. MS. fr. 18816, fols. 27v–28, 33, 37v, 41v–42.

the closed communal style of the office was supplemented with open public masses and processions to celebrate festivals. These complementary and sometimes conflicting styles of religious life generated considerable controversy. To understand why the monastic community participated in these activities, we shall have to consider the role of the abbey in the Faubourg St. Germain.

11

Neighborhood Leadership

At the time of its foundation, St. Germain des Prés ("St. Germain of the Fields") was still a rural place outside Paris. During the Middle Ages, however, an urban settlement or bourg grew around it.[1] By the mid-seventeenth century the expanding central city had absorbed this area, which acquired the names faubourg and quartier as progressive assimilation reduced its privileges to those of other neighborhoods. The population in 1675 has been estimated at 20,000: hundreds of new houses and 13 additional streets had been built since the tax census of 1637, which listed 1,331 houses on 57 streets.[2] Not only was the population of the faubourg increasing, but it was also becoming wealthier, as rich Parisians migrated westward and built opulent residences. Already in the late seventeenth century the Faubourg St. Germain had become one of the most aristocratic neighborhoods in Paris.[3] But here too was the annual Fair of St. Germain, a carnival of raucous amusements and trades that attracted both rich and poor.

Over all the aristocratic finery and lower-class squalor presided the Abbey of St. Germain des Prés. For centuries the abbot had exercised temporal and spiritual jurisdiction, which comprised powers to fix religious observances, to ordain priests and install bishops, to grant marriage licenses, to punish offenders, and to absolve sinners—in short, to regulate all religious matters as would a bishop in his diocese. Ordinarily the faubourg would have fallen under the authority of the bishops of Paris, but popes from the twelfth century onward had specifically granted exemption to the abbey. In this privileged enclave the bishops had no power, and the abbots

1. Françoise Lehoux, *Le Bourg St. Germain des Prés.*
2. Dominique Moyen, "Structures sociales du quartier St. Germain des Prés, 1675–1680," Mémoire de maîtrise, Université de Paris-Sorbonne, 1970, p. 1.
3. Claude Michaud, "Notariat et sociologie de la rente à Paris au XVIIe siècle," *Annales, E.S.C.* 32 (1977): 1154–87. Joseph N. di Corcia, "Parisian Society, 1740–1763," Ph.D. diss., Duke University, 1973.

were responsible only to Rome, a distant source of supervision. When commendatory abbots abandoned their role in administration, spiritual jurisdiction passed to the prior and the community. Acting in the abbot's name, they handled all the work of a diocesan chancery.

To the monks, therefore, belonged the control of religious life in their neighborhood. The abbey was the center of practice, the bureau to which priests and people looked for guidance. There was hardly a question of religious life that the monks did not touch, from the regulation of religious houses and banns of marriage to public festivals and literary censorship. Any exception to the rules of the church had to be approved by them: a marriage could take place in Lent, for example, only if the monks found "good and legitimate causes."[4] Persons who for reasons of illness or prestige wanted to hear mass in their own homes instead of parish churches had to ask the monks' permission first: foreign ambassadors, counsellors of state, even Queen Mother Marie de Medici respected their authority.[5] Permits to eat meat in Lent were given to old and infirm people; permits to preach and hear confessions went to visiting clergy.[6] The long lists of approbations, permits to officiate and to ordain, grants of absolution and the authority to absolve special cases, all testify to an energetic administration. Visits and ordinations of archbishops in the faubourg required the abbey's consent, and written acknowledgment of its authority from the high-ranking participants. Thus in 1649 Henry de Gondrin, archbishop of Sens, declared that he had consecrated Georges d'Aubusson de la Feuillade, archbishop of Embrun, in the Chapel of the Virgin at the abbey, with the approval of its officials.[7] If the abbey could consecrate priests and bishops, if it could convert heretics, indeed, if it could regulate all religious celebrations, then it fully deserved to be ranked with bishops. The crook and mitre on its coat of arms boldly emphasized this dignity, and in his formal appearances the abbot always bore them with pride.

The bishop of Paris could hardly look with comfort at St. Germain des Prés. Within the boundaries of his diocese, less than fifteen minutes' walk from his cathedral of Notre Dame, an independent authority held sway. Perhaps twenty thousand people thereby escaped his control. It was no small source of irritation to the bishop that his Parisian flock had a

4. In one case the couple had lived together for a long time and wanted to regularize their situation. Jurisdiction, A.N. LL 1135, fol. 123 (6 mars 1634).

5. Marie de Medici, A.N. LL 1135, fol. 42 (23 juin 1629); Marquis de Miranol, Spanish Ambassador, Ibid., fol. 94 (14 déc. 1631); Henri de Loménie, counsellor of state, ibid., fols. 107–08 (1633). About thirty other cases, ibid., fol. 291 (1628–59).

6. Meat eating, A.N. LL 1135, fol. 140 (1636); clerical licenses to Irish exiles, A.N. LL 1134, fol. 292 (1 juin 1658).

7. A.N. LL 1135, 239 (12 sept. 1649).

papally sanctioned example of religious independence right before their noses. Holidays and jubilees decreed in the diocese of Paris might well be celebrated on different days in the faubourg; when the bishop wanted to encourage fasting and closed butcher shops in the city, the abbey allowed its butchers to remain open. Worse still from the bishop's point of view was outright defiance of his orders. Even when commanded to attend, the clergy of the faubourg did not feel obliged to honor Parisian ceremonies; they preferred to hold their own. In vain did the bishop order his colleagues from the provinces not to confer holy orders in his diocese: the visiting prelates had only to obtain monastic permission—or, as often, monastic encouragement—to defy him.[8] Jealous of their privileges, the monks of St. Germain would not even permit the bishop of Paris to set foot on their territory, to say nothing of having him issue orders to their parish priests.

But in the seventeenth century Parisian episcopal authority was clearly ascendant. The kings of France, who had been quite content in medieval times with the see of Paris as a dependency of the archdiocese of Sens, now saw the grandeur of Paris requiring archepiscopal status in 1626.[9] The newly elevated archbishops set out to make themselves masters in their own house. In 1634 the archbishop proposed to visit the church of La Charité, a hospital in the faubourg. St. Germain was alerted, however; the unreformed prior, accompanied by officers of the abbot and a crowd of people, paid a visit to the archbishop, who declared under duress that he had no pretensions to jurisdiction over the church. Quite understandably, he was offended, and he complained to Louis XIII. The abbey chronicles note with relish that the king replied in a manner that shocked his courtiers: "My lord archbishop, I am sorry at the unpleasantness caused you by the monks of St. Germain des Prés, but the best and quickest way to deliver yourself from such annoyances in the future is never again to try anything prejudicial to their rights, nor in their jurisdiction."[10] The abbot of St. Germain des Prés, of course, was Henry of Verneuil, the king's half-brother. When the archbishop again wanted to visit the faubourg in 1641, he had to write to the abbey to ask permission, and to state his respect for their exempt jurisdiction.[11]

The battle lines had been drawn, in religion as in court politics. During the disorders of the Fronde, the struggle over jurisdiction was temporarily interrupted: Cardinal de Retz, the new archbishop of Paris, saw

8. The archbishop of Paris tried to prohibit the bishop of Belley from giving holy orders, but failed. A.N. LL 1134, fol. 148 (30 mai 1637).

9. *Gallia Christiana*, vol. 7; Jeanne Ferté, *La Vie religieuse*.

10. Choses mém., B.N. MS. fr. 18816, fol. 20v.

11. Ibid., fol. 21v. Henry of Verneuil's approval of the visit appears in A.N. LL 1134, fol. 203 (24 août 1641).

more advantage in a truce with the abbey than in renewed confrontations. But though Retz himself may have been friendly to the monks, his forced departure into exile did nothing to ameliorate the position of his vicars and successors vis-à-vis the abbey. Their discontent remained, and soon enough found a sympathetic audience. In national politics the tide of modern absolutism flowed over intermediate authorities to bring strong central government; there too the Fronde provided only a momentary relapse into judicial and aristocratic adventure and theatrical heroism. The weak minority of Louis XIV lasted only a few years, while his powerful majority from 1661 onwards exhausted decades. For a rebellious church Louis had the same remedy as for a rebellious aristocracy: the ecclesiastical form of absolutism ran exactly parallel to the reduction of provincial estates and magnates in the civil administration.

The chroniclers of the abbey proudly noted varying religious observances in city and faubourg as indubitable proof of the abbey's independence. They did not see the rise of a royal intention to overturn even the most ancient privileges in order to homogenize the state. Basing themselves on five centuries of accumulated precedent, the monks regarded every assertion of their power as another indication of its justice; meanwhile, diocesan officials could only look on in embarrassed impotence.

Ceremonies brought the competition between abbey and archbishop into the open. In troubled times people looked to their patron saints for help, and both parties had their heavenly champions. Ste. Geneviève, patroness of Paris, had repeatedly worked miracles to save the city. She could be invoked by municipal and diocesan officials only through elaborate formalities.[12] Appeals to St. Germain, on the other hand, were entirely within the jurisdiction of the abbey. In 1652, at the height of the aristocratic Fronde, young Louis XIV had to flee from Paris. Civil war had ruined the countryside, severely damaging the farms of the abbey, the cathedral, and the bourgeois; famine and plague loomed for the general population. Members of the city council saw the urgent necessity for divine aid, and therefore asked the clergy to organize a procession. On June 5, 1652, the archbishop announced that a procession of Ste. Geneviève would be held on June 11.[13] On June 7, the abbot of St. Germain des Prés scheduled his own procession of St. Germain in the faubourg for June 16.[14]

The competitive spirit became even fiercer as the days of procession

12. "La liste des miracles arrivés aux descentes de la châsse de Ste. Geneviève . . ." (Paris, 1652). See also M. Ultee, "Processions and Miracles of Ste. Geneviève, 1130–1725," paper read at the Society for French Historical Studies, Pittsburgh, March 1979.
13. Proclamation in A.N. LL 1134, fol. 352.
14. A.N. LL 1134, fol. 62.

approached. On June 10, the day before his procession, the archbishop prescribed fasting and abstinence from meat in Paris; but at St. Germain "even the butcher shops were open all day long."[15] Pamphlets containing French and Latin prayers for peace appeared for the edification of the public. On June 11, all the parish priests and regular clergy of Paris came to Notre Dame. Then, under the leadership of the archbishop, they crossed the Seine and walked up the Abbey of Ste. Geneviève, where the relics were kept. The archbishop expressly declared to the canons of Ste. Geneviève and their notaries that he merely requested their favor, and did not pretend to have any jurisdiction over them.[16] Once these formalities were completed, the actual procession with the reliquary of Ste. Geneviève could wend its way down to Notre Dame and back. Several hundred clergy, bourgeois porters of relics, judges of clerical and secular courts, the archbishop, the abbot of Ste. Geneviève, and the municipal authorities formed the "magnifique procession." A contemporary print takes pains to illustrate and identify them, and the poetic caption expresses suitable piety:

> Who would be able to prevent civil war
> From making a great desert of this great city,
> Ravaging its palaces with iron and fire?
> And who would save us from famine, and from plague
> If these holy priests by this heavenly shield
> Had not stopped the anger of God?[17]

Paris had sinned grievously, and its suffering was well earned. Anxious voices suggested that the procession might not be penance enough, that Ste. Geneviève might withhold her miraculous intervention. Antoine Godeau, writing as "un curé de la ville de Paris," observed that the patroness loved God more than she loved Paris, and that saints sometimes pray "against men, as much as for them."[18] Another pamphleteer agreed that the Parisians would have to mend their ways before they could expect a miracle, for Ste. Geneviève could not be content with a city that disobeyed its king. When the people of Paris led the kingdom of France to peace, God's bounty would soon return during the majority of Louis XIV.[19]

At the competing procession of St. Germain five days later, the monks

15. Choses mém., B.N. MS. fr. 18816, fol. 31.

16. "Ordre et cérémonie, qui se doit observer, tant en la descente de la châsse de Ste. Geneviève, . . . qu'en la procession d'icelle (Paris, 1652), p. 5.

17. See ill. 10, "La Magnifique Procession. . . ."

18. Antoine Godeau, "Advis aux Parisiens sur la descente de la châsse de Ste. Geneviève . . ." (Paris, 1652), pp. 19–20.

19. "Révélation de Ste. Geneviève à un religieux de son ordre, sur les miseres du tempts . . ." (Paris, 1652), pp. 5, 15–16.

also made every effort to achieve dignity and respect. Their pamphlets reported that processions of St. Germain had brought such good results as the defeat of the Norsemen; just as St. Germain ruled the hearts of kings in his lifetime, he could now certainly move Christians to a "general and particular peace."[20] Of course the monks had not attended the Parisian procession, and they certainly did not wish to have the archbishop of Paris present at their own; but in the absence of Henry of Verneuil, their abbot, they had to find another ecclesiastical dignitary. Their choice was the archbishop of Athens, the papal nuncio to France who represented their immediate superior in Rome. His presence underlined the abbey's independence of the diocese of Paris.

On June 13, preparations included gathering the relics of other saints that would also be carried in the procession; by the morning of the fifteenth they had all been moved to the choir of the abbey church, where they rested on tables covered with embroidered silk.[21] The nuncio spent the day before the procession with the monks, celebrating mass in the chapel, paying his respects to the relics, then eating in the refectory. After lunch the reliquary of St. Germain was moved to a specially prepared altar; then the nuncio, the monks, the Venetian ambassador, and other "persons of condition" revered and kissed it. By early evening the people of the faubourg wanted to satisfy their own desire to pay homage to the saint; they were allowed to visit until 10:00 P.M. The relics of St. Leu arrived from the abbey's seigneurie of Thiais, and all was ready for the next day.

At 6 A.M. on the sixteenth the monks had already been awake for hours when the first of the marchers received communion and dressed for the procession. These marchers included 80 bourgeois who would carry the relics, 40 members of the Brotherhood of Apostles and 120 small children. By 7 A.M. the children numbered over a thousand—Daughters of Providence in gray with white veils, girls carrying candles, and barefoot boys in white. The religious communities under abbey jurisdiction arrived in strength with their own relics. When the priests of St. Sulpice completed the gathering, the nuncio emerged from the sacristy, where he had been praying since six, and the procession began.

It must have been a colorful and inspiring sight: at the head, Daughters of Providence with flowers in their hair, children with candles, monks chanting hymns and prayers, dazzling reliquaries, the aged nuncio, and finally royal judges dressed in red robes. Four stopping places lay along the

20. "La descente et procession de la châsse de St. Germain, évêque et patron de Paris" (Paris, 1652), imp. in Choses mém., B.N. MS. fr. 18816, fol. 25v. This appears to be the source of the description in Bouillart, *Histoire*, pp. 246–48.
21. These details and others are taken from "La descente et procession. . . ."

route—the churches of la Charité, the Augustins, the Jesuit novitiate, and St. Sulpice. Each station was the site of more hymn singing and prayer in honor of the patrons. Soldiers and Swiss guards kept order among the multitudes packed in the streets. Not until three o'clock did the procession return to the abbey. After a mass and benediction for participants, the public streamed into the church. All day long the nuncio and the monks had honored St. Germain; once more, after vespers and compline, they kissed his relics before putting them away.

Prayers for the king, for peace, and for public necessity echoed through the faubourg with bell ringing, general tumult, and enthusiasm. "To serve as an authentic witness to posterity," printed accounts and engravings of the procession were distributed.[22] The engraving bears striking similarities to that of the procession of Ste. Geneviève: here too the artist has tried to include and identify every group of marchers, and the same printer has added verses that are enthusiastically royalist:

> We have suffered a disaster
> That has neither rules nor laws:
> Not being able to enjoy the beautiful star
> That gives the day to the French.
> But at the height of these tempests,
> The glory of our fleurs-de-lys
> Coming to shine over our heads
> Has dissipated all our worries
> Because the guardian saints of France
> And their Moses, St. Germain,
> Have given us back our hope,
> Louis, the love of humanity.[23]

Did the procession produce the desired effects? The monastic chroniclers saw more than coincidence in the procession and events that presaged better times. While the reliquary of St. Germain was being prepared for procession, the duke of Lorraine and his troops retreated from Paris. This news came to the nuncio during the procession itself. On the same day Parisians learned of the outbreak of war between Holland and England, those rebellious republics that had so long troubled France.[24] The monks and their supporters were convinced that their patron had worked a miracle.

22. Choses mém., B.N. MS. fr. 18816, fol. 31.

23. See ill. 11. The phrase "Moyse de la France" also appears in Henry of Verneuil's order for the procession, found in Mélanges, St. Germain des Prés, B.N. MS. fr. 16866, fol. 137.

24. Choses mém., B.N. MS. fr. 18816, fol. 31.

This contest between Paris and St. Germain des Prés ended with the abbey's independence and prestige intact.

Papal jubilees during the 1650s and 1660s occasioned further jurisdictional disputes. These jubilees promised indulgence to the faithful who visited and prayed at all of the designated stations in the city. When Pope Alexander VII sent news of a jubilee to Paris in 1656, the diocesan authorities wished to place several stations in the Faubourg St. Germain. Although the archdiocese offered to make a declaration respecting the rights of the abbey, the monks declined it and set their own jubilee. The year before they had held independent celebrations of Alexander's election to the papacy, and this time their friend the nuncio Nicolas, archbishop of Athens, had sent the abbot of St. Germain des Prés a separate letter announcing the jubilee.[25] Consequently, parish priests of the faubourg were ordered to ignore the Parisian festivities. In response, the Parisians allegedly sent two priests into the streets to tear down copies of the St. Germain ordinance. They also complained to Cardinal Mazarin and printed a protest pamphlet. In the faubourg the monks prohibited the sale of this offensive pamphlet and instructed their preachers to tell their flocks that the abbey's authority had been separate from Paris since time immemorial. This disputed jubilee was eventually celebrated in the Faubourg St. Germain fifteen days later than in Paris.[26]

In 1657 the struggle became more legalistic. Jean de Launoy, a theologian of the Sorbonne, published a Latin tract that cast doubt on the charters that exempted the abbey from the archbishop's jurisdiction. The Maurists chose Dom Robert Quatremaires to write a learned reply, which was published and placed in their strongbox with the most valuable charters and relics.[27] Although the monks considered Quatremaires' defense successful, he and de Launoy continued their pamphlet warfare for another decade. Still, there was no immediate change in the status quo. In 1661, on the occasion of a jubilee to obtain divine help against the Turks, St. Germain des Prés again scheduled its observance later than Paris. On the seventh day, just after the Parisian jubilee had ended, the great bells of the abbey were rung vigorously "to correct people who were saying that the jubilee had ended in our faubourg."[28]

25. Proclamation, A.N. LL 1134, fol. 487 (14 mai 1655); letter, ibid., fols. 258–59 (12 mars 1656).

26. Choses mém., B.N. MS. fr. 18816, fols. 63–64.

27. Sacristie, B.N. MS. fr. 18818, fol. 171; Bouillart, *Histoire*, p. 255. These first tracts were: Jean de Launoy, *Inquisitio in chartam immunitatis* . . . , (Paris, 1657), and Robert Quatremaires, *Privilegium S. Germain adversus J. Launoii* . . . (Paris, 1657).

28. Sacristie, B.N. MS. fr. 18818, fol. 191; Proclamation, A.N. LL 1134, fol. 43 (2 mars 1661).

As long as Cardinal de Retz was archbishop of Paris and in exile, diocesan authority remained weak. During the Fronde, Retz had offended both Cardinal Mazarin and the young Louis XIV. The canons of Notre Dame, acting as vicars for the exiled Retz, presided over his jurisdiction, but lacked the political influence of an interested magnate. Shortly after Retz resigned from the archbishopric in 1662, Louis XIV was able to appoint a powerful yet trustworthy figure, his former tutor Hardouin de Péréfixe. The king expected him to govern his diocese firmly, to restore the authority that had lain fallow since the Fronde. Where the absence of episcopal control had allowed dissenting opinion to arise, as at the Jansenist convent of Port-Royal, Péréfixe took direct action to bring back orthodoxy. The most serious and ultimately successful attacks on the exemption of St. Germain des Prés took place during Péréfixe's episcopate. His strong absolutist tendencies came to the surface in 1666, when he tried to suppress parochial holy days and standardize the diocesan calendar.[29] In this work he was encouraged by Jean-Baptist Colbert, the royal minister whose commercial schemes extended even to regulating traditional religious observances. To inspire people to work more, St. Germain des Prés was limited to one patron saint; with much regret the prior concluded that it was necessary to abolish the celebration of St. Vincent's day in order to preserve St. Germain's festival.[30]

When Péréfixe set about removing the irritating independent jurisdiction of St. Germain des Prés, he enjoyed royal support. Louis XIV was not as favorably inclined toward the monks' privileges as his father had been. But in supporting the authority of his archbishop of Paris, Louis XIV never showed insensitivity to the pride of the monks of his royal abbey. He ostentatiously honored them with his attention. In 1664, when Queen Marie Thérèse was ill, the monks obeyed a royal order to take part in a Parisian procession; afterwards they held two processions of St. Germain on their own. To show his gratitude when the queen was cured, the king and his brother Monsieur attended a service of thanksgiving at the abbey.[31] In later years he proposed the Comte de Vexin, one of his legitimized children, as successor to his legitimized uncle, Henry of Verneuil, commendatory abbot of St. Germain des Prés.[32] In the same manner that Louis reduced his unruly nobles to servile dependents at Versailles, passing over them for his admin-

29. J. M. Ultee, "The Suppression of *Fêtes* in France, 1666," *The Catholic Historical Review* 62 (1976): 181–99.

30. Sacristie, B.N. MS. fr. 18818, fol. 211.

31. Of course, the queen mother, pious Anne of Austria, had already been to the abbey several days before. Sacristie, B.N. MS. fr. 18818, fol. 208.

32. The child, Louis César de Bourbon, died at the age of ten in 1683; he was buried near Childebert at St. Germain des Prés. Reg. des Morts., B.N. MS. fr. 18818, fol. 349; Actes cap., B.N. MS. fr. 16857, fol. 178; Choses mém., MS. fr. 18816, fol. 136.

istrative appointments while scrupulously observing the formal points of politeness, so he reduced the independent authority of the abbey of St. Germain des Prés while his personal favor toward the monks continued undiminished. Their spiritual jurisdiction would go first, to the archbishop of Paris; later their temporal jurisdiction went to the Châtelet. The theoretical ground had been prepared by de Launoy's tracts; now the practical task of establishing control over spiritual jurisdiction fell to Hardouin de Péréfixe, who was nothing if not stubborn. Péréfixe doggedly went down the road to ecclesiastical absolutism.

The arrival of a special papal legate to France in 1664 provoked conflicting orders to the clergy of the faubourg, and resulted in the first erosion of monastic authority. On July 3 the legate was at Vincennes, awaiting the signal for a grand entry into Paris. Ten days later Henry of Verneuil and Prior Ignace Philibert went to ask the legate for help in protecting the privileges of the abbey. On the twenty-second, however, Archbishop Péréfixe ordered all the clergy of Paris, pointedly including those of the Faubourg St. Germain, to be at the cathedral at 6:00 A.M. two days later for the entry. But the day before the event, the abbot and prior of St. Germain tried to forbid their clergy from answering the archbishop's summons. Despite this order, all the faubourg clergy except the monks went to pay their respects to the legate. The attack on the abbey's privileges was clear. As the chronicler noted, the archbishop "wanted to oblige us or at least our clergy to attend. . . . God has appeased him somewhat in our favor; I pray that He may watch over the outcome and preserve our rights, which He has willed that we have for His greater glory." [33]

As long as Henry of Verneuil was abbot, Péréfixe's attacks on the St. Germain privileges faced a formidable obstacle. With the accession of Pope Clement IX in 1667, another jubilee and its accompanying dispute over jurisdiction in the Faubourg St. Germain seemed foreordained. Indeed, a papal brief announcing plenary indulgence and remission of sins was sent from Rome on July 18, and delivered in November to the archbishop of Paris and the prior of St. Germain des Prés by the nuncio. Péréfixe immediately adopted a rigid stance, contending that the brief was specially addressed to bishops: "We declare null and void all declarations and ordinances that may be made by others." [34] Since Henry of Verneuil was absent from Paris in his government of Languedoc, Dom Antoine Lespinasse, prior of the abbey, issued orders for the jubilee to the curé of St. Sulpice and others in his jurisdiction. On November 29, the archbishop threatened the curé with suspension if he obeyed the abbey, and three days later the

33. Sacristie, B.N. MS. fr. 18818, fols. 207–08.
34. Sacristie, B.N. MS. fr. 18818, fol. 215.

prior countered with a similiar threat if the curé obeyed the archbishop. In these confusing circumstances the parish priest appealed to Parlement for a declaratory judgment. Verneuil's influence with the court proved decisive, for when the members received a formal letter from him they chose to confirm the traditional privileges of the abbey. Péréfixe, however, continued the struggle by going to the king. He won a ruling of the Council of State that favored his position, although it also declared that he could not assert any new right of jurisdiction over the abbey. The monks were disappointed: "One cannot doubt that this order was given by surprise and on the basis of the false statement contained in the archbishop's declaration."[35] Yet most of the faubourg observed the jubilee according to the abbey's order, which the monks believed was the only valid one for the area.

More valuable than legal titles and briefs filed with the chancellor of France were the presence and support of Henry of Verneuil. While he was in Paris in 1665, the monks won a decision against Péréfixe; soon after, when Verneuil went to England on an embassy, the archbishop tried again to wrest away the privileges. If Verneuil had been present during the jubilee controversy of 1667, the outcome might have been different, as it appeared in Parlement. In April of 1668, the abbot was back from the estates of Languedoc, but his value to the abbey was waning. A dynastic ploy of his royal nephew threatened to neutralize his influence. Since 1623 Verneuil had been abbot of St. Germain des Prés; he had also been bishop of Metz and abbot of Fécamp. Though he never entered the priesthood, he lived in comfortable celibacy on his magnificent benefices. The abbacy of St. Germain alone was worth as much as the combined income of the monks, perhaps more under sound management. Unlike his half-brother Gaston d'Orléans, Henry of Verneuil stayed out of politics and kept to the church; but Louis XIV could not overlook his illustrious, if irregular, parentage. In 1668 the king ordered him to resign his ecclesiastical dignities and marry the widowed duchess of Sully, Charlotte Séguier, daughter of the chancellor. Possibly Louis intended to unite a high administrative family with the House of Bourbon in order to show that the legitimized children of France bore no social stigma, and to encourage administrators seeking to marry into the old nobility. Was this dynastic manipulation unreasonable? In the long run Louis failed, for the legitimized princes lost their privileges after his death.[36] But this marriage and others tying old and new nobility were contracted with royal blessing, and these couples were received at court. Absolute obedience, the sovereign's first requisite for increasing his author-

35. Sacristie, B.N. MS. fr. 18818, fol. 216. Copy of the arrêt of the Conseil d'état, A.N. LL 1134, fol. 133 (17 déc. 1667).
36. Franklin L. Ford, *Robe and Sword* (Cambridge, Mass., 1953), pp. 176–77.

ity, began with the royal relatives, and triumphed over Verneuil's religious commitments.

With Verneuil married, with Mazarin and Anne of Austria dead, and with Retz in exile, the abbey lacked protectors. "The archbishop believed that he could not encounter a more favorable occasion for renewing the litigation against us."[37] Between April and September of 1668, the monks of St. Germain were converted from intransigence toward the archbishop to acquiescence in his designs. At first both sides seemed determined to fight: the pamphleteers Launoy and Quatremaires had published additional tracts, written in French instead of Latin in order to seek a wider audience.[38] But in July the monks became conscious of their weakened position through a court decision that favored the archbishop over the abbey of Ste. Geneviève. This suit over jurisdiction had lasted two years; under the terms of the judgment, the abbot of Ste. Geneviève lost all trappings of independence: he was prohibited from wearing pontifical robes in processions, from giving benediction to the people, from promoting his canons in orders without the archbishop's consent, and from issuing any monitories except in cases referred by a secular judge.[39] If the canons of Ste. Geneviève, guardians of the most powerful relics in Paris, had lost their struggle with the archbishop, what chance did the monks of St. Germain have? St. Germain des Prés had stronger and better documents claims to quasi-episcopal jurisdiction, but the monks must have seen that by resisting the archbishop in the legal system they stood to lose more than in negotiations. During August they proposed conditions for surrender: they tried to keep the right of presentation to parish churches, but on this point and others they had to yield.[40] They had lost Verneuil, and they decided on a settlement to save themselves the costs of litigation. "It is more useful for the good of the monastery to listen to a just and reasonable accommodation."[41]

The final agreement was drawn on September 6, and approved by canonists, civil lawyers, and prelates before the formal signing in the abbot's palace on September 20. St. Germain des Prés retained the forms of jurisdiction while it gave the archbishop most of the substance. Within the abbey walls, monastic jurisdiction was essentially unchanged, but in the Faubourg St. Germain the monks became "vicars-general of the archbishop." Normally, the archbishop would exercise all spiritual authority in

37. Sacristie, B.N. MS. fr. 18818, fol. 219.

38. Jean de Launoy, *Examen de certains privilèges et autre pièces* . . . (Paris, 1665); Robert Quatremaires, *Défense des droits de l'Abbaye Royale de St. Germain des Prés* (Paris, 1668).

39. Félibien and Lobineau, *Histoire*, vol. 2, p. 1,496, preuves, vol. 2, p. 213.

40. Actes cap., B.N. MS. fr. 16856, fols. 290, 292.

41. Sacristie, B.N. MS. fr. 18818, fol. 220.

the faubourg. The abbey could still nominate the curé of St. Sulpice, but not those of other parishes. Only when the see of Paris was vacant were the monks restored to their former authority over the faubourg.[42] The following summer Hardouin de Péréfixe led a procession from Notre Dame de Paris to take formal possession of St. Sulpice. The curé, now released from his obedience to St. Germain des Prés, spoke with joy of his reunion with his true lord, from whom he had been separated for centuries.[43]

The ecclesiastical absolutism of Archbishop Péréfixe triumphed at Ste. Geneviève and St. Germain des Prés in 1668, but he did not live long to enjoy it. At the end of 1670, Hardouin de Péréfixe died.[44] An attempt by the interim administrators of the diocese to assert control over the faubourg, clearly contrary to the agreement, was squelched by Louis XIV.[45] At least the king maintained appearances of legality while continuing his campaign to reduce the independence of the church. His next nominee for the archbishopric of Paris, François Harlay de Champvallon, has been described by one historian as "a scheming and corrupt prelate, a true toady of power."[46] Throughout France bishoprics and abbacies passed to relatives of the king's ministers—the *cochon mitré* Le Tellier at Reims, Colbert at Rouen, Phélypeaux at Bourges. The docility of the Assemblies of Clergy under Louis XIV is understandable.[47]

What was the effect of advancing ecclesiastical absolutism on the abbey and Faubourg St. Germain? Before 1668, hierarchical relations between the abbey and the parish churches meant that orders came from the abbey, and observance was expected in the parishes. After 1668, parishes outside the walls of the abbey saw their observances conform to those of the archdiocese of Paris. The abbey church itself was reduced to a parish, grander perhaps than others, but a source of direction for them only during vacancies in the see of Paris. The monks still controlled special services at the abbey, whose relics and processions were far superior to those of other churches.

Without the reponsibility for spiritual jurisdiction, the monks could have turned inward, reducing their public observances to concentrate on prayer and scholarship. But even in scholarship the monks of St. Germain did not neglect the interested public. They met and corresponded with

42. Ibid., ff. 220–22; confirmations, fols. 223–25. Summary in Félibien and Lobineau, *Histoire*, vol. 2, p. 1,496; preuves, vol. 2, p. 214; Bouillart, *Histoire*, p. 262.

43. Sacristie, B.N. MS. fr. 18818, fol. 225 (7 juillet 1669).

44. Funeral orations in B.N., Coll. Clairambault, 1056, fols. 318, 354. Etienne de Martignac, *Eloges historiques des évêques et archévêques de Paris* (Paris, 1698).

45. Sacristie, B.N. MS. fr. 18818, fol. 225.

46. Hubert Méthivier, *La Siècle de Louis XIV*, 5th ed., (Paris, 1968), p. 84.

47. Pierre Blet, *Le Clergé de France et la monarchie* (Rome, 1959); as well as his later work, *Les Assemblées du clergé et Louis XIV de 1670 à 1693* (Rome, 1972).

scholars outside the cloister, and displayed a practical, outward-looking approach. From their initial compilations of saints' lives and works of the church fathers, they progressed to writing about the techniques of scholarly research. Their scholarship was not necessarily disinterested. Maurist monks wrote histories of cities and provinces with the help of official subsidies. Histories of monasteries themselves could be used to defend privileges. Monks combined their search for historical precedents with campaigns to increase the luster of the community, and to win royal patronage.[48]

Nevertheless, monastic contacts with the world were not limited to scholarship. The people of the Faubourg St. Germain formed the participating audience for special manifestations of spiritual life. The faithful souls who sought remission of sins during the jubilees had given ultimate meaning to the jurisdictional struggle. For their edification, special services and processions were held, and in their attendance lay the measure of spiritual vitality. The presence of the people at the abbey was a sign of God's favor. The monks had valued spiritual jurisdiction highly because it could be used to lead the people to the right observances. When that jurisdiction was taken away, voluntary attendance proved the continuing worth of public ceremonies. St. Germain des Prés fulfilled popular expectation by celebrating religious and stately occasions. It was as much in the interest of the abbey as for the benefit of the people that the contact between cloister and faubourg be maintained.

Consequently, defeat in the struggle with Péréfixe, while important in the general context of ecclesiastical absolutism, did not have a negative effect on spiritual life at St. Germain des Prés. Contact with the public through special services remained an essential monastic duty. The monks' participation in the faubourg after 1668 as well as before argues against those who would see the monastery (even in Paris) as "an escape from urban life," and the monks as "profoundly un-urban and uninterested in the traditional preoccupations of townsmen."[49] In fact the monks of St. Germain took an active part as upholders of urban traditions and privileges. One monk in 1616 might well have favored retreat: "My brothers, let us make ourselves of the elect by becoming alienated from the actions of the age, from the acts of parade, from vain and worldly works."[50] But these were the thoughts of Dom Laurent Bénard, an early Maurist theologian.

48. Note part 1. For reports on the Sunday night gatherings at the abbey, see E. de Broglie, *Mabillon et la société de l'Abbaye de St. Germain des Prés au XVIIᵉ siècle*, p. 53. On subsidies for research, see Madeleine Laurain, "Les Travaux d'érudition des Mauristes," *Mémorial*, pp. 231–71; Henri-Jean Martin, "Les Bénédictins, leurs libraires et le pouvoir," *Mémorial*, pp. 273–87.

49. Orest Ranum, *Paris in the Age of Absolutism*, p. 128.

50. Laurent Bénard, *Paraeneses Chrestiennes* (Paris, 1616), no. 27, p. 866.

While St. Germain des Prés had been careful to strengthen its enclosing walls in the 1630s, by the 1670s the community was encouraging the public to pass through the courtyard to the Rue St. Benoît, "to attract more people to our church and to facilitate the retail sale of wine in this monastery." But these worldly motives caused considerable inconvenience and commotion, and provoked the chronicler's lament: "Our [predecessors] did what they could to remove themselves from the world . . . and we do what we can to attract it toward us, as if our well-being and perfection depended on the presence of worldly people. . . ."[51] Perhaps this worldliness indicates the reduced spiritual vigor of an aging reform movement, becoming ossified into mere formal observance; we have noted demographic evidence for this view. Yet in a period renowned for scholarship at St. Germain des Prés and politeness at Versailles, the conservative, historicizing tendencies of both may have led the monks to observe ceremonial traditions more carefully.

In 1683, the governing council of St. Germain des Prés had an opportunity to express this attitude.

> God having called to himself the queen [Marie-Thérèse], it was necessary to decide whether a memorial service would be held for her, and it was concluded that one would be held, seeing as the same was done for their majesties Louis XIII and Queen Anne of Austria.[52]

Their desire to hold a service is noteworthy because civil duty and secular tradition appear to overrule monastic modesty and closure. Of course the monks had to honor their sovereigns and protectors: even if Marie-Thérèse had not shown as great an interest in St. Germain des Prés as had pious Anne, the abbey's place in society and precedents demanded a respectful commemoration of her death.

> Our reverend fathers, not believing that the private prayers they had said for the comfort of the queen's soul had absolved them from what they owed to her memory, judged that it was their duty to distinguish themselves in funereal pomp in proportion, as much as possible, to the merit of this great princess.[53]

---

51. ". . . who cannot but alter our regularity and inspire us with the sentiments of the age; we should close the doors of our monasteries and churches to [these people] as carefully as one would keep *dogs* out of an important place." Choses mém., B.N. MS. fr. 18816, fol. 133v (1678).

52. Séniorat, B.N. MS. fr. 18819, fol. 130v, 9 août 1683.

53. Sacristie, B.N. MS. fr. 18818, fol. 243.

What did duty require? For this service the monks had a monument built in the church, just in front of the iron grille of the nave. Around it were sixteen designs with Latin mottoes expressing the imagery of light and glory, themes that were continued in the statuary. At the top, the figure of the queen stood upright among gold-decorated children and a tutelary angel, "who pointed out to her the glory to which she aspired."[54] On a huge dais with four columns, amid smoking censers, sat a mournful figure of "Desolate Europe." All the sculpture was the work of Benoît, who had cast the queen's face while she was still alive. The entire church was draped with black and white fleur-de-lys bunting. On September 15, 1683, the abbey bells were sounded, and at 10 A.M. the next day the papal nuncio, bishops, and other invited persons of quality took their seats for the service. Dom Benoît Brachet, superior general of the congregation, celebrated the mass, and Dom Antoine Le Gallois gave the funeral oration. Le Gallois was hagiographic in the extreme, noting the late queen's attendance at mass two or three times daily, her absolute obedience to Louis XIV, and her general goodness: she was "a ripe fruit for eternity . . . a vase of glory, filled with good works, virtues, and graces . . . a ship filled with precious merchandise, departed to arrive happily at the port of eternity."[55] Everything would have gone well if the lamps in the choir and on the monument had not started fires! The sermon was interrupted, but the monks soon restored order. The persons of quality later gave satisfactory reports to the people, who were not able to attend; for three days afterwards, however, the decorations remained on display, and during that time "more than one hundred thousand persons" came to see them. "Never did France show more mourning and sadness. . . ."[56]

This style of public ceremony was reserved for funerals of royalty and those close to royal power. The church draped with black cloth, the allegorical emblems and coats of arms, the made-to-order statuary and specially composed Latin elegies: these were the last trappings of the great men and women honored publicly by St. Germain des Prés. Only once every few years did the abbey enjoy the privilege of memorial services for persons like Anne of Austria (1666), Henry of Verneuil (1682), the Comte de Vexin (1683), and Marie-Thérèse (1683). For some—Pomponne de Bel-

54. See ill. 8; the quotation is from the Sacristy book, ibid.

55. Antoine Le Gallois, *Oraison funèbre de . . . Marie-Thérèse . . .* (Paris, 1683). ". . . without flattery he established the eulogy of that incomparable princess, on principles that are the purest and holiest rules of the Christian religion." Sacristie, B.N. MS. fr. 18818, fol. 246.

56. Choses mém., B.N. MS. fr. 18816, fol. 139–40; Sacristie, B.N. MS. fr. 18818, fols. 243–46.

lièvre, *premier président* of the Parlement of Paris, and Anne of Austria—
the affection they had shown to the monastery during their lives merited
glorious services after their deaths.[57]

Yet obligation and desire to win political favors also figured in plans
to hold celebrations. On October 30, 1685, as soon as Superior General
Brachet learned of the death of Michel Le Tellier, chancellor of France, he
ordered every priest of the congregation to say a mass, and all other monks
to recite the office for the dead. In *each* monastery a memorial service was
held. As the Maurist headquarters, St. Germain des Prés decorated its
church with ribbons and crosses of the Order of the Holy Spirit, one of the
dignities held by the deceased. Emblems were specially painted for the
occasion, and a Latin prose elegy was printed for distribution to the audience.[58] But attendance was disappointing: neither of Le Tellier's powerful
sons, the archbishop of Reims and the marquis de Louvois, was present. Of
the entire family only the young Abbé de Louvois came, and it seemed that
the clan did not appreciate the great expense incurred by the abbey. The
monks had vainly hoped to persuade Minister Louvois to pay the king's
debt to the abbey for land taken in the expansion of Versailles. Yet, instead
of gratefully supporting the Maurists, Louvois soon forced them to leave
the monastery of Coulombs and converted it into a hospital. As for the
grand ceremony, the chronicler thought that "one would have done better
to use for alms the great sums spent on this service."[59]

While the Le Tellier service may not have been politically successful,
the careful records of attendance at all these events show the monks' social
and political aspirations. At the service for Anne of Austria, two duch-
esses, four bishops, and one foreign ambassador were present; even more
magnates would have attended if the court had not been at St. Germain en
Laye and if other bishops were not occupied with the Assembly of the
Clergy.[60] The service for Verneuil, held long after his resignation from ecclesiastical benefices, nonetheless drew twenty-three bishops.[61] The general
public was made aware of these gatherings by notices, bell ringing, and
processions; if they did not qualify for invitations, they could come after
the services to view the church. By their pomp, these infrequent ceremonials
may have attracted the largest crowds to the abbey.

Te Deum Laudamus, the Latin hymn of thanksgiving, was sung at St.

57. Pomponne de Bellièvre, Choses mém., B.N. MS. fr. 18816, fols. 72v–73 (14 avril
1657). Anne of Austria, Sacristie, B.N. MS. fr. 18818, fols. 209–10, 27 fév. 1666.

58. Sacristie, B.N. MS. fr. 18818, fol. 253.

59. Choses mém., B.N. MS. fr. 18816, fol. 148.

60. At this service the Swiss guards at the doors mistakenly denied entry to some
personnes de condition. Sacristie, B.N. MS. fr. 18818, fol. 209.

61. Choses mém., B.N. MS. fr. 18816, fol. 135.

Germain des Prés to celebrate the victories of the French monarchy and Christianity in general. The capture of Flemish towns and the defeat of the Turks were high ceremonial moments. Likewise, the peace treaties of the Pyrenees, Rijswijk, and Utrecht merited *Te Deum*, processions, and fireworks. Cardinal Guillaume Egon von Fürstemberg, abbot of St. Germain and also prince-bishop of Strasbourg in the 1690s, received personal advantages from the treaty of Rijswijk in 1697. He therefore sponsored "grandes réjouissances" at the abbey: an obelisk, symbolic medallions, and fireworks exalted the grandeur and benevolence of Louis XIV.[62] Still, it would be too severe to suppose that the monks sang *Te Deum* only out of particular or even royal interest. Rather, they wished to offer thanks to God in a manner edifying to the people so that religious and political interests were congruent. While yielding precedence to the cathedral of Notre Dame, whose services were attended by Parlement, the monks insisted upon their own place as the second most important church in Paris, and surely the most important in their neighborhood. Two days before their services, the monks announced their plans. The bells rang according to custom, and officers of the independent jurisdiction came to the abbey. Afterwards, the entire Faubourg St. Germain could view the fireworks and decorations and buy commemorative engravings. Whether the triumphs took place on the battlefields of Flanders or Crete, in the royal bedrooms where princes were born, or in the French countryside favored with good weather and plentiful harvests, St. Germain des Prés was prepared to lead the thanksgiving.

These arrangements flowed from the special situation of St. Germain des Prés, increasingly surrounded by urban life in the seventeenth century. While the archbishopric took certain rights away from the abbey, the public demanded more services from their ceremonial leaders. The abbey's shrine of Ste. Marguerite, patroness of pregnant women, imposed important obligations. Women of Paris came to her chapel to pray and to receive the sacrament. Peddlers at the doorway sold pamphlets in "vers gothiques" telling of the life and martyrdom of the saint. To increase her popularity the monks themselves prepared pamphlets and illustrations with prayers for a devoted public.[63] The relics of Ste. Marguerite were specially revered by the French royal family. When Queen Marie-Thérèse was about to give birth, Louis XIV summoned the prior of St. Germain. In October of 1661 the royal call came to Dom Ignace Philibert. Before leaving for Fontainebleau he arranged the display of the sacrament and public prayers. Then,

---

62. For details of the celebration, see Choses mém., B.N. MS. fr. 18817, fol. 14, 17 nov. 1697; fol. 15, 7 jan. 1698, 26 jan. 1698. A print showing the display is in B.N. Estampes, cliché 76 C 78202.

63. See ill. 9. Sacristie, B.N. MS. fr. 18818, fol. 179.

taking the silver reliquaries with Ste. Marguerite's chin and belt in a wooden box, the prior and one monastic companion left by stagecoach. Upon their arrival at the country palace, they were welcomed by Queen Mother Anne of Austria and lodged with her almoner. For the next three weeks the monks waited at Fontainebleau, and during the delivery itself the queen wore the sacred belt. News of the safe arrival of the dauphin was immediately communicated to the abbey, where Abbot Henry of Verneuil (great-uncle of the newborn child) and the assistant prior resolved to hold a general procession and *Te Deum*. By their orders, all clergy of the faubourg had to attend, and all houses along the route of the procession were hung with decorations. On the day before the procession, the monks placed tapestries in the church, and rang the bells for a full hour. The procession itself was another gala affair, traveling from the abbey to the Rue des Saints-Pères, along the river to the Rue de Seine, then back to the abbey via the Rue de Buci. For the actual service the church was packed, and nothing like it was seen in Paris.[64]

Devotion and honor: these were the immediate reasons for special services that benefited not only the rich and powerful, but also ordinary people with everyday concerns. Childbirth and illness, for example, represented dangers to all. In times of widespread illness among children, such as during the famine winter of 1661–62, popular devotion to St. Felix increased at St. Germain des Prés. Because of the crowds, the monks had to move devotions to a larger chapel. People believed that St. Felix would be most helpful to their children if the parents went begging from door to door to collect money for a special mass. Prayers were said over the head of the afflicted child, and he was encouraged to eat a piece of bread that had been blessed during the service. Although the monastic chronicler regarded these activities as "choses superstitieuses," the prior ordered full commemoration of January 14, the day of St. Felix. A painting of St. Felix with St. Maxim in the desert was produced and hung; it cost the abbey 100 livres, money well spent.[65]

Instead of escaping from urban life, the monks served as neighborhood ceremonial leaders, and their activity continued long after their loss of jurisdiction in 1668. Archbishop Péréfixe found it necessary to order people to stop asking St. Germain des Prés for spiritual advice;[66] when he and his successors died, the abbey immediately filled the jurisdictional gap. The monks returned to their practice of issuing marriage licenses, allowing

64. Sacristie, B.N. MS. fr. 18818, fols. 195–98. See also the abbot's order for street-cleaning, A.N. LL 1134, fol. 488, 4 nov. 1661; procession, 6 nov. 1661.

65. Sacristie, B.N. MS. fr. 18818, fols. 198–99.

66. Orders, A.N. LL 1134, fol. 490, 15 juil. 1669.

private chapels, inspecting religious communities, and setting observances in general. After 1690, the archbishopric of Paris even assigned certain spiritual matters to the prior of St. Germain: perhaps this cooperation was inspired when the influential Cardinal von Fürstemberg became abbot.[67] In 1715, at the close of Louis XIV's century, religious attitudes still pervaded urban social life. St. Germain des Prés through its public observances was inextricably involved with the entire ancien régime. The printed prayers to St. Germain for the regent and the young Louis XV were imbued with the same piety and royalism as those for his predecessor more than half a century earlier.[68] The visitations and permissions of St. Germain des Prés were just as numerous, and the abbey continued its pastoral work in the traditional pattern, though with the approval of the archbishop of Paris.

Ceremonial leadership, perhaps of lessened importance in modern times, cannot be taken for granted in early modern France. The monks of St. Germain des Prés told common people in the faubourg how to celebrate, and explained to them what to do and say. A modern reader may find in the carefully printed devotional tableaux little more than conventional sentiment, in the submissive prayers and poetry little more than prudent political manipulation. Yet the sincerity of those who listened then was no less than the devotion of those who pray now. Despite their apparent contradictions, the abbey's ceremonial politics and closed community went hand in hand.

67. Septième livre de la juridiction, B.N. MS. fr. 16862, fol. 31v.
68. Compare the procession of 1652 (ill. 11) with the annual tableaux of 1716–19, where the explanations honor, "Louis cette divine plante." Mélanges S.G.P., B.N. MS. fr. 16866, fols. 170–76.

Monastery and Society

"The religious house is always in part a product of the society from which it is trying to escape."[1] St. Germain des Prés stamped its character on the society around it. The monks saw as much religious and historical significance in their participation as in their retreat. Demographic, economic, and political forces shaped their lives. A review of these forces and their effects will emphasize the abbey's strong ties to the social order.

A number of lessons can be learned from monastic demography. First, the rate of growth of the Congregation of St. Maur was very high in the early years, when the work of spreading the reform throughout France required more manpower. Growth had to be commensurate with spiritual needs and economic resources. Several times during the century, sudden increases in deaths showed a correlation with subsequent increases in professions. In response to general demographic trends of French society, the superiors of the congregation made a conscious effort to recruit more monks. By the 1670s, however, the congregation had reached maturity: official attitudes were less favorable, and new professions were taken only to replace monks who had died or departed.

More monks came from the large northern French dioceses than from other areas; after compensation for size, however, there is no clear geographic pattern of monastic productivity. Local agricultural conditions and the presence of monasteries undoubtedly influenced recruitment, but the Benedictines of St. Maur seldom stayed in their native dioceses. The congregation's structure implied geographic mobility. Novices received their training at special centers, young monks completed courses of study at other houses, mature scholars and aged monks gathered at still others. Individual biographies often cite retreat from the spiritual dangers of worldly careers

1. R. B. Dobson, *Durham Priory, 1400–1450*, p. 388.

as the reason for entering the religious life. Most monks had bourgeois families and were aged between seventeen and twenty-five when they took final vows. The superiors preferred postulants who were several years above the minimum age because they tended to live longer and contribute more to monastic community, but the proportion of older men taking vows fell as the reform progressed toward maturity. While the founders had achieved great spiritual vitality by rebuilding monastic spirit, younger men who joined the congregation later saw hardened attitudes and more formal observance.

Monks had a better chance of living into middle age than did the general population, but fewer of them survived into old age. While monks were carefully selected during their early years, the hardships of cloistered life must have taken their toll of even the healthiest individuals. As the rate of growth of the congregation fell, monks were more evenly distributed in age groups and had greater average length of religious experience. For the mature Maurist congregation, reduced recruitment and aging were accompanied by stronger emphasis on external forms rather than innovative interior spirituality.

Monastic revenues, like other landed incomes, were tied to agricultural conditions. The aggressive management of St. Germain de Prés enabled the abbey to become over half a million livres richer in land during the Maurist century. Yet the records do not conceal fluctuations and times of difficulty. When pressed, the monks could adjust their income through sales of agricultural products and borrowing. With its excellent security, St. Germain des Prés could borrow on very favorable terms. The supply of capital was adequate for monastic projects, including purchases of land and buildings. In addition, the monks were frequently able to refund their debts on better terms as general interest rates declined. The lenders, older persons seeking life annuities or officials and merchants with surplus capital, were glad to lend to the abbey. Even during the financial crisis of the 1690s, when St. Germain required help from other Benedictine houses, the abbey continued its refunding practices. To sum up, in their handling of revenues the monks showed an astute understanding of worldly affairs.

The distribution of expenditures expressed conscious choices, yet was at the same time limited by fixed expenses. Taxes, debt service, wages, and seigneurial obligations represented one-third of the budget. The lands and buildings of the abbey required continual maintenance. Food and clothing for the monks were restricted by religious rules, but the Maurists nonetheless ate well in comparison with contemporaries. Only about half of the

4,600 calories that the monks consumed daily came from cereal grains, and the generally constant level of food prices meant that St. Germain could expect to pay about the same for community expenses each year.

Religious purposes represented a smaller portion of the abbey's budget. Charity, which may have been a general Christian obligation in medieval times, was given primarily to those who were related to the monks, dependent upon the abbey's lands, or bound to similar religious ideals. If the alms were small, the spirit in which they were given was correct and Christian, extending so far that the monks even borrowed money for this purpose in the most difficult years. The final category of spiritual expenses illustrates the abbey's sense of mission best. Their magnificent church imposed an obligation on the monks; devotion and honor required them to hold commemorative services, more for the public than for themselves. By this means the monks served as ceremonial leaders of their neighborhood, supporting the traditions of the monarchy and the church.

Demography and economics are useful in studying the community and the congregation, but impersonal statistics should not obscure important individuals. Claude Coton, an active proponent of the reform, was a sincerely religious and financially shrewd monk of St. Germain des Prés. Coton's successful administration of estates was a model for others, and his pious retirement showed the significance of preparing for death. Illness and advancing age may have increased his commitment, but did not lead him to ignore the events of the outside world. This faithful steward of the monastery thus embodied the combination of religious and secular interests that marked the community as a whole.

To write of St. Germain des Prés is to write of religious practice both inside and outside the cloister. The principle of closure created some tension between the monks' duties to God and their desires to play roles in external society. When social disturbances struck France, they appeared in religious orders as well: rebellion and apostasy also form part of the Maurist history. At St. Germain des Prés the struggle to keep spiritual jurisdiction demonstrated the monks' sense of responsibility for the faubourg—and their will to control it. As part of the movement toward ecclesiastical absolutism, Archbishop Hardouin de Péréfixe enjoyed royal support and emerged victorious over lesser authorities, including St. Germain des Prés. The dynastic politics of Louis XIV was the key to the monks' defeat. Yet their loss of authority did not mean that the monks had given up their ceremonial leadership. On the contrary, after 1668 as well as before, St. Germain des Prés was the leading ceremonial church of its neighborhood. Retreat into isolation was out of the question.

All of this may lead the reader to agree that St. Germain des Prés was very much part of French society of its time. What we hope to have achieved is a social and economic history of St. Germain des Prés. The Maurist reform made possible the concentration of scholars, the close guidance of superiors, and the aggressive expansion of the abbey's holdings, as well as its later rescue from crisis. Various secular trends in population and economy required conscious response from the monks: higher death rates, fluctuations in food prices, and lower interest rates all called forth monastic action. Likewise, the will of Louis XIV had its effects also.

The Maurist century at St. Germain des Prés was a great age of monastic scholarship and material expansion. The social and economic history of this abbey participated in full measure in the century of Louis XIV and the glory of France.

Bibliography

1. MANUSCRIPT SOURCES

Archives Nationales (*A.N.*)

H5 3700. Rentes, emprunts, quittances (manse abbatiale).

H5 4275. Recettes, 1661–70 (manse conventuelle).

H5 4279. Recettes, 1671–80.

H5 4274. Mises, 1660–63.

H5 4276. Mises, 1679–84.

H5 4277. Mises, 1691–95.

H5 4278. Mises, 1696–99.

H5 4280. Mises, 1711–16.

H5 4282. Mises, 1717–22.

L 750. Congrégation de St. Maur, professions.

L 751. Miscellaneous Benedictine papers.

L 810. Congrégation de St. Maur, letters, bulls, briefs.

L 811. Congrégation de St. Maur, constitutions.

L 814. Congrégation de St. Maur, règlements.

L 815. Avis pour ceux qui travaillent aux histoires des monastères (1677).

LL 989. Regula cum declarationis.

LL 990. Pièces justificatives.

LL 991. Misc. treatises, including Catalogus librorum non nullorum (books approved for reading), ff. 190–200.

LL 992. Diètes annuelles, Assemblées.

LL 993. Letters, Faron de Challus affair.

LL 1126–30. Cartulaire de la manse conventuelle, 1630–67.

LL 1131. Inventory of titles relating to spiritual jurisdiction, copies of bulls and royal privileges, contracts for reform (made by Claude Coton in case of contestation).

LL 1132. List of religious communities in the Faubourg St. Germain, 1659.

LL 1133. Copies of bulls and titles (mainly medieval).

LL 1134. Inventory of titles relating to spiritual jurisdiction, 1724—a very complete list referring to A.N. L 752–809, K 964–72; and B.N. MS. fr. 16862.

LL 1135. Spiritual jurisdiction, 1623–37.

LL 1136. ———   , 1637–41.

LL 1137. ———   , 1640–52.

LL 1140. ———   , 1652–59.

LL 1141. ———   , 1659–69.

> All of these volumes contain permits for ordinations, marriages, professions of religious communities, private chapels, baptism of heretics, etc.

LL 1139. "Direction de la juridiction."

LL 1141, LL 1142. Episcopal consecrations, abbatial benedictions, ordinations within S.G.P. area 1658–1735; 1640–58.

LL 1226. Abbey of St. Denis and Congregation of St. Maur, papers of union.

LL 1444. Monastery of Blancsmanteaux and Congregation, papers of union.

Y series. Insinuations of the Châtelet—a few notes of loans registered with the court.

Minutier central (A.N., M.C.)

Etude CX. Papers of Philippe Le Moine, notary for St. Germain des Prés (June 7, 1640–Oct. 15, 1976).

Liasses 95, 96, 97, 137, 155, 199, 200.

Bibliothèque Nationale (B.N.)

Manuscrits latin (MS. lat.)

11818, 11819, 11820, 11821. Monasticon Gallicanum.

11915. Papers and autobiography of Bernard de Montfaucon.

12789, 12790. Annales Congregationis Sancti Mauri.

12836. Acta visitationem, St. Germain des Prés.

13082, 13083, 13084, 13085. Catalogue of the library of St. Germain des Prés.

Manuscrits français (MS. fr.)

5871. Description of the revenues of the manse conventuelle, 1622.

8599, 8600. Necrology of St. Denis en France.

15714. Harlay collection—copies of memoranda, orders of bishops.

Actes capitulaires of St. Germain des Prés

16852. 1631–41.

16854. 1639–44.

16855. 1645–56.

16856. 1656–69.

16857. 1669–1722.

These contain minutes of chapter meetings, with discussions of finances, litigation, festivals, processions, etc.

16853. Claude Coton's Journal of Receipts.

16861. Necrology of St. Germain des Prés (published by J.-B. Vanel— see printed sources).

16862. Septième livre de la juridiction spirituelle, 1669 to eighteenth century—continues the series of A.N. LL 1135–41.

16863. Division of properties between the abbot and the monks; titles of acquisition.

16864. "Traité pour connaître l'état des biens" (written by Dom André Olivier, 1710); and other records of the temporel.

16865. Relics of St. Germain des Prés.

16866, 16867. Mélanges S.G.P., containing manuscript histories, orders and proclamations of abbots, explanations of tableaux and decorations, lists of monks, etc.

17669. "Origine de la Congrégation de St. Maur" (written by Dom Ange Nalet, ca. 1626).

17670. "Abrégé de l'histoire de la réforme" (possibly written by Dom Joseph Mège).

17672. Memoirs of Dom Bernard Audebert (see printed sources).

17806. Request for alms from St. Germain des Prés by the Recollects of the Faubourg St. Germain.

18816. Livre des choses mémorables, to 1695.

18817. Livre des choses mémorables, 1696–1743.

18818. Livre de la Sacristie, 1658–95. Registre des Mortuaires pour les personnes seculières ou regulières (other than monks of the Congregation of St. Maur).

18819. Deliberations of the Séniorat, 1649–1723.

18820. Professions of novices (convers), S.G.P.

18821. Receptions of novices (convers), S.G.P.

18822. Journal of Claude Coton (expenses).

19629. Instructions for the master of novices (by Dom Firmin Rainssant, 1651).

19630. "Les Devoirs des directeurs" (18th cent.?).

19857. Chronicle of St. Pierre de Solignac.

20846. Notes of Dom Germain Poirier, 18th cent.

20847. References to other documents, copies, etc.

20848. Declaration of Abbey properties, 1789.

21612. Delamare collection—"Etat des décimes, rentes, pensions. . . ." (Manse abbatiale, 1637).

24472, 24473. Notes of P. Léonard de Ste. Catherine on Parisian learned society (see Neveu, "La Vie érudite," in Works, below).

Monastic correspondence
The correspondence of the Maurists at the B.N. is so voluminous that I can indicate only a few volumes that were useful in this study: MSS. fr. 12764 (Montfaucon), 12804 (Michel Brial), 15793, 17680–17681 (Montfaucon, Pouget, Guillot), 17683 (Luc d'Achery), 17701–17713 (Montfaucon), 19644 (Mabillon), 19661 (Claude Martin), 25538 (Montfaucon and Martin). Some of these volumes have been inventoried.

Nouvelles Acquisitions françaises
9766, 9786. Portefeuilles A. Lancelot, containing an inventory of titles produced by S.G.P. in the jurisdictional dispute (9766, fol. 122) and some corrections to Bouillart's history (9786, fol. 193).

Collection Clairambault
1056. Funeral orations on the bishops and archbishops of Paris.

2. PRINTED SOURCES

Almanach Royal.

Audebert, Bernard. *Mémoires.* Edited by Dom Léon Guilloreau. Archives de la France monastique, 1911. Vol. 11.

Bénard, Laurent, *Paraeneses Chrestiennes, ou sermons très utiles a toutes personnes.* Paris, 1616.

Bouillart, Jacques. *Histoire de l'Abbaye Royale de St. Germain des Prés.* Paris, 1724.

Canons and Decrees of the Council of Trent. Translated by Rev. H. J. Schroeder, O.P. St. Louis, Mo. and London, 1941.

Félibien, Michel, and Lobineau, Guy-Alexis. *Histoire de la ville de Paris.* Paris, 1725.

Gallia Christiana in provincias ecclesiasticas distributa. . . . Paris, 1715–1865.

Gigas, Emile, ed. *Lettres des Bénédictins de St. Maur.* 3 vols. Copenhagen, 1892–93.

Isambert, François, et al., eds. *Recueil des anciennes lois françaises.* Paris, 1821–33.

Launoy, Jean de. *Examen de certains privilèges et autres pièces. . . .* Paris, 1665.

———. *Inquisitio in chartam immunitatis, quam B. Germanus, Parisiorum episcopus, suburbano monasterior dedisse fertur.* Paris, 1657.

Le Cerf de la Viéville, Philippe. *Bibliotèque historique et critique des auteurs de la Congrégation de St. Maur.* La Haye, 1726.

Le Gallois, Antoine. *Oraison funèbre de . . . Marie Thérèse*. . . . Paris, 1683.

Mabillon, Jean. "Réflexions sur les prisons des ordres religieux." *Opera posthuma*. Paris, 1724. Vol. 3.

――――. *Traité des études monastiques*. Paris, 1691.

Martène, Edmond, *Histoire de la Congrégation de St. Maur*, Archives de la France monastique. 1928–54. Vols. 31–34, 42–43, 46–48.

――――. *La Vie des justes*. Archives de la France Monastique. 1924. Vol. 27.

――――. *La Vie du vénérable père Dom Claude Martin*. Tours, 1697.

Martignac, Etienne de. *Eloges historiques des évêques et archévêques de Paris*. Paris, 1698.

Matricula Monachorum Professorum Congregationis S. Mauri. . . . Edited by Dom Yves Chaussy. Paris, 1959.

Montfaucon, Bernard de. *Diarium Italicum*. Paris, 1702. Eng. trans. *The Travels of the learned Father Montfaucon from Paris thro' Italy*. London, 1712.

Nouveau Supplement à l'histoire littéraire de la Congrégation de St. Maur. Edited by Henry Wilhelm, Ursmer Berlière, Antoine Dubourg, and A.M.P. Ingold. Paris, 1908.

Polyptique de l'abbe Irminon. Edited by Benjamin Guérard. Paris, 1836–44. Also edited by A. Longnon. Paris, 1886–95.

Quatremaires, Robert. *Défense des droits de l'abbaye royale de St. Germain des Prés*. . . . Paris, 1668.

――――. *Privilegium S. Germani adversus J. Launoii*. . . . Paris, 1657.

St. Benedict's Rule for Monasteries. Translated by Leonard J. Doyle. Collegeville, Minn., 1948.

Sanson, Nicolas. *Le Diocèse de Paris*. Map. Paris, 1679.

Tassin, René-Prosper. *Histoire littéraire de la Congrégation de St. Maur*. Brussels, 1770.

Vanel, Jean-Baptiste. *Les Bénédictins de St. Germain des Prés et les savants lyonnais*. . . . Paris, 1894.

――――. *Les Bénédictins de St. Maur à St. Germain des Prés, 1630–1792, Nécrologe*. Paris, 1896. An edition of B.N. MS. fr. 16861.

Pamphlets on the processions of Ste. Geneviève and St. Germain in 1652 are listed in the B.N. *Catalogue de l'histoire de France*. Vol. 2, pp. 159–60, Lb[37] 2620–28.

3. WORKS

L'Abbaye Bénédictine de Fécamp. Fecamp, 1959.

Anger, Dom Pierre. *Les Dépendances de l'Abbaye de St. Germain des Prés*. Archives de la France Monastique. 1906–09. Vols. 3, 4, 8.

d'Allerit, Odette. "Comment on travaillait à St. Germain des Prés sous la direction de Dom Claude Martin." *Revue d'Histoire Moderne et Contemporaine* 4 (1957): 212–28.

Anglim, Mary. "The Hôpital Général of Paris." Unpublished paper. University of Michigan.

Arbellot, François. "Les Bénédictins de St. Maur originaires du Limousin." *Bull. Soc. Arch. Limousin* 40 (1893): 644–70.

Ariès, Philippe. *Western Attitudes toward Death.* Baltimore, 1974.

Baudot, J. "Mauristes." *Dictionnaire de Théologie Catholique.* Vol. 10.

Baulant, Micheline, and Meuvret, Jean. *Prix des céréales extraits de la mercuriale de Paris.* Paris, 1960–62.

Bergkamp, Joseph U. "Dom Jean Mabillon and the Benedictine Historical School of Saint Maur." Ph.D. dissertation. Catholic University of America. 1928.

Bernard, Leon. *The Emerging City: Paris in the Age of Louis XIV.* Durham, N. C., 1970.

Bertin, Jacques. *Sémiologie Graphique.* Paris, 1968.

Beutler, Corinne. "Bâtiment et salaires: un chantier à St. Germain des Prés de 1644 à 1656." *Annales, E.S.C.* 26 (1971): 484–517.

Bezard, Yvonne. *La Vie rurale dans le sud de la région parisienne.* Paris, 1929.

Biver, Paul, and Marie-Louise. "L'Abbaye Royale de St. Germain des Prés." *Abbayes, monastères, et couvents de Paris.* Paris, 1970.

Blet, Pierre. *Le Clergé de France et la monarchie: étude sur les assemblées générales du clergé de 1615 à 1666.* 2 vols. Rome, 1959.

———. *Les Assemblées du clergé et Louis XIV de 1670 à 1693.* Rome, 1972.

Bloch, Marc. *The Ile-de-France.* Paris, 1913; Ithaca, N.Y., 1971.

Bolgar, R. R. *The Classical Heritage and Its Beneficiaries.* Cambridge, 1954.

Bourgeon, Jean Louis. *Les Colbert avant Colbert.* Paris, 1973.

Braudel, Fernand. *Civilisation matérielle et capitalisme.* Paris, 1967. Vol. 1.

———. *Ecrits sur l'histoire.* Paris, 1969.

Braudel, Fernand, and Spooner, Frank. "Prices in Europe from 1450 to 1750." *Cambridge Economic History of Europe.* 1967. Vol. 4.

Brice, Germain. "Le Quartier St. Germain des Prés." *Description de la Ville de Paris.* 9th ed. Paris, 1752. Reprinted ed., Geneva, 1971. Vol. 3.

Broglie, Emmanuel de. *Mabillon et la société de St. Germain des Prés au XVIIe siècle.* Paris, 1888.

———. *La Société de St. Germain des Prés au XVIIIe siècle: Bernard de Montfaucon et les Bernardins, 1715–1750.* Paris, 1891.

Butler, Cuthbert. *Benedictine Monachism.* London, 1919.

C***, Charles D.M. *Les Principes des rentes constituées.* Nîmes, 1758.

Carrière, Victor, ed. *Introduction aux études d'histoire ecclésiastique locale.* 3 vols. Paris, 1934–40.

Ceauneau, Chaoine A. *La Reforme de St. Maur à l'Abbaye de Notre Dame d'Evron (1640–1791).* Laval, 1949.

Charmeil, J. P. *Les Trésoriers de France à l'époque de la Fronde.* Paris, 1964.

Charvin, G. "Contribution à l'étude du personnel dans la Congrégation de St. Maur, 1612–1789." *Revue Mabillon* 46 (1956): 107–14, 200–30, 279–90; 47 (1957): 44–56, 115–29.

Chaussy, Dom Yves. "Le Mont St. Michel dans la Congrégation de St. Maur," *Millenaire monastique du Mont St. Michel*. Paris, 1966–71. Vol. 1.

Chavin de Malan, Emile. *Histoire de Dom Mabillon et de la Congrégation de St. Maur. Paris*, 1843.

Chill, Emmanuel S. "Religion and Mendicity in Seventeenth Century France." *International Review for Social History* 7 (1962): 400–25.

Coale, Ansley, J., and Demeny, Paul. *Methods of Estimating Basic Demographic Measures from Incomplete Data*. United Nations, 1967.

———. *Regional Model Life Tables and Stable Populations*. Princeton, 1966.

Constant, Jean-Marie. "Gestion et revenus d'un grand domaine aux XVIe et XVIIe siècles." *Revue d'Histoire Économique et Sociale* 50:2 (1972): 165–202.

Cottineau, L. H. *Répertoire topo-bibliographique des abbayes et prieurés*. Mâcon, 1936–38. S.v. Paris.

Couperie, Pierre. "Régimes alimentaires dans la France du XVIIe siècle." *Annales, E.S.C.* 18 (1963): 1,133–41.

———. "Les Marchés de pourvoirie: viandes et poissons chez les Grands au XVIIe siècle." *Annales, E.S.C.* 19 (1964): 467–77.

Cousin, Patrice. *Précis d'histoire monastique*. Paris, 1956.

Cox, John Rodda. "The Exempt Abbey of St. Augustine, Canterbury, and the Papacy, ca. 604–1406 A.D." Ph.D. dissertation, University of California, Berkeley, 1945.

Cox, Peter R. *Demography*. 4th ed. Cambridge, 1970.

Delamare, Nicolas. *Traité de la Police*. Amsterdam, 1729.

Delumeau, Jean. *Le Catholicisme entre Luther et Voltaire*. Paris, 1971.

Denis, Paul. "Les Bénédictins de la Congrégation de St. Maur originaires de l'ancien diocèse de Séez." *Bull. Soc. Hist. Arch. de l'Orne* 29, 30, 31 (1910–12).

———. *Le Cardinal de Richelieu et la réforme des monastères bénédictins*. Paris, 1913.

Dent, Julian. *Crisis in Finance: Crown, Financiers and Society in Seventeenth Century France*. Newton Abbot, 1973.

Deparcieux, Antoine. *Essai sur les probabilités de la durée de la vie humaine*. Paris, 1746, 1760.

———. *Traité des annuités*. Paris, 1781.

Deyon, Pierre. *Amiens, capitale provinciale: étude sur la société urbaine au XVIIe siècle*. Paris and The Hague, 1967.

di Corcia, Joseph N. "Parisian Society, 1740–1763: A Cross-Sectional Analysis." Ph.D. dissertation, Duke University, 1973.

Diderot, Denis, d'Alembert, Jean, et al. *Encyclopédie, ou Dictionnaire raisonné. . . .* Geneva, 1777+.

Dobson, R. B. *Durham Priory, 1400–1450*. Cambridge, 1973.

Dosh, Terence L. "The Growth of the Congregation of St. Maur, 1618–1672." Ph.D. dissertation, University of Minnesota, 1971.

Doucette, Leonard E. *Emery Bigot, Seventeenth Century French Humanist*. Toronto, 1970.

Douglas, David. *English Scholars, 1660–1730*. 2nd ed. London, 1951.

Dubourg, Antoine. "La vie monastique dans l'abbaye de St. Germain des Prés aux différentes périodes de son histoire." *Revue des Questions Historiques* 78 (1905): 406–59.

Dumoulin, Charles. *Sommaire du livre analytique des contracts, usures, rentes constituées, intérests et monnoyes*. Paris, 1547, 1586.

Dupâquier, Jacques, "Sur la population française au XVIIe et au XVIIIe siècle." *Revue Historique* 239 (1968): 43–79.

———. "Le Temporel et son administration du XVIe au XVIIIe siècle." *l'Abbaye royale Notre Dame de Jouarre*. Paris, 1961. Vol. 2.

Dupâquier, Jacques, Lachivier, M., and Meuvet, J. *Mercuriales du pays de France et du Vexin français*. Paris, 1968.

Ferté, Jeanne. *La Vie religieuse dans les campagnes parisiennes, 1622–1695*. Paris, 1962.

Finberg, H. P. R. *Tavistock Abbey*. Cambridge, 1951.

Fleury, Claude. *Institution au droit ecclésiastique*. Notes by Boucher d'Argis. Paris, 1767.

Floud, Roderick. *An Introduction to Quantitative Methods for Historians*. Princeton, 1973.

Fohlen, Jeannine. *Dom Luc d'Achery et les débuts de l'érudition mauriste*. Besançon, 1968.

Forster, Robert. "Obstacles to Agricultural Growth in Eighteenth-Century France." *American Historical Review* 75 (1970): 1,600–15.

Fourquin, Guy. *Les Campagnes de la région parisienne à la fin du moyen âge*. Paris, 1964.

Genestal, R. *Le Rôle des monastères comme établissements de crédit, étudié en Normandie du XIe à la fin du XIIIe siècle*. Paris, 1901.

Goubert, Pierre. *Beauvais et les Beauvaisis de 1600 à 1730*. Paris, 1960.

———. *Familles marchandes sous l'ancien régime: les Danse et les Motte de Beauvais*. Paris, 1959.

———. *Histoire économique et sociale de la France*. Edited by E. Labrousse et al. Paris, 1970.

Hamilton, Earl J. "Prices and Wages at Paris under John Law's System." *Quarterly Journal of Economics* 51 (1937): 42–70.

———. "Wages and Subsistence on Spanish Treasure Ships, 1503–1660." *Journal of Political Economy* 37 (1929): 430–50.

Heimbucher, Max. *Die Orden und Kongregationen der Katholischen Kirche*. Paderborn, 1932–34. Vol. 1.

Hémardinquer, J. J., ed. *Pour une historie de l'alimentation*. Cahiers des Annales, 28. Paris, 1970.

Hesbert, René Jean. "El Aggiornamento en la Congregacion de San Mauro." *Yermo* 7 (1969): 123–44.

———. "La Congrégation de St. Maur." *Revue Mabillon* 50 (1961): 109–56.

Hostie, Raymond. *Vie et mort des ordres religieux*. Paris, 1972.

Hourlier, Jacques. *A la recherche de St. Germain des Prés*. Solesmes, 1957.

"The Human Population." *Scientific American* 231:3 (September 1974).

Jacquart, Jean. *La Crise rurale en Ile de France, 1550–1670*. Paris, 1974.

———. "French Agriculture in the Seventeenth Century." In *Essays in European Economic History, 1500–1800*, pp. 165–84. Edited by Peter Earle. Oxford, 1974.

———. "La Fronde des Princes dans la région parisienne et ses conséquences matérielles." *Revue d'histoire moderne et contemporaine* 7 (1960): 257–90.

Jordan, C. E., *Histoire de la vie et des écrits de M. de la Croze*. Amsterdam, 1741.

Julia, Dominique. "Le Recrutement d'une congrégation monastique à l'époque moderne: les Bénédictins de St. Maur." Colloque de St. Thierry, October 1976. Article with Lin Donnat in *Saint-Thierry: une abbaye du VIe au XXe siècle*, pp. 565–94. Saint-Thierry, 1979.

Keyfitz, Nathan, and Flieger, Wilhelm. *Population: Facts and Methods of Demography*. San Francisco, 1971.

Knowles, David. *Great Historical Enterprises: Problems in Monastic History*. London, 1963.

———. "Jean Mabillon." *The Journal of Ecclesiastical History* 10 (1959): 153–73. Reprinted in *The Historian and Character and Other Essays*, pp. 213–39. Cambridge, 1963.

———. *The Monastic Order in England, 940–1216*. Cambridge, 1940, 1963.

———. *Toewijding en Dienst: Geschiedenis van het Monnikenleven*. Amsterdam, 1968.

Kossman, E. H. *La Fronde*. Leiden, 1954.

Krailsheimer, A. J. *Armand-Jean de Rancé, Abbot of La Trappe*. Oxford, 1974.

Leclercq, Henri. *Dom Mabillon*. Paris, 1953–57.

———. "Monachisme." *Dictionnaire d'archéologie chrétienne et de liturgie*. Vol. 11.

———. "St. Germain des Prés." *Dictionnaire d'archéologie chrétienne et de liturgie*. Vol. 6.

Leclercq, Jean. *The Love of Learning and the Desire for God*. New York, 1962.

———. "A Sociological Approach to the History of a Religious Order." In *The Cistercian Spirit: A Symposium*, pp. 134–43. Edited by M. Basil Pennington. Shannon, Ireland, 1970.

Lehoux, Françoise. *Le Bourg St. Germain des Prés depuis ses origines jusqu'à la fin de la guerre de cent ans.* Paris, 1951.

Lekai, Louis J. *The Rise of the Cistercian Strict Observance in Seventeenth-Century France.* Washington, D.C., 1968.

Le Roy Ladurie, Emmanuel, and Goy, Joseph. *Les Fluctuations du produit de la dîme.* Paris, 1972.

"Life and Death and Medicine." *Scientific American* 229:3 (September 1973). Special issue.

McHenry, E. W. *Basic Nutrition.* Philadelphia, 1957.

MacManners, John. *French Ecclesiastical Society Under the Ancien Regime.* Manchester, 1959.

Mandrou, Robert. *La France aux XVIIe et XVIIIe siècles.* Paris, 1967.

Marion, Marcel. *Dictionnaire des institutions de la France aux XVIIe et XVIIIe siècles.* Paris, 1923.

Martin, Germain, and Bezançon, Marcel. *L'Histoire du Crédit en France sous le règne de Louis XIV: Le Crédit public.* Paris, 1913.

Mémoires publiés par la Fédération des Sociétés historiques et archéologiques de Paris et de l'Ile-de-France. Paris, 1958, Vol. 9. Special issue with four articles on St. Germain des Prés.

Mémorial du XIVe centenaire de l'Abbaye de St. Germain des Prés. Bibliothèque de la Société d'Histoire Ecclésiastique de la France. Paris, 1959. Also published as vol. 43, no. 140, of *Revue d'histoire de l'église de France.*

Méthivier, Hubert. *Le Siècle de Louis XIII.* Paris, 1967.

———. *Le Siècle de Louis XIV.* Paris, 1968.

Michaud, Claude. "Notariat et sociologie de la rente à Paris au XVIIe siècle: l'emprunt du clergé de 1690." *Annales, E.S.C.* 32 (1977): 1,154–87.

Mols, Roger. *Introduction à la démographie historique des villes de l'Europe du XIVe siècle au XVIIIe siècle.* Louvain, 1955.

Moote, A. Lloyd. *The Revolt of the Judges.* Princeton, 1972.

Moyen, Dominique. "Structures sociales du quartier St. Germain des Prés, 1675–1680." Mémoire de Maîtrise. Université de Paris-Sorbonne, 1970.

Neveu, Bruno. "La Vie érudite à Paris à la fin du XVIIe siècle." *Bibliothèque de l'Ecole des Chartres* 124 (1966): 432–511.

Newton, William Ritchey. "Port-Royal and Jansenism." Ph.D. dissertation, University of Michigan, 1974.

Newton, William Ritchey, and Ultee, J. M. "The Minutier central: A Research Note." *French Historical Studies* 8 (1974): 489–93.

Noël, Albert. "Les Écrivains champenois de la Congrégation de St. Maur." *Revue de Champagne et de Brie* 5 (1878): 97–114.

Olivier-Martin, François J. M. *Histoire de la coutume de la prévôté et vicomté de Paris.* Paris, 1920. Revised ed., 1972.

Philippe, Robert. "Une Opération pilote, l'étude du ravitaillement de Paris." *Annales, E.S.C.* 16 (1961): 564–68.

Pillorget, René, and De Viguerie, Jean. "Les Quartiers de Paris aux XVIIe et XVIIIe siècles." *Revue d'Histoire Moderne et Contemporaine* 17 (1970): 253–77.

Pisani, P. "Histoire religieuse du Faubourg St. Germain." Paris, 1919–20. Typescript at the Institut Catholique.

Poisson, Jean-Paul. "L'Activité notariale comme indicateur socio-économique: l'exemple de la Fronde." *Annales, E.S.C.* 31 (1976): 996–1,009.

Ranum, Orest. *Paris in the Age of Absolutism.* New York, 1968.

Ravitch, Norman. *Sword and Mitre.* The Hague, 1966.

Richet, Denis. "Les Séguier: une famille de robe à Paris du XVIe au XVIIIe siècle." Thesis, University of Paris, n.d.

Roulland, Léon. "La Foire St. Germain sous les règnes de Charles IX, de Henri III et de Henri IV." *Mémoires de la Société de l'histoire de Paris* 3 (1876): 192–218.

Salmon, J. H. M. *Cardinal de Retz: Anatomy of a Conspirator.* New York, 1972.

Salzgeber, Joachim. *Die Klöster Einsiedeln und St. Gallen im Barockzeitalter.* Münster, 1967.

Schnapper, Bernard. *Les Rentes au XVIe siècle: histoire d'un instrument de crédit.* Paris, 1956.

Schroll, Sister M. A. *Benedictine Monasticism as Reflected in the Warnefrid–Hildemar Commentaries on the Rule.* New York, 1941.

Shryock, Henry S., and Siegel, Jacob S. et al. *The Methods and Materials of Demography.* Washington, D.C., 1971.

Smith, R. A. L. *Canterbury Cathedral Priory.* Cambridge, 1943, 1969.

———. *Collected Papers.* London, 1947.

Stein, Henri. "Le Premier Supérieur-Général de la Congrégation de St. Maur, Dom Grégoire Tarisse, 1575–1648." *Mélanges Mabillon.* Paris, 1908.

Tanon, Célestin Louis. *Histoire des justices des anciennes eglises et communautés monastiques de Paris.* Paris, 1883.

Thomassin, Louis. *Ancienne et nouvelle discipline de l'église.* Paris, 1678–81. Revised ed., 1725.

Thompson, James Westfall. "The Age of Mabillon and Montfaucon." *American Historical Review* 47:2 (1942): 225–44.

Ultee, J. M. "Perspectives on French Interest Rates in the Seventeenth Century." *Proceedings of Western Society for French History* 2 (1975): 2–11.

———. "Processions and Miracles of Ste. Geneviève, 1130–1725." Paper read at the Society for French Historical Studies, Pittsburgh, March 1979.

———. "The Suppression of *Fêtes* in France, 1666." *The Catholic Historical Review* 62 (1976): 181–99.

Van den Boren, Dom. "Bénédictins de la Congrégation de St. Maur originaires du diocèse de Versailles." *Revue Mabillon* 11 (1921): 178–205.

Vanuxem, Jacques. "The Theories of Mabillon and Montfaucon on French Sculpture of the Twelfth Century." *Journal of the Warburg and Courtaulds*

Institutes 20 (1957): 45–58. Reprinted in *Chartres Cathedral*, pp. 168–85. Edited by Robert Branner. New York, 1969.

Veissière, Michel. "Guillaume Briçonnet, abbé rénovateur de St. Germain des Prés (1507–1534)." *Revue d'Histoire de L'Église de France* 60 (1974): 65–84.

Venard, Marc. *Bourgeois et paysans au XVIIe siècle.* Paris, 1957.

Veyrassat-Herrer, Béatrice, and Le Roy Ladurie, Emmanuel. "La Rente foncière autour de Paris au XVIIe siècle." *Annales, E.S.C.* 23 (1968): 541–55.

Vogüé, A. de. "Travail et alimentation dans les règles de St. Benoît et du Maître." *Revue Bénédictine* 74 (1964): 242–51.

Whitmore, P. J. S. *The Order of Minims in Seventeenth Century France.* The Hague, 1967.

Wiegand, Friedrich. "Mathurin Veyssière de la Croze als Verfasser der ersten deutschen Missiongeschichte." *Beiträge zur Förderung der christlicher Theologie* 6 (1902).

Wolter, Maurus. *The Principles of Monasticism.* Translated by B. A. Sause. London and St. Louis, 1962.

Index